FEMINIST FREEDOM

ALSO BY MINNA SALAMI

Sensuous Knowledge: A Black Feminist Approach for Everyone

FEMINIST FREEDOM

An African Vision

MINNA SALAMI

Cornell University Press
Ithaca, New York

Preface to the Cornell University Press edition copyright © Minna Salami 2026

First published as *Can Feminism Be African? A Most Paradoxical Question*
in Great Britain in 2025 by William Collins

First published in the United States of America in 2026 by Cornell University Press

A version of chapter 11, "Individuation," first appeared as an article in *Feminist Formations* 36, no. 3 (2024): 17–32. Published by Johns Hopkins University Press.

Librarians: A CIP catalog record for this book is available from the Library of Congress.

ISBN 978-1-5017-8723-2 (hardcover)

ISBN 978-1-5017-8724-9 (pdf)

ISBN 978-1-5017-8836-9 (epub)

Set in Electra Lt Std by HarperCollins*Publishers* India

GPSR EU contact: Sam Thornton, Mare Nostrum Group B.V., Mauritskade 21D, 1091 GC, Amsterdam, NL, gpsr@mare-nostrum.co.uk.

*For those who believe that the invention of new language,
ideas and concepts is a vital tool of transformation.*

*And, for those who understand that language, ideas and
concepts are only a ripple of an even deeper insight.*

A bird doesn't sing because it has an answer, it sings because it has a song.

— Maya Angelou[1]

People say I sing politics, but what I sing is not politics, it is the truth. I'm going to go on singing, telling the truth.

— Miriam Makeba[2]

Language can either be an effective weapon in instilling conformity in people, especially in women, or it can serve as a wide-open doorway to intellectual and personal freedoms.

— Patricia McFadden[3]

Contents

III. BEING

Preface to the Cornell University Press Edition

My first encounter with freedom came through dance. Not by dancing myself but by watching a movie about it—*Flashdance*. The film tells the story of a young woman from a working-class background who dreams of becoming a ballerina but is held back by the gatekeepers of New York City's most prestigious schools, who reject her unconventional dance style. Instead she works in a welding factory while continuing to train and dream. In the welders' quintessentially masculine world, she is compelled to put on a kind of macho bravado. Her marginalization from both the elite ballet world and the industrial workspace symbolises the broader feminist struggle against systems that force women into predefined roles. Ultimately, it is only by moving entirely to her own rhythm that she sets herself free. In this sense, it is a story of feminist resistance.

As a little girl, I watched the film repeatedly until I knew every scene by heart. I did not yet see its male gaze—so obvious to me now—but I was captivated by its message: freedom comes from first learning the rules of the dance and then breaking them.

This remains my understanding of feminist freedom: that we must trace the logic of patriarchy—its norms, scripts, and structures—and then uproot them through the radical act of imagining otherwise.

This is also why, with all due respect to the unmistakable freedom teacher Martin Luther King Jr., I must gently counter when he says "freedom is never voluntarily given by the oppressor; it must be demanded by the oppressed."[1] Versions of this line are politically galvanising, but they presuppose a material reality in which freedom has a fixed, pregiven form. I prefer to understand freedom as a shifting quality—already and always present in our ecosystem. A birthright (as King indeed also affirms in *"Letter from Birmingham Jail"*).

This view refuses to centre the oppressor by implying that he owns freedom and could, but will not, "voluntarily give" it. I prefer, therefore, the sociologist Avery F. Gordon's line: "Freedom is the process by which you develop a practice for being unavailable for servitude."[2]

This book can be read as a response to Gordon's definition. At its core lies a question both urgent and open-ended: How do we become unavailable for servitude? What kinds of seeing, being, and meaning making might such refusal demand?

The book suggests that developing such a practice requires carefully examining and unravelling the narratives, scripts, and imaginaries that sustain what I call *Superiorism*—a concept I develop in the book to describe the belief system that legitimises racism, sexism, and classism through a logic of superiority—and then reimagining them.

What could be identified as mainstream feminism, whether in the United States or elsewhere, has sometimes risked servitude by adopting the posture of certitude. In its pursuit of legibility, it has explained itself in palatable, textbook-like terms. But the insistence on fixity and unassailable conviction can echo the very logic of patriarchy it seeks to resist.

Rather than offering a formula or prescription, this book is an epistemic intervention grounded in the possibilities of African feminist political philosophy. It suggests that meaning must be transformed not through linear or materialist modes alone, but—like a dance, through backflips, pirouettes, even twerking—with language. That is: inventing language for realities long misnamed or not yet imagined. It means giving language to experiences that existing concepts cannot yet hold because to make freedom is to make meaning, and also the inverse: to make meaning is to make freedom.

When I watched *Flashdance* as a child, I was growing up in a society—and indeed a world—in which everything around me spelled confinement. Nigeria—and Africa—were locked in systems of neocolonial imprisonment. Women around me were living under varying degrees of patriarchal control. I sensed I had to break away from conformity and learn to dance to my own tune. How? I had no clue.

Years later, I found the answer: feminism. It was an encounter with antiestablishment thinking—with dancing the world open, with freedom. Feminism offered the metaphorical dance shoes, the tools with which to deconstruct and reinvent the dance itself.

This book is, you could say, a choreography of that deconstructing dance. I hope that by the time you reach its final page, you will not only think differently about what freedom might look like but also recognise that African feminism has much to say about it. And in a world where freedom is increasingly coopted, surveilled, or commodified, such rethinking is liberatory and necessary.

Prologue: The Glitch

Africa is a European invention.

— Wole Soyinka[1]

A writer's heart, a poet's heart, an artist's heart, a musician's heart is always breaking. It is through that broken window that we see the world; more mysterious, beloved, insane, and precious for the sparkling and jagged edges of the smaller enclosure we have escaped.

— Alice Walker[2]

Perhaps the most important thing to say about feminism in relation to Africa is that, if taken to its fullest purpose, feminism shakes up the already unstable identity of being African. If referring to African identity as unstable seems objectionable, then that is only further proof that it isn't a stable identity in the first place; for what is firm is not threatened by what is breakable, and what is true cannot be proven untrue by false claims.

Africans are often unwilling and unable to speak about the precarious nature of African identity because there are great psychological risks involved. Imperialism and colonialism not only exploited African soil but also troubled the collective African psyche. The word 'Africa' has become a verbal altar that addresses these wounds, a shrine of pride and meaning, as well as a site of sorrow and shame. Europe colonised the continent in brutal and unjustifiable ways, and still today Africa is sucked dry of its riches by greedy elites. The colonists' best weapon was never military but mental – sieging lands and increasing hegemonic power by destabilising the spirit of self-inquiry.

Africans understood that the deeper target of the attack was the mind, and retaliated with a fitting mode of defence: not a military apparatus but rather an army of sages, griots, revolutionaries, artists, storytellers, mystics and sangomas, who could counter the forces of harm with mythologies of self-regard. The problem, however, is that mythology can either give you wings, or it can keep you stuck – solidifying like cool wax into a specific shape. We of our current time face the task of differentiating which myths make us fly and which myths keep us stuck.

A sign that a myth holds us back is its claim to unquestionable 'truth'. There is no true Africa. Anyone who sets about finding a 'true Africa' will eventually realise that Africa is a fiction, or a 'European invention', as Wole Soyinka says in this chapter's epigraph. Moreover, Africa is a fiction built, paradoxically, precisely upon the shaky foundation that there is a truth about Africa, and that one of the defining qualities of Africanness is to find this truth. This premise is not only false but also circular; for if we believe that there are fundamental truths about Africa, we will try to identify those things, solidifying the idea once again that there are absolute truths about Africa. When this circular reasoning comes to characterise Africanness, it locks us into a mental struggle where the alleged truth and reality are called into battle. This internal conflict produces a defensive posture, presenting African truths as solid and fixed. From the 'solid Africa' emerges a kind of self-inflicted Othering that carelessly assumes ownership of qualities that are poisonous to the well-being of Africans collectively, while dismissing others that might be nourishing.

However, the contradictions that shape the foundational frameworks of African identity also present a *glitch*. It is 'true', for example, that Africans possess virtuous qualities, such as magnanimity and big-heartedness, as one of these solidified myths-as-truths suggests. In fact, it is remarkable how gracious and generous Africans genuinely – and generally speaking – are, despite the continent's hardship. There's an idiosyncratic uprightness about the continent's descendants, as though blessed by the Orisha with infinite dignity. It is rare, in my experience, to meet an African who hates their country in the way that you may come across a Brit, American or German, say, who feels a strong aversion towards theirs. Africans feel frustrated, disenchanted and occasionally dismissive of their roots, but these emotions coincide with a strange and slippery longing that has nowhere to go. I have come upon this Africa in the simultaneously hopeful and woeful way that Africans nostalgically relay their relationship to the continent. But it is also not 'true' that magnanimity and big-heartedness, to stay with the example, are what make Africans African. It certainly is not a truth that is locked in stone. Nor is it even particularly helpful – since such statements are often a posture masquerading as a fact to counter the negative image that the West has imposed on the continent, and demanding virtuous behaviours of Africans that others need not comply to. As a West African proverb says: 'The chameleon changes colour to match the earth, the earth doesn't change colour to match the chameleon.' The circumstances of Africanness might – and should – change according to that which does not change, namely: change itself.

The more we leave the Western gaze in the past, where it belongs, instead of giving it a front-row seat in the continent's narrative, even if it's to provide a counter-myth to it, the more we come to see Africa for what it is, rather than what it has been or even what it could be. We come to see the present as the secret superpower; changing with the seasons of Nature.

If the mystical tone of this prologue seems surprising, then that is precisely why I am writing it. We stand on the threshold of a new world where, in addition to the vast injustices that already adversely impact Africa, technological shifts are set to have unprecedented social ramifications on people's lives. Artificial Intelligence, programmed on Europatriarchal desires, shapes our futures without regulation. The colonisation of space is likewise tied to imperialist, patriarchal and capitalist goals. The ramifications of these new developments are even vaster for Africa and its people. Global narratives are already dominated by the West and tied to military and economic imperatives, which in turn reinforce gender, racial and colonial orders. These legacies leave little room for Africa-centred feminist visions in the global imagination.

Yet African feminism, with its history of determined resistance that includes theory and praxis, and also embodiment, imagination and community spirit, provides a unique portal of possibility for shifting and moulding contemporary narratives. African feminism is a school of thought that is genuinely equipped to do the critical, analytical and imaginative work that is required as a response to the evolving world, and it is genuinely equipped because it is truly willing.

African feminism takes the narratives about Africa and reimagines them so that, like the ever-seasonal chapters of Nature, their roots and branches remain the same but suddenly they look, sound and feel different, like the chameleon. African feminism shifts the gaze from Europe to Africa, and from maleness to the female experience of Africanness. It moves the narrative from greed and exploitation to resistance and fertility; from violence and domination to exploration and equality; from scarcity to abundance; and to radical imagination, conscious empowerment and transcendent love. It does so by rattling our accepted perceptions of what Africa means. Once our minds, bodies and souls are activated from the stirring up of perceptions, we are better positioned to formulate new stories that are truly empowering and transformative for all Africans – and not only its male elite, or for that matter, the foreign elites that can easily exploit rigid self-image through 'divide and conquer' tactics. African feminism offers what every transformative formulation needs: a language and a vision which articulates and conjures the new way. However, African feminism gives more than language or vision. It recalibrates our values, opens our hearts, expands our senses and our dreams. It is like the fire that melts the solid wax and reshapes it. The candle is still the candle, its flame remains but its shape is transformed.

Suppose Africa is Othered by the West, and African women are Othered in the male-dominant defining of African identity, both statements which I will continue to validate throughout the coming pages. In that case, feminism in Africa makes a glitch in the foundations of Eurocentricity and patriarchy.

That the foundation and the glitch so closely intermingle, however, is why African feminism is, as we shall see, a political philosophy that is both tremendously challenged and magnificently enriched by the enigmatic domain of the paradox. So much so that it might itself be a paradoxical thing.

Introduction: Questions and Paradoxes

I view my own activity as a writer as a kind of participation in the thought of the whole world. No other occupation provides for such an international outlook as writing. I have my national, my African side but I am also very much an international kind of person.

– Bessie Head[1]

Questions

If there is one question I am most frequently asked when writing and speaking about African feminism, it is simply: 'What is African feminism?'

Of course, the question isn't simple because there is no single African feminism. African feminism is a political movement and a school of thought within the broader feminist movement, and like all branches of the movement at large, it defies a straightforward definition.

Another common question is: 'What is the aim of African feminism?' Well, like all feminism, African feminism wants an end to patriarchy. Yet, in the context of Africa, people seem to expect something different than the deliberate dissolution of male rule, in all its various forms, that feminism strives for.

What precisely the different expectations are becomes apparent with the third question I commonly receive concerning African feminism, namely: 'How does African feminism address humanitarian issues in Africa?' Given some of the grave circumstances faced by women in Africa – female genital cutting, polygamy, child marriage, displacement, violence, poverty, conflict, etc. – it is perhaps unsurprising that people expect African feminism to focus on these urgent issues. With so many humanitarian crises, how could African feminism *not* focus on these most piercing circumstances?

Even so, I will address all three of these frequently asked questions straight away by clarifying that this book will not answer the question of what African feminism is; nor will it spell out the aims of African feminism; and – despite their urgency – this isn't a book about humanitarian issues. The leading question of my book is not what African feminism is or does, but rather, can feminism be African?

It's not that the above questions aren't valid or worth asking. My intention is not to categorically dismiss any of them. For almost two decades I have advocated for African feminism and, through this work, I have visited platforms and institutions across the globe to engage with the topics and themes that African feminism raises. It is on these occasions that such questions, as described above, are typically raised. Often, conservative-minded Africans (mostly male) who view feminism disapprovingly are those who ask them. White feminists whose worldviews are strictly shaped within Western borders also frequently pose them. Mostly, however, people are genuinely curious and intrigued about African feminism, and I have received their queries enthusiastically. There is nothing wrong with wanting to learn about a new concept, discover new feminist arguments, or learn how to be in solidarity with feminists of African heritage. The many conversations I have contributed to and participated in inform this book. I feel hugely privileged to engage in these discussions, not least because they give me a pulse of the attitudes, fears and hopes that African feminism gives rise to.

Yet these conversations also put me in a position of concern about the stymieing of the development of African feminism. By endlessly being tasked to respond to these three questions, and variations of them, as well as the biases that are often masked by them, the scope of African feminism is narrowed to proving itself. The truth is that there is no monolithic African feminism, and even if there were, those wishing to maintain the status quo will hear what they want to hear.

Instead, I have come to think about African feminism as a way of responding not only to feminism, or Africa, but also to the world-at-large and the African woman's entanglement within its sphere, a sphere about which African feminism has plenty to say. Echoing Bessie Head, quoted in this chapter's epigraph, I too view my activity as a writer, and an African and a feminist, with an international outlook. It is consequently impossible for me not to view the questions that African feminism is concerned with as informing a robust political philosophy that dissects the apparatuses of power, and speaks to the spirit of dissent for everyone, everywhere.

Nonetheless, my desire for simultaneously specific and world-making African feminist conversations has, lamentably, opened my eyes to the persistent disinterest in African feminist perspectives in the mainstream discussion about feminism, Africanness and other global conversations. Aside from African women, to whom the movement should be of direct interest, everybody would significantly benefit from the insights of African feminism. Take any significant issue of our times: gender inequality, climate change, neocolonialism, fundamentalism, extractivism, authoritarianism – you name it, and African women's relation to it is uniquely immediate. Africa lies at the intersections of issues impacting all our lives today, and its feminist thinkers have contributed important things to these pressing topics.

Yet although feminism is unprecedentedly mainstream today, with new feminist books published at an unparalleled rate, and although intersectionality (a concept coined by the black feminist legal scholar Kimberlé Crenshaw to describe how multiple modes of oppression impact women's lives) is, thankfully, a consistent theme running through the wealth of feminist literature, African feminist perspectives remain underrepresented. This is a disservice to knowledge production.

And so, in the first instance, the question is one that I have often asked myself, sometimes exasperatedly adding the word 'already' to its end. Can feminism be African already? Meaning: can there be more curiosity and more engagement with the timely and expansive world of African feminism, at least by the feminist movement at large?

In the second instance, the question is directed – in a roundabout way – at African nationalists, traditionalists, conservatives and populists who, since the rise of African feminism in the 1970s, continue to form a forceful backlash against African feminism with claims such as: 'Feminism is an ideology created by white women for white women'; 'African societies are historically matriarchal and don't need feminism'; and 'Africans see women and men as complementary rather than equal'. Suffice it to say at this stage that it is profoundly sexist and colonialist to think that black women need white women to point out their oppression. The popular argument in public discourse in Africa – that feminism is 'white' – also gives away feminism – an international movement from its inception – to the West, and in so doing immediately and automatically categorises it as undesirable for Africa. As for discussions about a matriarchy, where women rule and govern over men in an equivalent way to how men rule and govern over women today, even if there had been evidence of matriarchies in Africa's past, so what? They do not exist any longer. Moreover, if matriarchies did exist in the African past, then what should interest us is not that they existed per se, but how to revitalise the political power that they would have made available to women in ancient and later precolonial Africa. This is never the preoccupation of the 'Precolonial Africa was matriarchal' brigade.

The argument that African women and men are 'complementary', rather than equal, is similarly full of holes. It is a tender-sounding argument that implies that complementarity is inherently positive.

Yet the dynamics of Master and Slave, Oppressor and Oppressed, and Coloniser and Colonised are also 'complementary' relationships, but they are far from equitable or desirable. Asserting that women and men in African culture are 'complementary' is typically a way to dismiss the feminist demand that women and men should be equal, and to encourage women to accept fewer privileges so as to preserve a false sense of equilibrium. It is semantic too, as equality and mutuality are congruous. Equality does not communicate that an entity is greater, lesser, weaker, stronger, or anything of that nature. Certainly, it does not insist that the entities must be clones. It means the same value, and so to dismiss equality and promote mutuality is to admit to wilful ignorance.

Yet I am inclined to immediately debate my own statements above about equality. Yes, I believe the statement to be accurate in so far as the tactics of the backlash go. But admittedly, the notion of equality is not as straightforwardly progressive as it appears in mainstream feminism. If you looked up feminism in a lexicon, you would come across definitions such as: 'Feminism is the belief in social, economic and political equality of the sexes', and slogans like equal pay, equal opportunity and equal representation.

Even though equal rights are hugely important for feminists, they are not feminism itself. What the lexicon doesn't immediately say, but should, is that feminism connotes resistance to patriarchy in *all* its forms. Feminist transformations to legislation, policy, politics, government, and so on, do not end patriarchy. Women can be equal with men before the law, have equal pay with men, or receive an equivalent education to men, and yet experience discrimination in every other part of their daily existence. This clarification is crucial to Africa, where the focus on equality has resulted in the inevitable co-opting of feminist discourses into neoliberal economic models underpinned by pacifying and techno-bureaucratic thinking. If feminism is reduced to a struggle for equal rights, then in a continent where many rights are violated, and where so many people are also impoverished by unjust economic systems, it is no surprise that African feminism is becoming increasingly technical and administrative. These threads will be picked up later in the book.

What matters here is that precisely because feminists have had to pay so much attention for decades to the opponents of feminism, it has detracted from efforts to critically explore the ideas, contentions and radical potential of African feminism itself. Rather than to persistently disprove the orthodoxy of patriarchy in Africa and, more importantly, how to end it, the opposition turned the feminist focus to proving that we can be both African and feminist by appealing to the suggestion that for feminism to be African, it must have roots in historical Africa. African feminists have put huge effort into unearthing the home-grown roots of feminism in historical Africa, but less on developing the political philosophy of African feminism itself – or to explore its world-making capacities. The motivation behind asking the question, can feminism be African? in this second instance is, therefore, precisely to continue positioning African feminism as an ideas space that, yes, addresses proto-feminist patterns in African history, but also engages with the sociopolitical and cultural global order. How can African feminism shape the collective social imaginary, pan-Africanism, the post-pandemic world, populism, Artificial Intelligence, the human, and her sovereignty? These are some of the topics addressed in this book.

Much of feminist history has fought patriarchy as a concrete and external system, in which men use culture and politics – family, tradition, law, language, customs, education and the division of labour – to dominate women in apparent ways. For example, feminism has opposed the ways that women are discriminated against in the law, sexually objectified by the media, unjustly compensated in the labour force, harmed by violence and underrepresented in leadership. This description of patriarchy as it manifests in external structures and institutions is, of course, still a necessity. However, patriarchy is also a clandestine system. The feminism of our times is called to expose and then oppose (critique, resist, dissent, transgress) the new hiding places of twenty-first century patriarchy and how it shapes attitudes, dispositions, fears, desires, griefs and beliefs. In short, how patriarchy defines reality as we know it.

The rise of neo-authoritarianism is an example of such a clandestine hiding place, into which patriarchal ideology seeps. Authoritarianism is a form of governance where leaders exercise unchecked control over society. Its deep-seated patriarchal roots are evident: every authoritarian system is intrinsically patriarchal, and every patriarchal system harbours elements of authoritarianism. Authoritarianism and patriarchy go hand in hand. In times, as in ours, when authoritarianism spreads, its roots stretch into people's private thoughts, creating a kind of subterranean patriarchy that infiltrates political, psychological and societal thought.

Unlike overt manifestations, this concealed form of patriarchy is evasive, lurking at the boundaries of our consciousness and societal norms with its traps. It subtly undermines women's sense of security, joy and kinship. It pervasively influences not just political and bureaucratic spaces but also language, symbolism and personal aspirations. It plants fantasies of submission in the depths of our being so that they sit side by side with our quests for belonging, equity, justice, voice, safety, joy, pleasure, power, love, leisure time and freedom, unleashing their control as we pursue these desires. Subterranean patriarchal manifestations render women to perpetually strive for two contradictory things at the same time: to celebrate women's achievements within patriarchal structures, and also to oppose patriarchal structures. The cyclical critique of male-dominant patterns, juxtaposed with the applause for women who excel in them, opens old wounds, heals them, reopens and heals them, activating the trauma repetitively. My aim in *Feminist Freedom* is to expose the bones of local and global patriarchy – and how we break through them to flesh out a healing and critically aware body.

One last question – this time a question that has frequently come up while writing this book: is the book only for Africans or women?

I have written this book for anyone interested in the themes it addresses, which encompass feminism, African studies, imperialism, race, decolonisation and classic feminist topics such as power, oppression, resistance and liberation. The book also exists to give a sense of African feminist discussions and concerns to a wider audience, while moving away from strict academic textbooks and journal articles. Also, as readers of my previous writing will be aware, I am interested in ways of knowing – philosophies, systems, and, generally, writing that transcends the rigid disciplines and disturbs the power-laden dualisms of what in my previous book, *Sensuous Knowledge*, I referred to as 'Europatriarchal Knowledge'. One of the characteristics of Europatriarchal Knowledge is that it diminishes deeper human values with its mechanistic and deterministic worldview. It forces things that defy logic or measurement, such as freedom, imagination, justice and other qualities into rigid boxes. Obviously, these are qualities that are of immense significance to the feminist cause.

This book challenges the conventional Europatriarchal prism by synthesising the material and concrete world with social imaginaries, paradoxes and other nonmaterial factors that are shaping the post-pandemic, neo-imperialist, surveillance capitalist world in which African women find themselves. As a work of creative non-fiction, *Feminist Freedom* aims to be thought-provoking and expansive to read. Nothing in the book is speculation or fantasy, except if presented as such. Yet, as the (paradoxical) main question implies, the book does have a playful nature.

The impulse to be inventive and creative may not seem apt for the serious nature of issues that African feminism addresses; however, in fact, rigid and dogmatic certainties lie at the root of domination and stagnation. Knowledge that devalues experience, devalues aliveness. Life consists of stories, narratives, metaphors, relationships and, sometimes, if we are honest, also a touch of magic. To understand any topic deeply, we need to enliven the faculty of imagination. By imagination I do not mean entertainment. Entertainment can be imaginative, but it can equally be formulaic and algorithmic. Entertainment is not what this book is about.

Paradoxes

I titled the UK edition of this book *Can Feminism Be African?* because there is a sense in which the question is paradoxical. Depending on your political views, you might indeed have wondered how feminism cannot be African. You might have asked: why I would insert a modicum of doubt into the relationship between feminism and Africanness by asking such a question?

The answer is that it is because the inquiry invites paradox into our exploration. When the mind comes upon a paradox, it encounters a contradiction and must prod deeper to engage the tension within the question at hand. Paradoxes are therefore provocative and generative, as this book aims to be, too.

Paradoxes are conducive not least because we are living through times that are themselves of a subliminally contradicting and puzzling nature. Paradoxical questions and statements are, therefore, useful devices to ignite dormant insights and illuminate unconventional places within the social imaginary, where both comrades and adversaries to African and feminist progress can also be found.

Often overlooked, paradoxes are a crucial force in feminist history. Consider some of the statements that have shaped feminism in groundbreaking ways. For instance, by the revolutionary feminist and poet Audre Lorde in the classic feminist book *Sister Outsider*, that: 'The master's tools will never dismantle the master's house.'[2] Was Lorde wondering if the oppressed should fight for power within oppressive systems, or if they should invent new ways of thinking about power? There is no straightforward interpretation of Lorde's statement, which is why it continues to generate discussion many years after she formulated it. She was, in some sense, grappling with the conundrum of whether to infiltrate or invalidate the 'master's' world. Infiltrating patriarchy will only ever benefit small groups of privileged women who are lauded for adopting the same male-dominant behavioural patterns which they themselves oppose.

Invalidating patriarchy, on the other hand, means disqualifying a social order, where women nevertheless must carve out their lives. My point is that the statement is generative because, as with all paradoxes, it provides no simple answers.

Or think of another hugely impactful feminist statement, namely the one made by the French feminist philosopher Simone de Beauvoir, in her trailblazing book *The Second Sex*: 'One is not born, but rather becomes a woman.'[3] This quote highlights the paradoxes and complexities of prescribing gender identity, but also the between of being and becoming.

When it comes to identity, there is a difference between being something and becoming something. To become any given identity implies that that identity has fixed parameters. It implies that there are distinguished actions to that identity which one can strive towards. For example, to become a writer, you must write, read, research and schedule your life in a way that enables you to become a writer. By contrast, being something does not require any specific activity. To be a writer, to stay with this personal example, is not something you actively do; it is something you are. To become a woman, then, implies that there are predetermined parameters of womanhood (which in a patriarchal society are mostly disadvantageous to women) that a woman must meet to 'become a woman'. To be born a woman, on the other hand, would mean that no matter the choices or behavioural patterns one later adopts in life, one's womanhood would not be at question. This paradox in Beauvoir's statement is what makes it so endlessly thought-provoking and rich with meaning.

One of my favourite paradoxical feminist statements is Virginia Woolf's words in *A Room of One's Own*, where she says: 'As a woman I have no country. As a woman I want no country. As a woman, my country is the whole world.'[4] Here again, as in all paradoxical sayings, lies a productive tension. To declare, as Woolf does, that one 'wants no country' as a woman, yet has a country 'in the whole world', points towards the simultaneous exclusion and nostalgia that feminists often harbour with respect to the nations that we come from.

The list of feminist statements that have had a huge impact on the movement, and that are in some sense paradoxical, is long. There's Betty Friedan's 'The problem that has no name' – referring to the sense of ennui felt by white and middle-class housewives in 1950s and 1960s America; or Audre Lorde (again) with the very title of her famous book *Sister Outsider* – a phenomenally paradoxical and enigmatic title! If you feel inspired, you might like to recall other paradoxical feminist statements that you know.

The last one I shall mention is the one that this book's central question probably has the most in common with, namely: 'Ain't I a Woman?' It was the question asked by the American freedom fighter and previously enslaved woman, Sojourner Truth, when she gave a speech of the same title at a women's right's convention in Ohio in 1851. Truth presented some of the richest and most piercing paradoxes to her audience by saying:

> *That man over there says that women need to be helped into carriages, and lifted over ditches, and to have the best place everywhere. Nobody helps me any best place. And ain't I a woman?*
>
> *Look at me! Look at my arm. I have plowed [sic], I have planted and I have gathered into barns. And no man could head me. And ain't I a woman?*
>
> *I could work as much, and eat as much as any man – when I could get it – and bear the lash as well! And ain't I a woman?*
>
> *I have borne children and seen most of them sold into slavery, and when I cried out with a mother's grief, none but Jesus heard me. And ain't I a woman?*[5]

The paradox in Sojourner Truth's 'Ain't I a Woman?' addresses both the contradictions of being excluded from the category of womanhood due to her race and the broader contradictions inherent in what it means to be a woman. Truth challenges the assumption that to be a woman is to be weak and in need of protection, as expressed in the belief that women are damsels in distress who must be helped into carriages and lifted over ditches. Yet, at the same time, she presents herself as stronger than the men who define those convictions: a woman who can plough fields, bear the lash, and endure hardships, yet still not be recognised as fully woman. She then adds another layer by expressing her grief as a mother whose children were sold into slavery – yet no one but Jesus hears her. The paradox here is double: womanhood is portrayed as both fragile and resilient, vulnerable and invincible, but if you are black, these traits still don't affirm your womanhood.

Truth's paradox reveals the layers of exclusion and contradiction that black women in antebellum America faced, challenging the audience to rethink both race and gender. Similarly, I ask 'Can feminism be African?' to question not only the intersections of African and female identity, but also what it means to be African in the first place. Just as Truth's womanhood is thwarted because of her race, African identity too is often defined in ways that obstruct an empowering understanding of what it means to be African. Within African identity, moreover, the experience of being a woman is even more compromised. Much like Truth's question, the central question of this book unsettles assumptions about identity and belonging.

You can think of the paradox in the question 'Can feminism be African?' like the 'Ship of Theseus' story, where ancient Athenians gradually refurbished the worn-out vessel one part at a time. Eventually the question arose: if all the parts of the ship are replaced, piece by piece, is it still the same 'Ship of Theseus'? Similarly, once you ask whether feminism can be African, it becomes necessary to explore what you mean by African, what you mean by feminism, and even what the tiny but profound word 'be' in the question represents.

—

Before we jump straight in and look at the implications of Africa, Feminism and Being in the following corresponding sections, I'd like to share a few words on the writing of this book as the process also informs the content. Some mornings I'd wake up and feel it would be too painful to continue writing it. Someone had asked me what the book was about and its 'topic', and I wanted to say: 'It doesn't have a topic, it has a "wound".' I began to imagine the question: 'Which wounds are you writing about?'. Other days I could barely wait to explore the captivating worlds I was articulating.

I was aware, as I wrote, of an oscillating, contradicting relationship to the work, even as I also feared reaching a limitation where I could no longer find new parts to replace the old Theseus-like ones that supported me. The speed of the shifting world and the political effects of this seismic shifting, juxtaposed with the timeless and immemorial commitments of the non-conforming woman to freedom, liberation, transcendence, awakening – you name it – has always been challenging to reconcile, but it now was full of traps. I felt like Tom in *Tom and Jerry*: as soon as I thought I had a strategy to capture the tiny mouse, I instead became its victim. A word like 'resistance', which only yesterday seemed to mean one thing, had seemingly overnight come to mean something entirely different. I found that hiding beneath the language of resistance, to stay with the example, were shadows, elements of market economics, neocolonial developmental-speak and patriarchal dogmas that are adversarial to the cause of resistance.

Don't get me wrong, the language of resistance still plays a vital role in social change. There is no doubt about that. Think of resistance groups and freedom fighters such as the Black Panthers, the Contras in Nicaragua, the Zapatistas, Frelimc in Mozambique, Malcolm X, or Patrice Lumumba, who all opposed imperialism, state tyranny and dictatorship using various forms of resistance, such as civil disobedience, guerrilla warfare and physical defiance. It is no accident that the actions of such political dissidents are defined as 'resistance' – a term stemming from the clandestine networks that emerged in the Second World War – and resistance movements have gone to war against the social order.

But in the current moment, with all its risks of co-option and elite capture, and where even political dissidents are frequently faced with allegations of sexism, homophobia and transphobia, and use their authority and power to undermine critical opinion, or where organizations championing radical change are also corrupt, and where allies claim solidarity while perpetuating privilege, the conventional language of resistance is more complex and to some degree unsuitable for the aims of African feminism in our times. When we talk about 'technologies of resistance', for instance – referring to the same technologies that also reinforce and enlarge the problems of militaristic capitalism, patriarchy, classism and heteronormativity – it makes this a treacherous path to change. I sought some other quality, something that destructive mechanisms had not co-opted, and which was apt for the glitches to the foundation presented by African feminism.

But I found a way to navigate the vessel at every turn: language. I ultimately realised that the waves of doubt and insecurity, on the one hand, and rapture, on the other, also nourished the spirit of paradox that I had invited to shape my words. In that tension, a voice whispered from the depths of my worries and vexations, urging me not just to find words but to reshape them, to rearrange language and forge new expressions. I would make a new lexicon of sorts, born from the knowing, the magic, the wounds and fractures that are embodied by the idiosyncrasies of African and female experience.

As most writers, I am obsessed with this power of language. It is an all-consuming fascination that includes an appreciation for the meaning, rhythm and structure of words. It also reflects their ability to leave a lasting impression and convey complex ideas through devices such as conceptualisation, analysis, metaphor, theory, polemic and argument – devices that repeatedly feature throughout this book.

Language is a product of instinct, nature and culture, and it is, in countless ways, a gift from our near and far predecessors. Insofar as it is a gift, I owe much of the language in this book to those who continue to celebrate the ways that the struggle is also beautiful, and not only painful – including all marginalised groups who, like ectopic plants, irradiate the possible worlds at the edges. But as I mention in the dedication of this book, language and ideas are not the ultimate destination; rather, they serve as the vessel that carries us toward the horizon of deeper knowing.

I hope that by the time you finish this book you will have a greater understanding of African feminism – of the differences and similarities it has with Western feminism; of gender in African history; of extraordinary women; of African feminist ideas, art, aesthetics and culture. But I primarily wrote this book as a book of feminist theory that I hope will be politically illuminating and thought-provoking. More than anything, I wrote it in the hope that others might pick up some of its questions and paradoxes, and stitch them into their own endeavours to understand and interpret the world.

I

AFRICA

1.

Metaphysical Africa

So, like Diogenes looking for an honest man at the gates of Athens, I would have liked to arm myself with a lamp and run shouting: 'Africa, where are you?'

— Maryse Condé[1]

We are all Africans trying very hard to be Ghanaians or Tanzanians. Fortunately for Africa, we have not been completely successful. The outside world hardly recognises our Ghanaian-ness or Tanzanian-ness. What the outside world recognises about us is our African-ness.

— Julius Nyerere[2]

We need more people to see Africa for what it is and not just what you guys have learned in textbooks and on National Geographic.

— Tyla[3]

Can feminism be African? Well, it depends, firstly, on what you mean by African.

Is it to be one of the 1.3 billion people from the African continent? Does African mean the same as black? If you are an African descendant from the UK, USA, Brazil or Cuba, are you still African? Furthermore, are only black Africans African? Or are white Zimbabweans and Arab

Egyptians also African? Are foreign citizens who naturalise through marriage or work, African? In any case, is Africa a biophysical location, a historical project, or perhaps a political identity?

Most people, when asked to perceive Africa, conjure its biophysical landmass of about thirty million square kilometres bordered by the Mediterranean Sea to the north, the Red Sea and the Indian Ocean to the east, the Atlantic Ocean to the west, and the Southern Ocean to the south. They will have seen the outline of this landmass not only in maps and the news, but replicated on T-shirts, earrings, tattoos, you name it; the figuration of the African continent is almost as symbolic as the Cross. Others hear the term 'Africa' and they think of the continent's rivers and lakes, deserts, rainforests, savannahs and, of course, its famous wildlife. They may then move on to picture the different regions of the continent: the Sahara in the north, the Sahel that divides the Sahara from the imperiously labelled Sub-Saharan Africa; the meandering Great Rift Valley, the abundant Congo Basin with the second-largest rainforest in the world; and the steep Drakensberg Mountains. Those with roots in the continent may further picture a specific country out of Africa's fifty-four, and zooming in further, their minds might conjure particular cities, towns, villages, and even more specifically, they may envision family homes, beaches, nightclubs, shrines, gathering sites, shopping malls, farmland, bus stops, food stalls and carnival-esque markets where people don't only exchange goods but also arguments, ideas and laughter.

Then to some, Africa may primarily be, from all appearances, an unchanging and non-complex geopolitical object. This reductive objectification of Africa is especially the case in Western media, where global affairs – be they pandemics, new technologies, or conflict – are typically reported as affecting 'Africa' as a whole. But Western media is not alone in the fossilised view of Africa as one 'country' where issues such as corruption, Big Man politics, extraction and tribalism form equally static and interminably plodding diagnoses for the entirety of Africa. Westerners frequently travel to 'Africa', or have watched an 'African' movie, or eaten 'African' food. But these phrases have absolutely no meaning whatsoever, e.g., 'African' food does not reveal what they might have ingested.

There are some phrases though, which do merit 'African' as a general qualifier, such as 'African literature', where rather than narrowing, the phrasing almost has the opposite effect of signalling that the continent contains a broad and diverse range of countries.

Pan-Africanism, African liberation, or institutions like the African Union, may also feature as reactions to the mention of Africa. Some may associate the continent with specific African peoples – the Zulu, the Khoi, the Maasai. They may think of individual Africans – leaders like Nelson Mandela or Kofi Annan may appear in their mind's eye. Or they may be less specific and conjure physical traits of Africans – the various shades of brown or the tightly coiled and curly hair of Africans, or their facial features or physiques.

It should be obvious that these biophysical and phenotypical associations are not the defining characteristics of the word 'African' in the phrase 'African feminism'. My shape or form does not influence my feminism, nor can I attribute my feminist politics to the river streams meandering through the continent's interiors. There isn't any singular, unchanging spatial narrative that defines my feminism either. There is something more to the summoning of Africa in African feminism.

Nor is this 'something more' to do with another common assumption that people think about when they think about Africa, namely: underdevelopment. It is true that a vast number of Africans are disenfranchised people on whom interconnected injustices have had a particularly grave impact. But Africa is not defined solely by its challenges. There are elements of Africanness that, in contrast, reflect characteristics that are effervescent, joyful and unburdened by the weight of suffering.

'What is Africa to me:', the African American writer Countee Cullen begins his famous 1925 poem 'Heritage'. 'A book one thumbs/ Listlessly, till slumber comes,' he responds.[4]It seems there might be only one way left to describe what Africa implies, and that is – history.

Africa is a book of history one may listlessly thumb, like Cullen. To be African is, after all, to have an ancestral history that is a dizzying page-turner of wealth and dynamism, as well as exploitation and plunder. It is to share a mutual history with people who, in some way or the other, call the continent home. It is to share ancestry stemming from ancient kingdoms such as Nubia, Ghana, Mali, Songhai and Zimbabwe. It is to possess an affinity with the descendants of these kingdoms even as they have dispersed across the globe. Undeniably, Africanness is entangled with the inescapable history of human greed, loss and sorrow.

Still, even the historical associations don't quite satiate the meaning of African when coupled with feminism. Recorded history is an extraordinary tool, offering us a window into the past and helping to shape our understanding of the present. However, because history has often been shaped by power dynamics that marginalise women's voices it becomes a complex and tricky foundation on which to ground feminism. Only 0.5 per cent of the last 3,500 years of recorded history is women's history.[5] When we learn about history, yes, we learn about what generations have fought for, resisted, and dreamed of. But under patriarchal rule, history is largely a text on generational male experience. It is men's drives and motivations that are reflected in the shared human story. Aiming as it does to elucidate and eliminate the roots and effects of oppression, a feminism that is African must be in the search for something more than chronologies of events.

For women, history is instead a chronicle of stymying. Through the ages, in every part of the world, women have struggled against their exclusion. They have developed ways to share knowledge, fought to control their bodies, battled for positions of power, and struggled against male-dominant traditions and laws. But it was not until around the turn of the twentieth century that those longstanding struggles consolidated into perhaps the truest history women ever had – the international feminist movement. As historian Karen Offen writes: 'The history of feminisms is, in fact, women's political history.'[6]

The politics of chronology also means that what we know as history, focuses on Europe. Due to the disruptions of colonialism and violence there are gaps in the history of the African continent. As Antonio Gramsci said: 'The history of subaltern social groups is necessarily fragmented and episodic.'[7] Even when we discuss African history we, by and large, delineate it into three periods: Precolonial Africa, Colonial Africa and Postcolonial Africa. These designations are problematic as containers of African history because they suggest that colonialism is the defining story of Africa. The German philosopher Martin Heidegger, for example, went as far as to suggest that Africans (along with plants and animals) have no history.[8]

Without a doubt, European colonisation has shaped the course of African history. But the above periodisations erase Africa's history before Western colonisation. The continent did not only have its own pivotal shifts and turns, it also had sustained periods of interactions with other continents and regions, such as Asia and the Muslim world, before its encounter with Europe.[9] It is grievous that we render all the centuries of sprawling trade routes, religious connections and empire expansions, enduring through epochs and civilisations – the Aksumite Empire trade (first to seventh centuries), Trans-Saharan trade (eighth to seventeenth centuries), Islamic Expansion in Africa (seventh century onward), Swahili Coast trade (eleventh to sixteenth centuries), Great Zimbabwe and Southern Africa trade (eleventh to fifteenth centuries), to name only a few, and all the captivating and rich narratives, the innovations, the cultural exchanges, the philosophical systems, the arts and creativity, the architectural monuments, the judicial practices, the legacies of oral storytelling, the histories of alchemy, hieroglyphics, metallurgy, geometry – to a footnote in Europe's colonial project. It is hard to picture a similar scenario when it comes to Europe: that instead of distinguishing Europe's history by markers such as the Classical Antiquity, Renaissance, or the Industrial Period, we signposted Europe with the periodisations: Precoloniser Europe, Coloniser Europe and Postcoloniser Europe (when that day finally comes). That would equally reductively obscure other important patterns in Europe's development, even if it would be more true of Europe's context.

As a result, reducing Africa to a series of pivotal moments in history confines it to tangible, measurable and recordable 'events'. Historical milestones like the transatlantic slave trade or the independence struggles are all signposts in Africa's chronology, but to think that they are Africa is a mistake for which we pay a steep price. For example, because many events in 'Precolonial' Africa are not written down, there is often the illogical reasoning that they therefore did not exist. It is like Schrödinger's cat, where a cat in a box is considered both alive and dead at the same time until you open the box to check. Just because we can't always read it, doesn't mean it didn't happen.

——

This is distinctively the case with philosophy, a discipline where claims that philosophical discourse could not exist without writing are common. For example, the influential Italian philosopher of the eighteenth century, Giambattista Vico, described the trajectory of philosophy in his book *Scienza Nuova*: 'First the woods, then cultivated fields and huts, next little houses and villages, thence cities, finally academies and philosophers.'[10] Vico's statement implies that philosophy can only take place in cities and, further, in universities. It also suggests that philosophers cannot be illiterate, which is untrue. The written word is a technology that is not in itself philosophical nor required for the search for wisdom. Plenty of non-philosophical writing sees the light of day (thank goodness). And plenty of philosophical discoveries are made outside of the written text. One could make the case that the written word can even diminish philosophical open-mindedness by dogmatising it. There is a conceivable future where the merging of humans and technology warrants new interpretations of philosophy, which will subject literary techniques to critiques of similar shortcomings. What we now regard as canonical instruments of philosophy may then be exposed as limited and static representations of thought, insufficiently immersive or adaptive for the evolving consciousness of that future age.

One of the African philosophers to pointedly refute reductive claims about Africa and (il)literacy was the feminist public intellectual Professor Sophie Bosede Oluwole, who contended that African philosophy could be discovered via an interpretative approach to the oral canon of the continent. African philosophical thought, as Bosede Oluwole argued, was relayed through proverbs, ritual texts, epic poems, musical traditions, creation myths, life histories, historical narratives and recitations, rather than through written works, and it was through studying these sources that ancient Africa's philosophical thoughts could be understood. In her book, *Socrates and Ọrúnmìlà: The Two Patrons of Classical Philosophy*, Oluwole offered a groundbreaking comparison between Socrates, the founder of Western philosophy, and Ọrúnmìlà, a persona around whom there is both historical analysis and legend, but who is nevertheless attributed as the author of the 'corpus of Ifa', which is the quintessential Yoruba compendium of philosophical themes such as wisdom, justice, time, destiny and purpose. If the allegedly illiterate philosopher Socrates could be considered the father of Western philosophy, having left behind no written work of his own, then why shouldn't Ọrúnmìlà, who is believed to have predated Socrates, be considered the father of African philosophy? Ọrúnmìlà's words too, like Socrates', were not written down but transmitted by his disciples. Where Socrates famously said: 'An unexamined life is not worth living', Ọrúnmìlà said: 'The proverb is a conceptual tool of analysis.' Where Socrates said: 'The highest truth is that which is eternal and unchangeable', Ọrúnmìlà said: 'Truth is the word that can never be corrupted.' Where Socrates said: 'God only is wise', Ọrúnmìlà too addressed the limits of human knowledge in the statement: 'No knowledgeable person knows the number of sands.'[1]

None of this is to say that literacy isn't powerful. That would be a rich claim coming from an author! Rather, my point is that when we shift our focus away from a monolithic framework of knowledge production, historical approaches of doing philosophy in Africa are not only relevant in their own right, they are feasibly also futuristic in their integrative and multi-sensory perspective.

Nor do I mean to suggest that the classifications of African history into the Precolonial, Colonial and Postcolonial periods are altogether unsuitable. Work of tremendous value, scholarly and otherwise, has been generated using these periodisations. I am not dismissing that work. Furthermore, I am not saying anything which hasn't already been stated. Whether these designations are useful or harmful has been a widely discussed topic among Africanists.[12]

The wider argument here is that history, as a broad association of African in African feminism, does not quite cut it. The anti-colonial spirit that informs African feminism demands a dissection of Eurocentrism that historical accounts alone can't achieve. The anti-patriarchal temperament necessitates a destruction of androcentrism (the belief that, in the broad scheme of things, the human male is the primary sex and the human female is the secondary sex). That involves history, yes, but it also transcends accounts of the past to consider Africa's layered, present-time meanings, its extant conceptual and symbolical values, as well as its nature beyond the physical world and what we can see.

If both women and Africa have a long history of being excluded from 'history', then to be a woman from Africa, in reference to the passage of time, is to inhabit a kind of 'negative space'. By this I don't mean 'negative' in the sense of being undesirable but rather, as in the artistic sense – the space on a canvas that remains unfilled, yet conveys meaning through an absence and contrast with what is filled. *Girl with a Pearl Earring* by Johannes Vermeer is an example of a famous painting that uses negative space. The empty, dark void in the background of the painting illuminates both the face of the girl with a pearl earring and the focal pearl she wears. Just as negative space often defines the objects and figures in an artwork and gives them meaning, the exclusion of African women from 'history' is an absence that paradoxically shapes and informs the narrative arc of history.

What, then, is this mysterious Africa in African feminism? What is its negative space?

When followed into the depths of its implications, combining the words 'Africa' and 'feminism' means taking an obstinately closer look at both terms. It means making each term – in this chapter, 'Africa' – say something exact: did Africa exist before it was named Africa? If so, what truly defines Africa? If the Africa in African feminism is not simply a material place that we can examine empirically, geographically or historically, then what is it? Is there an Africa beyond what can be observed, a construct that eludes plain sight?

—

My answer is yes, there is an Africa beyond sensual perception. Africa is not only a tangible place that we can map out, but is also a non-material 'place' populated with beliefs, ideas, desires, emotions and ideas that we have yet to articulate. It is a matrix made of lived experiences, narratives and events that, while not strictly observable, can be understood conceptually. In African feminism, Africa is a paradoxical denominator: contrasting and synthesising; concrete and abstract, grounded and transcendental, tangible and imagined, political and personal, evolving and enduring; real and symbolical. In its totality, the Africa in African feminism is metaphysical. It is a Metaphysical Africa.

What I am proposing here is not that there is such a thing as 'African metaphysics'. That would be awkward, seeing that there is an established field of African metaphysics that includes some of the continent's most brilliant philosophers and that, as we speak, is one of the most inspiring emerging scholarly fields.[13] To give an example of an invigorating approach put forward by African metaphysicians in recent years, consider the Conversational School of Philosophy (CSP), which has been at the forefront of conversationalism – or 'arumaristics' – as one of the influential philosophers of the school, Jonathan Chimakonam, defines the 'intellectual engagement between or among proponents (called *nwa nsa*) and opponents (called *nwa nju*)'. Arumaristics is a term derived from the Igbo language, 'that describes the act and the mechanism of engaging in critical and creative conversation, on a specific thought in which critical and rigorous questioning and answering are employed to creatively unveil new concepts and open up new vistas for thought'. According to Chimakonam, CSP is a philosophy that 'could well be our best bet for a universal, ethnically non-committed method for a true intercultural discourse'.[14] This dialectic manner of transcending identity and cultural boundaries, is one that resonates deeply with me.

However, what I am exploring here is more open and creative-theoretical than the detailed examinations of African metaphysicians. My aim is less about complicated philosophical debates and more about exploring new pathways for speculation and a reimagining of Africa. What I am proposing is that Africa itself is metaphysical. The prefix 'meta', meaning 'beyond' in Ancient Greek, signals that Metaphysical Africa transcends the physical. While Africa is a material thing that can be observed with our senses, it is also a container where intellectual, spiritual, historical and experiential realities converge. Metaphysical Africa escapes material measurement, but it profoundly shapes identities, politics and worldviews. Metaphysical Africa has a different type of knowledge – one that cannot be formulaically assessed – but that is conjured in perceptions, evocations, symbolism, language, and the sensitive appraisal of temporality. It is both a living idea and an embodied experience, present in ways that defies categorisation but undeniably real.

If Metaphysical Africa has a location, it is in the 'social imaginary', a place that, as the phrase implies, involves both the social and images. The word 'social' can imply varying things – human characteristics (the social animal), events (social gatherings), or civic organisation (social politics), to give a few examples. Images on the other hand connote visual, mental, or symbolic representations – in this case those that are embedded in collective consciousness. Combined, social imaginary suggests the behaviours, interactions, cultural practices, institutions, laws, symbols, etc., through which societies construct a shared idea of themselves and around which they shape their norms. The feminist epistemologist Lorraine Code defines the social imaginary as: 'effective systems of images, meanings, metaphors and interlocking explanations-expectations within which people, in specific periods and geographical-cultural climates, enact their knowledge and subjectivities and craft their self-understandings'.[15] Her definition of the social imaginary – as the frameworks that inform how people in specific times and cultures understand their knowledge, identity and sense of self – is useful in this context too. Metaphysical Africa – in this mental picture where the social imaginary influences actions, strategies and choices that in return impact the material truths of the continent – is simultaneously the canvas, the paint, the brush, the artist, and the act of painting.

Planes, Cats and African Time

I will use three examples to explain Metaphysical Africa further. Firstly, picture yourself on a plane flying back home from a work trip. Picture all the things onboard that you can touch – the upholstery on the passenger seats, the mechanism that folds and unfolds the tray in front of you, and the toy-like interior of the aircraft. Visualise the plane landing, and picture yourself walking through customs, eventually arriving at your home, and turning the key in your door. Your journey is made of tangible and material objects with names: Boeing 737, brass, plastic, polyester, paper, Kotoka Airport, etc. You are likely to consider these things to be 'real' precisely because you can empirically observe and name them.

But you could also describe your journey home through things that you cannot empirically observe. Let us imagine that throughout the flight you had a sense that you'd fundamentally changed following your trip away, but you could not yet describe why or how. Or looking outside the oval window at the clouds, you might have felt an expansive sense of awe and transcendence, accompanied by an overwhelming feeling of oneness. Perhaps you have a fear of flying that caused you to undergo a panic attack, which you experienced as a near-death experience. Or perhaps, as often happens to me, slight turbulence lulled you to sleep as though you were in a giant cot, and you had a dream in which you were both on the plane and in the clouds, altering your perceptions of time, space and self. These kinds of events and experiences may not be tangible, but they are 'real'. Together with the material objects such as those mentioned, they make up the experience of your return journey. Metaphysical Africa, similarly, encompasses both the material and non-material aspects of Africa that shape its reality.

The second example to help describe Metaphysical Africa is learning how to read. Do you recall what this experience was like? In my case, I can remember the very moment it happened. I was four years old (this my mother later told me) and was lying half-naked on the dense, dark-brown woollen rug in our family living room (which now strikes me was an odd habit given how hot and humid it was in Lagos). I was looking at pictures in a children's book that my mum usually would read aloud to me when, suddenly, even though she wasn't there to read the words accompanying the images, they formed right before my eyes. The word 'cat' emerged as the same word that I knew to describe the illustration of a cat on the adjacent page. I tasted each letter like a mouth-watering sweet whose flavours my tastebuds could suddenly and gluttonously explore. I read the word aloud: C-A-T. It was exhilarating. Now that I could read the word 'cat', a world of expression to fuel my imagination was released.

Metaphysical Africa emerges in a similarly activating manner. In the beginning, there's the materiality of Africa, with its fifty-four countries, country-by-country colonisation, and all the depressing facts and stats we know about this process. Empirical Africa is not only negative, mind you. We also see shapes and images that enchant: festivals, beach parties, tropical fruit, monsoons and adorable animals such as the gorilla Ndakasi, who famously posed for a selfie with her friend and park ranger Andre Bauma in Congo's Virunga National Park. Like the image of the cat in my childhood storybook, material Africa – let us inversely call it 'Empirical Africa' – represents something perceptibly real. But then you notice that the representation is just the arrow pointing to ever more complicated textures, sounds, colours and threads that can only be described by the revelation of time from one second to the next. You realise then that Africa is fluid, dancing with substance, exploding with energies and purring with metaphysical allure. Then you notice that there are cognitive, emotional and societal states reflected in the images we create and the language we use about the continent, constantly reshaping how we understand and express ourselves. Eventually, you read A-F-R-I-C-A. Not just a place on a map, but a living, breathing entity with a body of desires, textures and teleological purpose.

My last example will likely be incredibly familiar to you if you are of African heritage. It is the notion of 'African Time', which is not just a relaxed approach to punctuality, as is often assumed, but when you truly consider it, is a way of life that is rooted in a deeper understanding of both the orderly and chaotic nature in which life inevitably unfolds. There is much to be said concerning the elusive physics about time. Most of us don't quite grasp the mysteries of time despite our efforts to (physicists themselves are mystified by it). But intuitively we know that time is both wild and structured; sometimes cyclical, at other instances, linear. Personally, I've come to see time as a substance that mediates between the known and the unknown: time reveals that the 'known' is sometimes more mysterious than we think, and that the 'unknown' is sometimes very familiar. I think of time as the force that unites science and spirituality, connecting the cognitive with the elusive.

In ancient African cosmology, time had female years and male years. Months were defined by the moons; days by concepts such as victory, consolation, deadlock and unity; hours by sunset and sunrise; seconds by the twinkling of a crab's eye. 'African Time' points to the contrasting relationship between such intuitive understandings of temporality, on the one hand, and the quantitative arrangement of existence into units as microscopical as zeptoseconds, measuring a trillionth of a billionth of a second, on the other. African Time acknowledges all modes of the temporal, including chronological (events unfolding consecutively), anachronistic (events deviating from chronological time), and isochronous (events all happening at once). It alludes to the mysterious temperament of time, like the ancient Greek notion, *kairos*, that conveys when something happens at the right moment rather than at the orchestrated moment. When we say African Time, it is to acknowledge that, at times, the crab is slowed down by wet sand and sometimes the prospect of a potential mate makes the crab scuttle fast. As the Ghanaian writer Ama Ata Aidoo said: 'Time by itself means nothing, no matter how fast it moves, unless we give it something to carry for us.'[16]

Contrastingly, in Western thought, time is industry, and industrialisation is progress. And so, since Western thought dominates, the more industrialised Empirical Africa becomes, the more it is perceived to progress. But things other than industry can signify progress. The abiding to one's ethics, the practice of love and compassion, the edification of future generations, the act of slowing down...

In the circus of modernity as we know it, there is no escaping the noise of excessive information, surveillance, competition, surplus. Slowness is difficult to attain. But slowness in Africa can be, as Bessie Head said, 'like a broad, deep unruffled river [where] no new idea stands sharply aloof from the social body, declaiming its superiority'.[17] In Africa, the Colombian novelist, Gabriel García Márquez, wrote: 'There were men so intelligent and peaceful that their only pastime was to sit and think.'[18] To sit and think, or as Head continues to describe the rural town in Botswana to which she self-exiled: 'A world that moves so slowly that it seems to be asleep within itself.'[19] Assigning status to such a calm and reflective stance is also progressive.

I have no intention of creating a hierarchal relationship between industrial time and African Time (or, for that matter, materiality and non-materiality, or empiricism and metaphysics). Metaphysical Africa exists both in contrast and in tandem with Empirical Africa. Some things need to be on (industrial) time, such as that imagined flight you caught earlier. And some things require a more relaxed approach to time (personal transformation or creative endeavours, say). We need chronometrical time to farm, travel, build, deduce knowledge, and sometimes even to make poetry and dream. But when we apply rigid chronometrical measurements to the messy experience of life, we end up as the god Kronos eventually did, defeated, and sentenced to an eternity of counting time, which is why the term 'chronic', from the Greek *khronos*, is not only used to describe 'of time' but also to imply a pathological condition.

I certainly am not suggesting that Africa is categorically slow as per a conventional understanding, equating slowness with a lack of progress. Of course, many of Africa's cities are just as tirelessly and pulsatingly fast as anywhere else, and people across the continent, as anywhere else, are as consumed with the optimisation of life that such a tempo demands. The distinctions between African Time and industrial time nonetheless reflect the problematic nature of conflating Empirical Africa with Africa *in toto*, and the limitations to our understanding that the conflation demands.

Empirical Africa

When most people think about the continent, they think about Empirical Africa, the Africa that we can observe concretely and measure physically. The Africa that is composed of data, hard facts and chronological events. The Africa which has a fecund material landmass from which natural resources – iron, coal, petroleum, bauxite, manganese, copper, gold, diamonds – are ravenously extracted in an endless race to amass resources from the continent. Africa has one-third of the world's untapped mineral resources; it hosts almost half of the world's biodiversity, with significant forest reserves and unique ecosystems that are vital to global environmental health. Additionally, Africa has more than half of the world's untapped energy potential. Yet these riches are grossly exploited by external powers while Africans are deprived of their benefits. The consequences of this impoverishing exploitation by international actors of the continent's resources can be empirically known, as can detailed statistics about GDP, infrastructure, demographics, corruption, education, health. You name it, Empirical Africa charts it. Take these examples: Africa's combined GDP is approximately $3 trillion. It has rapidly developed urban centres with fast-growing sectors like technology, innovation and telecommunications. Demographically, Africa is the youngest continent, with a median age of nineteen years. However, the continent faces challenges with corruption, affecting various aspects of governance and economic development such as education. Africa's literacy rate is around 65 per cent, and infectious diseases like malaria and HIV/AIDS impact its healthcare infrastructure.

We also know historical facts about Africa. For example, that the Portuguese explorer Prince Henry the Navigator initiated the Age of Discovery and the exploration of the African coast in the fifteenth century. That the Berlin Conference, where the rules were formalised for the 'Scramble for Africa', the division and annexation of African territory by European nations, was organised in 1884 by Chancellor Otto von Bismarck of Germany and attended by representatives of multiple European powers and the United States. And we know that the term 'Africa' was not used by black people of the continent until the eighteenth century, when African heritage authors and activists like Ignatius Sancho and Phillis Wheatley began to present themselves as African to propagate Christianity.[20]

It cannot be doubted that such technical information and historical records are of immense value, even if they often are discouraging. So much of what is wrong in global politics today is connected to facts and figures and should not be ignored. Africa exists, empirically so. We can measure and map Africa, and we can codify and systemise it. The dictum among African heritage communities that 'You can't know where you're going until you know where you've been', speaks to the acute need for these contexts. To transform material reality we need, after all, the capacity to measure, observe and keep track of it. Empirical Africa is real, just like the continent's landmass is real.

But the emphasis on Africa's sociopolitical data obscures that African realities – crises and blessings alike – are not simply made of physical matter. Thinking truthfully about Africa should not only mean thinking practically about Africa. Yet Africans are dissuaded from thinking about their continent beyond a measurable thing and are subsequently encouraged to only be concerned with verifiable observations that can be put into practical use. We focus on the 'facticity' of African existence, as Simone de Beauvoir may have put it.[21] That is, we turn to all the concrete details against the background of which human freedom exists and are unable to see that Africa is also a metaphysics: a sentiment, an atmosphere and a language, that reaches for attention.

Viewing Africa through these repeated and familiar empirical lenses omits a smorgasbord of equally important and legitimate ways to understand the continent. The tragedy of Empirical Africa is that we are not only denied our rightful fraction of the world's material resources but also our fraction of the world's collective social imaginaries. The interior of Metaphysical Africa has riches up for grabs, too. There we find stories, images, representations and ideas that play essential roles in outlining Africanness. We cannot sail these numinous waters with the unbending oars of empirical knowledge. As Aimé Césaire said: 'Poetic knowledge is born in the great silence of scientific knowledge.'[22]

For Empirical Africa to 'develop', it needs Metaphysical Africa. It is in the metaphysical – and not science, economics, traditional history, and the like – that we can ultimately transcend the limitations imposed not only on our material existence but also on the factors that impose those conditions in the first place. For example, if Empirical Africa is exploited, it is because it is simultaneously Othered. But to absolve Empirical Africa of Othering is an abstract goal that largely is shaped out in the configurations of Metaphysical Africa. It is, therefore, in metaphysics that the African phenomenon – whatever it ultimately may be – can be reimagined.

Yet even if I'm conjuring Metaphysical Africa as a way to bypass the development-speak of Empirical Africa, we should not conflate Metaphysical Africa with a romantic view of Africa. By contrast, to think of Africa as metaphysical brings to the fore hurts and traumas that we quickly sweep aside by focusing on material reality, as the next chapters will substantiate.

African Feminism in Space and Time

When it comes to African feminism, we also typically think of its socioeconomic, material and political dimensions which contain disempowering layers of African women's political reality, such as misogyny and exclusion of women from decision-making; violence against women by men, including rape, domestic abuse, sexual harassment, and other violations. We are speaking of a continent whose biodiversity is declining, and women bear a disproportionate brunt of the climate crisis, even though Africa's contribution to global carbon emissions is a mere 2–3 per cent.[23]

It is true that what I have described as Metaphysical Africa cannot give a complete account of such situations and their political weight. Here too we need empirical analysis, surveys, studies, facts, statistics, figures, graphs, charts, policies, and other technical knowledge to do that. But facts and objects don't convey meaning in themselves. And feminism ought to be in the business of shaping Africa's labyrinth of meanings.

An African feminist political philosophy must unpack, deconstruct, dismantle, build and rebuild reality. This work has metaphysical dimensions, prodding into immaterial elements of life. However, the structured understanding of Empirical Africa encourages us to categorically break down African feminism into 'issues' that can be 'fixed', often by funnelling them into processes we refer to as 'NGOs', 'development work', 'women's empowerment', etc. I am always left cold when I read the policy-speak that increasingly shapes the African feminist narrative, and turns our struggles, dreams and hopes into techno-bureaucratic jargon. In the dominant equality theory of today, policymakers, lobbyists, entrepreneurs and NGOs dictate freedom, and women are free only when we become economic and empirical (equated as rational) individuals.

Except (thankfully) it is not really feminism that is becoming infested with technical jargon. Instead, it is the sector known as 'Gender and Development' (GAD). GAD operates on a near-industrial scale, funded mainly by the West, and its neoliberal and materialist disposition to Africa has taken over the discussion on equality in the continent. The language of GAD – gender policymaking, gender public programmes, gender resource allocation, gender-bargaining, gender ministries, etc. – is everywhere.

On the surface, it is a language that seems aligned with feminism. Feminists, too, want parity in decision-making, resource distribution, and so on. Still, it is not feminists who shape these expressions but rather administrative institutions like the World Bank, the African Union and the World Trade Organization. Believe you me, if these institutions paid homage to the feminist origins of terms such as empowerment, or for that matter gender, they would not propagate strategies such as 'smart economics' – the credo that institutions such as the World Bank ties to its gender equality initiatives with the central idea being that expanding women's economic opportunities is 'nothing more than smart economics'.

Boris Johnson is not someone I would typically quote in a text about African feminism, or anywhere else for that matter, but he nailed it when, in a 2002 *Spectator* article, as former editor of the magazine and the then foreign secretary, he said:

> *Almost every dollar of Western aid seems tied to some programme of female emancipation – stamping out clitorectomy, polygamy, bride price, or whatever. While some readers may feel vaguely that the African male should not be stampeded into abandoning his ancient prerogatives, one cannot doubt the care – bordering*

on obsession – with which Western workers pursue their ends. In the depths of the bush, in halting English, recipients of aid will tell you how 'empowered' they feel to be 'stakeholders' of 'social support programmes'. It is no surprise that the aid industry is by far the biggest in Uganda and the one that attracts all the brightest and most ambitious. In the course of five minutes, while driving down a Kampala dirt track, I noted signs boasting the HQs of the following organizations: Uganda Centre for the Development of Marginalised Children; Kampala School for the Physically Handicapped; Send a Cow Uganda; Uganda Network of Aids Service Organizations; Centre for African Development Initiatives; the Uganda Women's Finance Trust for the Economic Empowerment of Women in Uganda.[24]

Johnson's motivation for writing the passage was very different from mine (touché). He also wrote it with characteristic condescension, as revealed by phrases such as 'or whatever', 'African male', and 'ancient prerogatives'; but he certainly was right about one thing – the grotesque enormity of the GAD industry.

The point here is not that GAD does not do important work. It would be insensitive and plain wrong to claim that organizations that are working on issues like girls' education or maternal health care are not contributing in caring ways. But as a creation of the development sector, GAD, like much of the institutionalisation of Empirical Africa, has become difficult to distinguish from the debris of colonialism. To justify Europe's colonisation of Africa, colonisers propagated the idea that African people could not sustain their interests. They then used these propagations about 'backwardness' to justify their grim actions and build institutions to validate their prejudices. These discourses are now sanitised but reproduced by developmental institutions and the charity sector.

When it comes to African feminism, relating it to GAD is the opposite of feminism, which, after all, has always been about making clear arguments for ending the domination of women, which consequently results in actions. The suffragettes went on hunger strike because feminist discourse showed how patriarchy oppresses them. The freedom fighters of countries like Algeria. South Africa and Mozambique joined liberation fronts because of activists' conscience-raising work. Without the critical arguments behind these acts, there would be no feminism. The most important thing about feminism is, therefore, to create the conditions where women can resist patriarchy by exposing the deceptions of patriarchy to women.

Feminism has three tools to help with this: analysis, critical argument and imagination. These three qualities are present in all the great feminist works and achievements. We need analysis to fully comprehend the predicament of living in the 'familial-social, ideological, political system in which men – by force, direct pressure, or through ritual, tradition, law, and language, customs, etiquette, education, and the division of labour determine what part women shall or shall not play, and in which the female is everywhere subsumed under the male', as Adrienne Rich defined patriarchy in the classic feminist book, *Of Woman Born*.[25] Analysis causes us to prod into even fundamental questions, such as why humans have created cultures where several millions of nuclear families repeat similar behavioural patterns directly and indirectly favouring boys and men to the detriment of girls and women? Does that culture, furthermore, expand outside of the intimate nuclear family, into the broader human family, stamping its prototype on every living organism? Is it the penetration of a sexist perspective into the fabric of social organisation that causes us to believe that we are living in patriarchy? Such transcendent questioning is hardly the business of the development sector.

'There are two sides to development,' systems thinkers Edgar Morin and Anne Brigitte Kern argue. 'On the one hand, there is a global myth wherein societies, having become industrialised, attain well-being, reduce their extreme inequalities and dispense to individuals the maximum amount that a society is capable of dispensing. On the other hand, development is a reductionistic conception which holds that economic growth is the necessary and sufficient condition for all social, psychological and moral developments.'[26]

Perhaps there is also a third side. The development sector rests upon a fundamental misunderstanding of human nature: that change comes from the outside. It is arguably the other way around: the idea of change comes from within. It is like a drop of water falling from the tip of a mountain until it visibly gains momentum and swells into a river. But while external factors are often the environments for inner transformation, whether individual or collective, the deepest shifts occur in the incongruous and multidimensional interior realms.

One night while writing this book, I had a strange and (*ahem*) primal dream that I was in a physical confrontation with someone. In the dream, my combat style was nothing short of badass. I effortlessly and quickly took down the unidentified object of my wrath. The sheer force of my extraordinary dexterity jolted me awake, only to find myself gracelessly and frenetically tugging at my pillow. I am quite sure that the dream came before my attempt to butcher the poor, innocent pillow.

My uninhibited dream amused me because it was the perfect example, in my personal life, of how the metaphysical can be 'real'. There I was in the most abstract of realms – the dream world – and what was happening there also produced a physical reaction here. On a societal scale, our ideas and perspectives can also become 'real' in this sense. Our interpretations of the world shape the world. The way we understand Africa forms Africa. How we think about African women creates the sociopolitical reality of African women.

I don't mean to suggest that Africa is a 'manifestation' or reification of any single individual's, or groups of individuals', ruminations. Sure, synchronous relationships between perception and reality are not rare – think, for instance, of conditions such as insomnia, erectile dysfunction or panic attacks, and how they can be physical manifestations of mental factors. But we cannot assign all reality to somatics. Other factors too, of course, are involved in such conditions. For example, it is possible to experience sleeplessness without any apparent cause, or due to hormones; and impotence can also have physiological causes.

Nevertheless, we can safely assert that whichever ideas we hold to be true of ourselves – such as gender, religion, profession, disposition – have material consequences in the 'real' world. Think of the transformation of body language, for example, when Africans meet in a distinctly African space, especially outside the continent. In such spaces, there is a nearly palpable transformation, a sudden tactility and relaxed posture seemingly catalysed by nothing other than being in the presence of fellow Africans. Moreover, Metaphysical Africa can also have an adverse embodiment. In a white-dominated setting, its racialised spatial presence can cause the body of the African to shrink in posture or to puff the chest defensively. It is for reasons such as this that the sociologist Akwugo Emejulu emphasises that engagement in traditionally white spaces, be they universities, media or politics, should not always be the end goal for black people. She argues for 'underground spaces' that aren't 'as vulnerable to harm and hostility'.[27]

What I am saying is that 'Can feminism be African?' is not a materialist question. If it were, then there would be no need for this book. Then, we could focus on economic empowerment and structural transformation, and feminism would be doing its job. Feminism with Africa would be about ending poverty, improving education, bolstering healthcare and pumping funds into GAD.

Perhaps I am wrong to suggest that feminist concerns aren't developmental, though. After all, what could be more foundational than probing into the scaffolding of Africa, not only into its material side but also into its metaphysical composition consisting of collective ideas about time, experience and meaning?

I conclude this chapter by reiterating that I am not concerned with African metaphysics in the technical sense, discussing concepts like properties, substances and causality in relation to Africa. Instead, I am examining Africa itself as a metaphysical concept, exploring its deeper, non-material character and how it shapes our understanding of identity and experience. People sometimes refer to me as a philosopher, and whilst that bestowal humbles me, the only thing I am, or at least that I professionally aspire to be, is a feminist writer.[28]

Were I a philosopher, I might proceed to strictly focus on the metaphysical assumptions that have shaped Africa's making in the social imaginary. But I will leave any attempts to engage Metaphysical Africa with technical expertise to experienced philosophers who may be inclined. The purpose of feminism is to offer a political critique. My interest in Metaphysical Africa, as you will discover through the following chapters, is that it is a helpful tool in both exposing and challenging the monstrous unreasonableness of two oppressive systems that African feminism opposes: patriarchy and neocolonialism. Both hegemonic systems are anchored in what I call 'Superiorism'.

2.

Superiorism

Personally, I believe the European has a god in whom he believes and whom he is representing in his churches all over Africa. He believes in the god whose name is spelt Deceit. He believes in the god whose law is 'Ye strong, you must weaken the weak.' Ye 'civilised' Europeans, you must 'civilise' the 'barbarous' Africans with machine guns. Ye 'Christian' Europeans, you must 'Christianise' the 'pagan' Africans with bombs, poison gases, etc.

— Nnamdi Azikiwe[1]

Latin America, China, and Africa. From all these continents, under whose eyes Europe today raises up her tower of opulence, there has flowed out for centuries towards that same Europe diamonds and oil, silk and cotton, wood and exotic products. Europe is literally the creation of the Third World.

— Frantz Fanon[2]

In the previous chapter I made clear that, while humbled by being referred to as a philosopher, I do not necessarily assign myself this label. However, I do undeniably think I'm a conceptualist. In *Sensuous Knowledge*, I referred to notions such as Europatriarchal

Knowledge and exousiance to describe robotic epistemologies and alternative ways of looking at power, respectively. The title of the book itself, *Sensuous Knowledge*, was conceptual. This book is cut from the same cloth.

A concept is not merely an intellectual device; to me it is visceral, a means for giving birth to new realities. Few things reveal the distinctiveness of human existence more clearly than a well-articulated and keenly sentient concept, which can reveal deeper layers of our shared reality, the dynamics of power, and how to escape them, and the conventions that teach us what matters and what does not. To conceptualise is to participate in the very creation of thinking. One of my all-time favourite books is Raymond Williams's *Keywords*, a text that, through its careful dissection of terms like 'Democracy', 'Art', and 'Culture', reveals the evolution of our shared vocabulary. In Williams's approach, one finds a dedication to understanding not just words, but the world they signify. This is what drives me to conceptualise too: to engage with the world critically and curiously, with wonder, play and astonishment, as well as with revolt and resolve. Concepts are helpful compasses for wandering through the kaleidoscopic world of knowledge; they are my tools to question not only what is, but why it is that way, and how it could be otherwise. But ultimately the aim is to release the 'compass' of knowing and to roam even deeper into the presence of being. As I allude to in the dedication of this book, there are ways of knowing which have more depth than even the most brilliant and visionary concepts and ideas. These ways of knowing can sometimes be found in the simplest of the most mundane experiences – eating a pear, or gazing at a tree or listening to music.

I say all this because I want you to read this book knowing that the concepts it offers are here to help us make sense of the world so that we can reimagine it. But in developing new concepts, I don't intend to narrow complex issues into abstract ideas. By contrast, I am engaging in a form of storytelling, as I see it, and the stories that I tell in this book are intended to both expand and inspire. This prospect is also how the story of 'Superiorism' begins, with a traditional form of story.

Don't Be So Emotional – A Short Story

Imagine that all of existence was, once upon a time, a sandbox. Imagine that the sandbox contained, every experience, every observation and every object that exists. In this sandbox there was electricity, magnetic particles, chuckles, cuddles, atom bombs – everything. One day, a young girl was building sandcastles in this sandbox-of-everything, when a boy joined her.

As they played, the boy suddenly lifted his arms high up in the air and shouted triumphantly: 'I won! I am the king of the sandbox!'

'What do you mean?' asked the girl, bewildered by the boy's assertion.

The boy replied, proudly: 'I have built seven sandcastles and you have only built three.'

'But, I was not rushing to build sandcastles,' said the girl. 'I didn't even realise that we were competing.'

'It doesn't matter,' the boy jubilantly chanted, 'because I am the *king* – I am the king of the sandbox and all your sandcastles too.'

The girl shrugged. 'Look,' she said, 'you may be the king of the sandcastles, but you are not the king of the sandbox There is more in this sandbox than your basic and unimaginative castles.'

The boy looked away. He had noticed how elaborate the girl's castles were.

'For example,' the girl continued, unaffected by the boy's hurt pride, 'there is time. There is language. In fact, the word "king" is something that exists in the sandbox but not in any of the castles. There are the sand grains with their warm and padded texture they provide under our bare feet. There is, or perhaps I should say there *was*, shared delight. You cannot be the king of those things.'

Defiantly, the boy sneered: 'Don't be so emotional. You're just upset because girls are not as fast, smart and powerful as boys. I can prove my superiority because I can count the number of sandcastles I built. This is not anecdotal; it is a rational conclusion. This sandbox is now mine.'

—

I share this little story as it mirrors the current structure of social relationships which I call 'Superiorism'. The logic of Superiorism is as follows: assert difference; rank and vilify the Other; justify competitiveness, with violence if necessary; defend your actions with a biased interpretation of rationality; and assert control. These are the tactics of what I refer to as Superiorism.

Another way to put it is that Superiorism has five defining features. The first is difference. The second is that difference is hierarchical. Consequently, Superiorism entails competition. The fourth feature of Superiorism is the human skill that is instrumentalised to defend the previous three, namely: *rationality*. The concluding characteristic, and intended goal, of Superiorism is *control*. Superiorism can be summarised as: I am different to you. I am better than you. I am in a competition with you. I am more rational than you. *I control you.*

The logic of Superiorism is deeply embedded in Europe's identity. Which is not to say that Europe is the only continent to exhibit the features described above. Across time and place, all members of the human species are, to varying degrees, territorial and judgemental. You may be challenged to find a society that doesn't feel an instinctive or learned behaviour of defending, marking, or asserting ownership over a specific geographical area. You would also be hard pressed to find a culture that doesn't, in some regard, have a condescending view of at least one other culture. Every society, at least according to my observations, believes itself in some way or other to be superior to at least one other society.

Europe's situation is unique, however. Named after the Phoenician princess Europa, whom Zeus abducted to ancient Greece, Europe has viewed itself with a distinct air of regality since its formation. From its conception in the Classical Antiquity Period to its later expansion, the fundamental psychological feature of Europe in relation to the rest of the world was the belief in its superiority. If Europe did not perceive itself as better than other parts of the world, its identity would be altogether altered. As the political scientist Hans Kundnani says: 'As long as Europeans have thought of themselves as

Europeans, they have thought of themselves as being better than the rest of the world.'[3]

In medieval times, when the label Europe (or Europa) first became a recognised term, Europe defined its identity in contrast to the 'barbarian' – originally a term meaning 'foreigner', and comparable with how we today use the term 'Other'. The Europa of that period was interchangeable with Christendom and so the perceived 'barbarian' of this era meant Europe's (or Christianity's) two rival religions – Islam and Judaism.[4] The crusades against Muslims were, for example, taken in the interest of Superiorism. In 1212, Europa sent children as young as six to reclaim Jerusalem in what is known as the 'Children's Crusade', using the rationale that children had not been sullied by life and were therefore better suited for such actions. Jews, similarly, were persecuted across Europe in waves of intensity. Through the codification of an adverse disposition towards the 'barbarian', Jews were expelled from England in 1290, from France multiple times from the twelfth to the fourteenth centuries, and from Spain in 1492.[5]

The year 1492 was also when the Italian explorer Christopher Columbus, under the Catholic Monarchs of Spain, led exploratory missions to the Americas. These expeditions would catalyse the Age of Discovery, and the debased state of plunder and colonisation that Europe descended into. With the onset of the Age of Discovery and Europe's forays into the 'New World', Europe's antagonistic 'barbarian' naturally and gradually expanded to include the populations of Africa, Asia, the indigenous Americas, and anywhere non-Europeans were encountered. On the back of other regions, Europe became not only the 'king' of its own sandcastles but perceived itself as the all-powerful dominator of the sandbox-at-large.

There was never a time in Europe's history where it did not perceive itself as better than the Other. But this is not the only reason that Europe and Superiorism are tied up. As I have already argued, there is no society that doesn't hold a superior view at least towards one other group. What distinguishes Europe in this regard are the last three tenets of Superiorism: I am in a competition with you. I am more rational than you. *I control you*. No other continent has seized control and dominance over so much of the world's resources using this triumvirate rationale as Europe. And no other continent has invented a methodical system of knowledge and power to institutionalise these premises. Whereas other regions have also exhibited the sentiment in the first two sentences, 'I am different to you' and 'I am better than you', this particular continent turned the sandbox into sandcastles in order to claim power over them. When it comes to Europe, its culture has been shaped around the instructive psychology of control: to control Nature and everything within it. It is the unique combination of this bloated and solipsistic attitude of Europe towards the rest of the world, and the subsequent convoluted practice of justifying control over non- Europe, that I call Superiorism.

I am by no means suggesting that Europe was so rational that it was able to strategically and logically position itself as superior to other continents. The opposite could not be truer. Bias, by definition, is the opposite of objectivity, and objectivity is a hallmark of rationality. You could not get a more supreme bias than Superiorism: to position oneself above objectivity. The weaving together of Europe with Superiorism has been so spectacularly ego-inflated that even Narcissus would crumble in the face of its God-complex.

Nor am I in any way hostile to rational thinking. Quite the contrary, rationality is a sacred quality (in the most rational sense of the word 'sacred', of course). It is something to cherish and guard, hone and nourish. What I am opposed to is rationality being used as an instrument of control and a means to propagate supremacy. This is the case when one specific understanding of rationality is positioned as doctrine. Truth is that no society lacks rationality, even if the way it is practised varies across cultures and regions. Every society has developed its own set of logical frameworks, technologies, decision-making processes and interpretations of their environment that satisfy their day-to-day needs and beyond.

In the context of Europe and Superiorism, however, rationality transcended simply being a cognitive skill and assumed the role of a value system. By system, I mean how 'a set of things – people, cells, molecules, or whatever – inter-connect in such a way that they produce their own pattern of behaviour over time', as the environmental scientist, Donella Meadows, defines it.[6] In this case, the pedestalling of reason and rationality over all other epistemic methods became the motor (system) of Superiorism because it could be manipulated to defend the moral logic of Superiorism in Europe's making. Stemming from the philosophies of Aristotle, and later of Thomas Hobbes, John Locke, Francis Bacon – intellectual giants who profoundly shaped Europe's thought – the foregrounding of rationality gradually became central to Europe's story, and thus to Superiorism.

The convoluted Superiorist logic developed as follows: rationality is what imbues value in humans. If rationality could produce advanced sciences and industrial technologies such as ocean-going vessels, steam engines and weaponry then it was only rational to use these technologies to plunder, enslave and colonise those who hadn't utilised the metric of rationality to produce such technologies. Rationality therefore proved that the Other was inferior, and was used to justify and difference, impose hierarchies, and to legitimise and actualise control. In other words, rationality was weaponised.

How? Through the art of illusion. The creation of illusions is the oldest tactic used by con artists. To fool the spectator, the magician creates an illusion that distracts from what is truly happening. A classic example of this is the card trick, where the magician presents a deck of cards to a crowd and invites a participant to select a card, memorise it and then return it to the deck. Despite the apparent randomness of the selection process, the magician then manages to locate the chosen card. The trick is carried out using tactics such as sleight of hand and diverting the participant's attention while discreetly hiding the chosen card, or by subtly influencing their decision to select a predetermined card while creating the illusion of free choice.

So too has the experience of rationality become reduced into a trick of massive proportions. To justify the ranking of humans, the trickster needed a tool – a metaphorical deck of cards – to draw people's attention. This tool became the argument that rationality is the defining quality of humanity. When everyone focused on this feature, then all other human qualities could be recast as irrelevant or inferior, and thus undesirable. When qualities such as emotion, intuition, instinct and sense perception were undesirable, the audience gradually became more robotic and could more easily be controlled. Furthermore, someone had to represent these other inferior qualities; cue women, non-Europeans, children, indigenous peoples, gay people, or any other subjugated group of people, as well as animals, fungi and plants. If the con artists could accuse dominated groups of being emotional, instinctive, illiterate, etc., and consequently irrational, they could also claim that they weren't quite as *human* – and dominate them based on those grounds.

You may have noticed that I am using the term 'Europe' rather than 'Europeans'. This is because I am not categorically referring to the citizens of Europe, a group to which, despite our shortcomings, I also fondly belong. Nor am I referencing the geographical boundaries that define Europe, within which lie countries such as Finland (where, together with Nigeria, I share my heritage), or Sweden (where I am a naturalised citizen), or England (my beloved home of soon two decades), or Hamburg (the city where I have written much of this book).

The aim in focusing on Europe rather than Europeans is not to make Europe entirely symbolical, and consequentially detach it from the actions of Europeans in other parts of the world. Rather I'm using the term 'Europe' as I am using the term 'Africa', in a metaphysical sense, with an emphasis on its real-world ramifications. Even if you take the hardest of biophysical facts about Europe – that it is the second smallest continent by surface area, covering about ten million square kilometres, or that it was the hub of two world wars – you would be honing elements that are shifting, and being reinterpreted by the second, reconstituting what Europe means. Europe is a concrete place, but it is also the materiality of an idea. Europe is a somewhere, but it is also a somehow.

As I use the term 'Europe' here, I am thus not strictly thinking of the landmass of Europe, but I am referring to the behemoth force that seeps into all corners of the Western hemisphere – the US, Canada and Australia and, in a world where Western dominance is ubiquitous, into parts of the non-Western world too. Europe is not merely a geographical entity but a potent confluence of ideas and ideals that have shaped the course of human history with cultural, technological, political, social and historical means.

I'm making these clarifications because, in an age where arguments about place and identity are immediately drawn into identity politics, and incessant culture wars between the political left and the political right, my intention isn't to enter these divisive discourses.

I refer to the systemised tendency to differentiate, condescend and control the Other 'Superiorism', rather than the more familiar 'Eurocentrism', because although Superiorism is a mindset whose seed lies in Europe's origin story, it is now a global phenomenon. And so Superiorism describes not only Eurocentrism but also racism, sexism, classism, heteronormativity, or any of the other power dynamics that African feminism necessarily responds to.

Racists do not only perceive brown and black people as different but as inherently inferior. Elites, regarding the working classes as beneath them, use similar tactics to fortify their positions. And sexists of course view women as inferior to men. All these oppressive 'isms' are grounded in some version of Superiorism, but the opposite is not necessarily true. A sexist is not always racist, as obviously there are many black men who are sexist but not racist. A gay elitist may not be homophobic, and so on.

Should the human animal, against all odds, survive the Anthropocene, the truth that will inevitably be laid bare is that it was not racism, sexism or any other bigotry that was the capital 'P' societal Problem. The real difficulty would be that we did not escape the very patterns of thought that inform Superiorism. Understanding the underlying currents of historical patterns seems the only way left to prevent their repetition. If we lived on another planet, we might be able to continue the same path, but we have reached a critical juncture of increasing droughts, melting glaciers, and a natural environment undergoing rapid and threatening transformation. We can no longer deceive ourselves that the destruction of the planet, democratic decline, economic recession, growing social inequality, global health scares, and immense mental and emotional suffering are not connected. They are interwoven with a bright red, harmful thread: Superiorism.

The logic of Superiorism is marvellously, if unintentionally, depicted in the 2023 film *Oppenheimer*, directed by Christopher Nolan. The film follows the life of the 'father of the atomic bomb', Robert Oppenheimer, and his central role in developing the atomic bomb which was eventually unleashed on Japan by the US president, Harry Truman, during the Second World War. In the film, we see how both science and politics are manoeuvred to dominate and control, and the disaster that arises from these intersections.

The events that unfolded through the establishment of the Manhattan Project, which enabled Oppenheimer to develop the atomic bomb, can only occur when we conflate existence with quantifiability, quantifiability with power, and subsequently justify immense acts of violence – in this instance, made possible through material resources such as uranium ore and plutonium, deep in the material reserves of our planet. As the White House statement following the bombing of Hiroshima tellingly said, the atomic bomb 'is a harnessing of the basic power of the universe'.[7]

Oppenheimer is inadvertently a film about the psychology of Superiorism. Of course, the film and let alone my summary of it, are zoomed-out views of history, touching only on broader and superficial elements. If you zoom in on the story of Oppenheimer, for example, you see that his involvement in politics and in the Manhattan Project aside, he also made contributions to quantum physics, and quantum physics is of course a field that engages precisely with how matter can behave in surprising, mysterious ways. Even the quantifiable world, it turns out, is a place of wonder and poetry.

Yet, we live in a world governed by a mindset that seeks to annihilate the beauty and the mystery of the deep order of the universe for the sake of territorialism and occupation.

If the president, Harry Truman, is our figurative 'king of the castle' from the story about the little girl and boy in the beginning of this chapter, then perhaps the feminist philosopher, Elizabeth Anscombe, at least in the case of the atomic bomb, can represent the little girl's wisdom. In *Metaphysical Animals: How Four Women Brought Philosophy Back to Life*, authors Clare Mac Cumhaill and Rachael Wiseman describe the instance when, in 1956, Anscombe opposed the awarding of an honorary degree to the warmongering US president by the University of Oxford. 'I am not seizing an opportunity to make a "gesture of protest" at atomic bombs,' Anscombe said in her speech where she made the pronouncement. 'I vehemently object to our action in offering Mr Truman honours, because one can share in the guilt of a bad action by praise and flattery.'[8]

Truman not only received the award, but he also remained defiant – like the little boy – in the face of Anscombe's remarks. When the *New York Times* wrote about her public opposition to his prize, Truman was asked by a journalist what he thought about Anscombe's argument. 'I made the decision on the facts as they existed at that time,' he said, 'and if I had to do it again I would do it all over again.'[9]

We have addressed the features and consequences of Superiorism, but Truman's remark speaks to what I believe are some of the key causes of Superiorism: necessity, desperation and primitive fear. Did Europe calculatedly set out to violate people in other parts of the world in the interest of Superiorism? This is not my interpretation. At least not at first. Did Superiorism arise because the Europeans (and here I use the label Europeans intentionally) are essentially immoral? No, there is no innate wickedness to Europe and its people. Rather, Superiorism took root in Europe because its harsh environment made it a place marked by a hollowing darkness and bitter scarcity.

Prior to the Age of Discovery, large parts of Europe were poor and the quality of life in the continent was low. The cold winters in many of the continent's regions resulted in disorienting agricultural failures, which in turn led to famines and guerrilla wars. During the

Little Ice Age, starting around the fifteenth century, grains would not grow, leading to widespread hunger and increased mortality. There were floods, water-borne diseases, droughts and other natural disasters. It is plausible that Europe's freezing, unlivable climates were a prime contributor to the brutish mindset that many of the people who inhabited the continent had. There were witch-hunts that led to the execution of tens of thousands of women and some men; lynching was frequent, and children were sent off on crusades.

Perhaps it is no wonder, then, that amidst this stark and unforgiving landscape, Europe developed such a bloodthirsty view of human nature, which places the human as master of His destiny, capable of wielding dominion over His environment and any other groups. Europe was constantly desperate for new sources of wealth. Once Europe found such resources outside of its borders, its bleak reality served as a primer for raw and predatory greed.

Yet, that Superiorism became the defining story of Europe doesn't mean that there weren't other conceivable routes. Necessity is not the same as justification. It would have been plausible for Europe to respond differently to the scarcity it faced than with brute violence, and for that response to have consequently shaped world history in a different manner. In fact, Europe contains some of the movements, ideas and people that have most powerfully challenged and resisted Superiorism. Instead, tragically, the suffering and destitution that drove Europe to enact some of the most toxic acts of human history now plagues vast parts of the world that Europe expeditiously impoverished.

By the time Europe encountered other continents and peoples, Superiorism was already so interwoven with Europe's identity that there was no other way for Europe to approach them than with a grim logic. By contrast, the regions of the world whose land Europe entered, and went on to plunder, were ensnared in a sequence of events which, unless they too had been shaped at core by the logic of Superiorism, there simply would have been no way for them to prepare for.

We are now, thankfully, living in times when growing numbers of people are awakening to the biased and destructive nature of the premises of Superiorism and seeking out new social narratives. They are turning away from a materialist way of thinking that is conducive to the possession, domination and control of matter – be it territory, land, natural resources, buildings, cities, art, technology, political institutions, armies, weapons, bodies, minds, objects, animals, plants, seas, or trees. More people are rejecting a worldview where the metaphorical sandcastles, rather than the sandbox itself, constitute reality. Superiorism is looking at Superiorism in the mirror and, for the first time since its inception, it does not necessarily like what it sees.

Today's markers of status are often practices that revert Superiorism, where the opposite was once true. More individuals and institutions are nurturing a worldview where, in contrast to Superiorism, difference is insightful, where hierarchies are undesirable, where violence is not acceptable, and where rationality is not corrupted to justify destruction. Celebrities who once flaunted their wealth now boast about their charitable contributions. Men, who like Don Juan used to brag about their seduction skills, now read bell hooks and intersectional feminism. Powerful white individuals embrace inclusivity rather than exclusivity. Even the conservative class frames their traditional beliefs as contributing to the greater good, rather than as expressions of allegedly meritocratic entitlement. The wealthiest people, their corporations and foundations are ever-increasingly engaged in some form of social philanthropy. In fact, those who don't object to Superiorism, of whichever manifestation, are more and more seen as outcasts.

Such societal developments, where values once seen as radical and militant are now not only acknowledged but celebrated, indicate a positive transformation in broader society. Yet, hope unchallenged is wishful thinking, which is antithetical to change.

A legacy as institutionalised as Superiorism has anticipated its destruction. It has planted appropriate preventative measures to its annihilation. Superiorism is still enacted out of a sense of fear and desperation. It is a trickster. Those who oppose Superiorism must therefore learn to spot its tricks, and to see through the illusion before it catches. We ought to ask: what does Superiorism mutate into when challenged?

3.

The Trickster Dualism

Traveller do not shrink from them, or seek to vanquish them. Let them haunt you, steal from you, deceive you, and unsettle you, for the trickster brings gifts deeper than safe arrival, wider than homecomings, and finer than destinations. Cast a stone in honour of her/his presence; pay homage to these emissaries of transience. And as you cross the boundaries, you might notice that it isn't you that has done the travelling at all, but the very nature of things.
— Bayo Akomolafe[1]

One day, I found myself watching the slate-grey water of the Atlantic swelling back and forth against the coast of Lagos, as though Earth were in labour. I have stood by the shores of many seas but only in Africa does the water strike me as a feature of simultaneous beauty and horror. Gazing out towards the demarcation between water and sand that marks Nigeria's boundary, I had the disorienting sense that rather than the outline of Africa, I was witnessing the makings of Europe. After all, it is Europe that named this outline Africa and, in so doing, drew an image of Africa that its people can neither reconcile with, nor escape.

The 'inescapable' Africa that I am speaking of is not, strictly speaking, the actual continent, which countless Africans do not want to leave, and which they are happy and proud to call home. Rather, I am referring to a narrative that spans into the deep and oceanic mirror of Africa like a *mise en abyme*, as two mirrors facing each other, so when you stand between them and look you see yourself reflected repeatedly ad infinitum – like a picture inside another picture, inside another picture, and so on, in a never-ending tunnel of frames. Even those Africans who literally escape the landmass that is Africa, often as refugees risking their lives in the tides, find that the narrative that accompanied Africa's inception has also followed them beyond place and time, swelling, like the ocean, into their lives.

When Africans first encountered themselves as Africans, they simultaneously gazed into this infinite mirror and abruptly found themselves as Other. Whatever it meant to be African was not, initially, their story to tell. In the story of Africa, they had no voice, only silence. To speak about this Africa that was theirs but also not theirs, they had to pay a weighty and often incriminating price. They had to accept a tongue that was alien, a foreign script about themselves, and dissociate with whatever else they knew to be true about who they were and where they came from. Paradoxically, the more they dissociated from their indigenous ways and developed an alienated sense of identity, the more they unwittingly became African; for the inception of Africanness required only one set parameter: Otherness.

Africa, as we think of it today, was conjured adventitiously, by people like the first Chancellor of the German Empire, Otto von Bismarck, and the colonial Prime Minister of the Cape Colony, Cecil Rhodes, and the German philosopher, Georg Wilhelm Friedrich Hegel. Its narrative was enacted and crafted with a notably pejorative character. James Hunt, the president of the Anthropological Society of London, in his unbearable 1863 book *On the Negro's Place in Nature* – where he examined the alleged inferiority of Africans down to their bones, teeth, hair, heels, every last detail – wrote: 'the Negro is inferior intellectually to the European ...[and] can only be humanised and civilised by Europeans. The analogies,' he said, 'are far more numerous between the Negro and apes, than between the European and apes.'[2]

Hunt was far from alone with his reckless postulations. But there were some Europeans who viewed Africa as a place of magnificence. For example, some of the first Portuguese who arrived on the continent were in such awe of the culture they encountered that they recruited Africans to share their knowledge with their kings.[3]

Whichever angle they took, Europe reduced Africa to a conundrum. Africa's people were something to be gawked at and something to be deciphered. Sometimes, they were observed in awe, at other times with disdain. Some Europeans found them striking, others appalling. Africa was split apart, divided and broken into pieces.

The contrasting sentiments of fascination and condescension still shape the continent's narrative today. Every myth about Africa has an equally pervasive counter-myth: it is viewed as the cradle of humanity, but also as a place that has not contributed to human development. Africa is ancestral, but also outside of history. Africa is mystical and spiritual but also earthy and simplistic. It is intermittently strong, weak, sometimes familiar, and yet always Other.

To be African is, consequently, to traverse dichotomies. It is to come from the land of 'double-edged swords', 'challenges and opportunities', 'promises and perils'. It is to dodge conversations about the continent in non-African environments (at times even in them), knowing how likely it is that the discussion they will be characterised by sensational absolutisms and extreme generalisations. Whether it is a new technology such as AI, a global movement such as Me Too, a scholarly field like philosophy, a social media app like TikTok, or a health discovery like the Covid-19 vaccine, once it reaches Africa – literally or figuratively – the opposite tends to become its defining characteristic. Will the new thing be a challenge, or an opportunity for Africa? Will it save, or destroy Africa? Will Africans contribute to it or 'import' it from Europe? The continent is a kind of Rorschach test about whether a phenomenon is a saviour or a villain, or a measure of the continent's progress or backwardness. For example, when discussed in relation to Africa, AI is either devastatingly destructive or promisingly impactful. On the one hand (a phrase which is often used to convey the dichotomous nature of everything Africa-related), with its deep fakes and privacy compromises, AI poses a threat to stability and peace in Africa. In a region already burdened by conflicts and violence, AI is 'certain' to be weaponised for spreading misinformation. Also, with Western companies at the helm, AI exacerbates negative biases and discrimination towards Africans. And with men as the major developers of AI, it further marginalises African women and hinders an already teetering path towards gender equality. AI systems are, in short, bad news for Africa.

But hey, on the other hand, they aren't! Rather, AI promises Africa opportunities without which it would crumble into annihilation. After all, the continent needs rapid development and what better technology than AI to develop education, agriculture, healthcare, transportation. In addition, AI in Africa can be used to preserve the continent's rich culture, and its natural resources. AI is possibly the best thing that could happen to Africa.

The reflex to neatly classify African affairs into opposing categories obfuscates the fact that every society has opportunities, challenges, promises, perils – the one hands, and the others. AI, to stay with the example, has the potential to disrupt jobs everywhere; algorithmic biases are problems in all societies, as are the threats to peaceful and democratic civic structures, and it is hardly the case that there is gender equality in engineering and technology in any continent. In Silicon Valley, the global hub of innovation, half of startups have no women on their leadership teams.[4]

So why is the African narrative shaped by extreme dichotomous and binary, either/or, 'good' or 'evil' thinking?

To respond to this question, I first need to clarify how I use the terms 'dichotomy' and 'binary', which we tend to use interchangeably, however they are not the same. Think of the notions hot and cold. It is a dichotomy to state that Africa is hot, and Europe is cold. Of course, this is not entirely true: Africa is cold sometimes and Europe is seasonally hot. But most of Europe experiences varying degrees of chilly weather and the vast part of Africa experiences a largely hot climate. There is nothing inherently troubling about a dichotomy per se.

If, however, you were to add a value judgement and state that Africans are 'dirty' because Africa is hot and Europeans are 'clean' because Europe is cold, then you would be making a binary statement. This particular binary opinion about cleanliness in Europe vs a lack of hygiene in Africa is one that I've come across on several occasions, and it never fails to remind me of exactly how ignorant binary thinking is. The point I am making is that binaries are simplistic and often prejudiced adaptations of a dichotomy.

However, despite their irksome simple-mindedness, even binary statements are not the ultimate hazard. A binary is not necessarily entangled with power, and so its damage is not systemic or institutionalised. On some level, the binary harms the person who sees the world through an either/or lens more than it harms the subject of their narrow-mindedness. Their arbitrary but privileged identity may bestow them with some power, but when it comes to the opportunity to be expanded and stretched by the world – the richest opportunity life bestows anyone – they hold the shorter end of the stick.

It is another notion, also easily confusable with dichotomies and binaries, that goes a step further to infuse the binary with hierarchical power – to institutionalise it. This notion is dualisms.

The conventional understanding of dualisms is that they represent a worldview where two things are together seen to constitute a whole. From a dualist standpoint, all there is to understand about a phenomenon can be broken down into two clear and contrasting pairs of opposites – say, the masculine and feminine, heaven and hell, or life and death. The little boy in the previous chapter is a dualist. He has is a limited world in which there are either sandcastles or no sandcastles.

But even more so, the boy's is a world where that dualist view empowers him with the status of a king. Power dynamics are not a typical concern of the non/dualist debate, but from a feminist perspective it is precisely the contention with power that makes dualisms so destructive. In the example about cold and hot weather contrasts, the dualism would postulate in absolute terms that not only is Africa hot and dirty, but that Africa should, therefore, be the loser in the race. If this formula sounds familiar, and to be clear this example is an artificial one, it is because it mirrors the premise of Superiorism.

The dualism is, indeed, the 'Master Idea' of Superiorism. Dichotomies and binaries are primordial and exist in cultures, but the dualism as I have defined it above, is a companion to Superiorism. Substitute 'hot' and 'cold' with other attributes such as 'developed' and 'undeveloped', 'educated' and 'non-educated', 'wealthy' and 'poor', and then think of how these dichotomies infer power in relation to Africa. Of course, the power relationship connoted by dualisms, or Superiorism for that matter, is not exclusive to the Europe–Africa relationship, but it has a particularly defined nature in relation to the two continents. Consider the wealthy vs poor dualism, for example. It is not simply that there is a dichotomy between the state of wealth and the state of poverty. There is, although as with most dichotomies, there are nuances. Nor does the trouble straightforwardly start when you apply binary thinking to the wealthy/poor dichotomy. Sure, there are people who narrow-mindedly perceive a wealthy person (or country, region, city, etc.) as better than a poor person (or country, region, city, etc.). In their limited view, a wealthy person might be better than a poor person because they see them as hard working and view the poor person as lazy. Of course, what is lazy is such all-or-nothing thinking! Still, although binary thinking is frustratingly myopic, it's ultimately the dualism that engraves oppression into the split. Europe is not only wealthier than Africa, the dualist says; it is also therefore better and deserving of more wealth. Not only that, but institutions also that configure assets and resources should for this reason serve the interests of Europe first.

The dualism, like the binary it is derived from, does not grapple with spectrums, complexities and paradoxes. It does not complicate what it means to be rich or poor in the first place. Are poverty and wealth material or experiential? What role does luck play in a person's wealth, and a person's misfortune in poverty? It also doesn't pay attention to cause and effect, or it would know that Europe's wealth is contingent on the impoverishment of Africa. The famine and poverty that existed in Europe before it exploited other continents is now what those continents experience as a reversed result of Europe's extracting of their resources.

The Self and the Other

If the 'Master Idea' of Superiorism is the dualism, then the 'Master Dualism' of all dualisms is 'the Self and the Other'. This dualism was popularised by Hegel in *The Phenomenology of Spirit* (1807) where he developed his popular 'Master–Slave' dialectic, which rippled into multiple schools of thought, including postcolonial thought, Marxism and feminism. Hegel, of course, did not champion anti- colonial or anti-patriarchal ways of thinking. It was the Martinique thinker Frantz Fanon who popularised a version of 'the Self and the Other' in postcolonial studies to infer 'the Coloniser and the Colonised', and it was Simone de Beauvoir who famously applied the polarisation to gender, and who suggested that: 'He is the Subject, he is the Absolute – she is the Other.'[5]

You might be thinking that the leading dualistic divide of Superiorism should not be 'the Self and Other' but rather 'the Superior and Inferior'. The formula might then go as follows: a wealthy person is superior to a poor person, who thus is inferior. But that would be tautological, as superiority and inferiority are already embedded in the nature of dualisms that I have described so far. Conversely, the Self and Other require a dualistic value judgement before conveying a hierarchy of superiority and inferiority.

You can superimpose the dualist power dynamic that informs the relationship between the Self and the Other onto all the other binary dichotomies that have shaped the modern world: Man and Nature, Masculine and Feminine, Science and Emotions, Public and Private, Master and Slave, Coloniser and Colonised, etc. 'Man' is conflated with the rational Self and viewed not only as separate but also as better than 'Nature', which then becomes Other. The 'Masculine' is not only distinct from the 'Feminine', but also equated to the subjective Self, making the Feminine, Other.

People take dualisms seriously because they give the illusion of complementarity – and complementarity is a quality that humans are drawn to. Yet the truth is that the Self and the Other, and all its mutations, not only are not complementary, but they are also not even real. Dualisms are constructs. In fact, I would argue that dualisms underlie the notion 'social constructs', the theory that some ideas, concepts, or phenomena are created and maintained by society, rather than being inherent in nature. Consider a phenomenon that may typically be referred to as a social construct, such as 'gender'. If it weren't for the fact of the dualism 'women and men' – and recall that by dualism I don't mean dichotomy or binary but rather the power infused into them – then there would be no need to discuss gender in the way that we do, as a construct enmeshed in a battle for power.

Across the world are knowledge paradigms that are more searching and shifting. Yoruba philosophy, for example, traditionally denounces separation. Instead, it propagates 'a world in which animals, birds, trees, the entire creation is looked at as our own brothers and sisters'.[6] It also does not prescribe any form of absolutism. In Yoruba cosmology, rigid stereotypes are seen as anti-intellectual because everything is always changing. This attitude is well encapsulated in a simple proverb: 'Wisdom this year is folly next year.'[7] There is a recognition of dualisms without a corresponding impulse to reduce knowledge into the prism of an 'either/or' mindset. Goodness and evil are inseparable, for instance. There is even a divinity that protects non-dualism: 'Eshu Elegbara, *onile orita*', ('Eshu, the powerful one, owner of the crossroads'). Eshu is 'The Trickster', the progenitor of paradox, whose role is to protect and nurture the crossroads where decisions and actions are never straightforward. Eshu baffles us, sometimes in ways that push our buttons. In a story from the Yoruba pantheon shared by the prolific and prophetic philosopher Bayo Akomolafe, rather than resist the violent enslavers – as the other divinities did – Eshu travelled with the captives to the New World, 'living in the lower decks of the ships ... using the epistemologies of the coloniser, Eshu eats the slave ship, eats the shore, and climbs into the body of the slave driver. There are no traumatic binaries here: no victim and no perpetrator.'[8]

To be sure, dualisms are not straightforwardly static either. They travel spatiotemporally. The Other is not only black African, and the Self is not always white European. The relational pattern between the Self and the Other exists between ethnicities, identities and entities. It exists among different groups of people of colour and between humans and other animals. What never changes, as far as dualisms go, is the asymmetrical power dynamic between the pair.

I grew up in a part of the world called the 'Third World', which later was dubbed the 'Developing World'. Then I also lived in 'Sub-Saharan Africa'. At one point, the place I inhabited was named 'Postcolonial Africa'. The labels may change, but whichever socioeconomic neologism you use, the fact remains that they all signify the same thing: occupation, exploitation, neoliberalism, militarism, neo-imperialism, and the consequent suffering that these paradigms cause.

I have now moved from this country of multiple names, and the name has changed too, to the 'Global South', the popular terminology used to describe one of the uneven two blocs that make up the whole today. Although the phrases are useful when it comes to describing geopolitical contexts and identifying instructive relationships such as 'South–South Cooperation', where countries in Africa, Latin America, Asia and the Middle East circumvent dominant nations in economic trade, the 'Global North' and the 'Global South' also are transpositions of the dualistic Self/Other polarity. After all, there are many countries and regions that don't fit into the Global North or Global South boxes. Is China in the Global North or Global South? What about Japan, or some of the Caribbean Islands? Furthermore, serious thinking today is oversaturated with technocratic language, and lacking in more profound and complex ways of understanding our world. The popularity of the Global South and Global North dualism is connected to the established domination of policy-speak, bureaucratese and technical language, precisely because these are the institutions that tend to be infused with dualist thinking.

A non-dualist and more hope-inducing term for those regions (Africa, Latin America, Asia and the Middle East) could be 'Places of Colour' (to riff off 'People of Colour'). This they vibrantly are! Each of these continents are characterised by a plethora of colourful features – their striking landscapes, lively markets, electric street life, hypnotic art and warm, welcoming communities.

As a non-dualist feminist, I inhabit and view society and knowledge through a lens that is pluralist in all senses – hybrid, cosmopolitan, collaborative, genre-crossing, border-crossing, synthesising, non-divisive and fluid. This is true not only in this book, but generally in life. These sensibilities influence my life choices, from the mundane to the intimate and the spiritual, and my writerly imagination is therefore similarly drawn to stitching worlds together – mythology and science, psychology and history, creation stories and evolutionary theory. I am not speaking of interdisciplinarity, a notion which is often invoked to develop a holistic understanding of a topic by addressing a problem through various disciplines, but which is often unable to meet these expectations because it emphasises the idea of 'disciplines', an idea informed by a worldview of neat categorisation.

Nor, per se, is it transdisciplinary – that is, transcending or going beyond disciplinary thinking (which is indeed a holistic and integrative approach that involves groups from various fields and backgrounds collaborating to transcend disciplinary boundaries). But this incentive still inadvertently centres the 'disciplines'. Rather, you could refer to my approach as the way of Nature, or what I call 'Sensuous Knowledge'. It is messier; more disobedient, and 'epistemically polyamorous'. (Thank you to my friend and colleague, the philosopher Jonathan Rowson, for this phrase describing 'Sensuous Knowledge'.) It is an approach that is multi-perspectival, branching not only into disciplines but also experiences, senses, textures and environments. It is a mindset that derives more of the polymath than the expert, more of the artist than the scientist, and more of the poet than the reporter. I am not saying that experts, scientists and reporters, for example, are not important roles in society. That would be ludicrous.

It is possible, however, for individuals and groups in such professions to also be artistic, creative, etc.; you can approach science with a poetic disposition, like the marine biologist and environmentalist, Rachel Carson, or the physicist, Carlo Rovelli. But you can also approach poetry 'scientifically' in terms of rhyme, metre, length, etc. A sonnet is, for instance, a fourteen-line poem typically written in iambic pentameter. A traditional haiku follows a 5–7–5 syllable pattern. These nuances don't compromise the scientific work of Carson or Rovelli, or the poetic allure of sonnets and haikus. What I am conjuring is a disposition, an inclination to pursue knowledge with a contemplation of the known and an eye towards the unknown. To see that knowledge is not only orderly stacked; it is also stretched, fugitive, wild and alive.

When seen from this prism, dualisms are not only limited, but they are also banal. There is one dualism, however, that has the depth and breadth required for deeper knowing, namely: 'the Observer and the Observed'.

Except the Observer and the Observed are not really a dualist pair. They appear to be so on the surface, but in truth they are neither dichotomous, binary nor dualist. For one, the Observer can only know itself through observation, which concurrently makes it the Observed. Someone, or something, must also see the Observed, which means it is an Observer, too, watching whoever or whatever is watching them. This is why the Observer and the Observed 'dualism' exposes the deceptive nature of the Self/Other illusion by blurring the sense of separation that informs the power relationship between the Self and the Other. There is an Observer and an Observer within the Self, as well as within the Other. If the Observer and the Observed are the same, so are all the variations of the Self and the Other. This is why I call 'the Observer and the Observed' dualism a 'Trickster Dualism'. It is a dualism from the crossroads, or from Eshu.

A scene from Céline Sciamma's stunning film *Portrait of a Lady on Fire* helps explain the seamless relationship between observing and being observed further. The movie tells the story of Marianne, a young female painter, who in eighteenth-century France is commissioned to paint a wedding portrait of Héloïse, a young woman who has just left the convent. But Héloïse does not want to get married and refuses to pose for the portrait, and Marianne must paint her in secret. Marianne decides to observe Héloïse by day and to paint her at night. An erotic energy builds between the two women, as Marianne spends time watching Héloïse – one that the viewer assumes is made from their designated roles: Marianne as Observer and Héloïse as Observed. However, in the scene that I am referring to, Héloïse has allowed Marianne to paint her. The atmosphere is charged with sexual desire when Marianne, flirtatiously if smugly, reveals to Héloïse how she perceives her. She describes Héloïse's mannerisms and habits in detail, down to how she bites her lip and looks away when she wants to smile. Rather than become self-conscious, Héloïse penetratingly responds: 'When you're observing me, who do you think I'm observing?'[9]

The scene speaks to a revelatory moment when the Self recognises that it also is the Other to another Self.

This pattern is infinite and repeating: Selfother, Otherself, Selfother, Otherself. And this revelation, if one has it, is what leads to an end to thinking in dualistic ways, and to engaging in true dialogue. But such moments are rare because the dissolution of the Self would inherently mean the undoing of the Other. Like the fates of two trees that have intergrown inseparably, the Self cannot simply discard the Other without facing its own demise.

If the relationship between Europe and Africa were interpreted through the prism of the Observer and the Observed, rather than the Self and the Other, what would the relationship look like? Who would be the Observer and who would be the Observed? The answer is not straightforward. Don't extrapolate what may seem an obvious answer based on the current algorithm of the Self and the Other. If you look deeply at this paradox, you will see that everything about the relationship between the two continents would change.

4.

Ally Fever

The most important part of teaching = to teach what it is to know.

— Simone Weil[1]

Teacher and Student

Colonisation is never 'simply' occupation and the theft of land. The coloniser must also assume control of the interiority of the colonised. He must enter those chambers of the soul where power and agency are bolstered and transform them into bewilderment and mistrust. As the South African revolutionary and writer Steve Biko is attributed with saying: 'The greatest weapon in the hand of the oppressor is the mind of the oppressed.'[2]

The role of the teacher in ancient African cosmologies is a reciprocal one. Before the introduction of the Western school system, the teacher was someone whose talent to elucidate was acknowledged by others in the community before they assumed the role of an educator.[3] For example, in the Yoruba repository of practices and beliefs known as Ifa, the role of a Babalawo or Iyanifa are first bestowed after more than a dozen years of training. The first five years of training are spent learning plant medicine and assisting the teacher. Then the Babalawos and Iyanifas begin the years-long journey of learning the 256 *Odu* (the history, culture, medicine, mythology, philosophy, great poems, etc. of the Yoruba people) by heart, their verses, stories and all their implications. At this point Babalawos and Iyanifas become not simply 'priests' and 'priestesses', as these roles are translated into English, but scholars and custodians of the compassionate Ifa tradition.[4]

Indigenous knowledge is not always better than Western knowledge. It can be overly pious and too focused on rules. It can also be judgemental and essentialist. It can be patriarchal, as we will see later. But if one can maintain discernment and an independent mind, then indigenous and traditional knowledge can offer a pure form of wisdom that is hard to find in modern Western and dominant thinking. There is no methodical strategy to discerning when you encounter this wisdom. We intuitively know when a teacher (whether formal or informal) adds value to our individual and collective existence. That intuitive discernment is of great worth in times when multiple competing forces seek our attention.

There are elements of these types of instinctive teaching also in modern society, when teaching is seen, among other things, as a 'confrontation with our past selves', to quote the philosopher Amia Srinivasan.[5] Teaching in this sense is reciprocal, humbling and sympathetic, enriching both teacher and student. But increasingly, the teacher role is instead facilitated through bureaucratic course materials, market forces, networks and privileges. Those teachers who burn with the passion for knowledge dissemination are reduced to being administrative servants. Teachers (be they schoolteachers, gurus, priests, or any other such authority figures) have in many instances become the very problem obscuring our individual and collective edification.

One of the most deleterious dualisms that marks the relationship between Africa and Europe concerns the role of the Teacher and the Student. In this dualism, the Teacher is the archetype of an all-knowing authority figure. They are pontifical and pretentious, with an exaggerated perception of their positive qualities and a conceitedly moralistic and sermonising attitude. Crucially, the power held by this archetypical Teacher is such that, no matter the topic taught, the Teacher is, above all, a moral authority figure and their goal is not simply to teach the Student maths, sports, science, you name it, but also how to behave and what values to hold in life. For centuries, Europe seized power over Africa by placing itself in the role of this Teacher.

Note that I capitalise Teacher and Student. By Teacher, I don't here mean the role of actual professional teachers in modern educational institutions. The Teacher role I am referring to is an archetype.

Archetypes can be traced back to Plato, who believed that archetypes (or 'forms' as he called them), are ideas underlying all phenomenal appearances. Even if archetypes are 'only' ideas or constructs, Plato reasoned, they are as real as everything else in our phenomenal world because they influence concrete actions. His view was co-signed by later developers of archetypes such as René Descartes, who described an archetype as a 'perception belonging to the divine mind', or as John Locke described them, 'real beings'. But it was the Swiss psychoanalyst Carl Jung who eventually developed archetypes as we think of them today. Jung argued that archetypes followed primordial themes and images (e.g., the Mother, the Hero or the Shadow) that lie deep within the unconscious mind. He asserted that these archetypes could be found across all temporalities, and that they influence both the mental and the physical world in both individual and collective ways.

The imposition of the Teacher/Student dualism was an accomplice to colonisation in Africa. In the Teacher/Student dualism, the corresponding Student archetype with a capital 'S' is not the critically thinking, interested and curious student but rather the innocent, naive and persistently inferior student. It is the lazy student who, deep down inside, can feasibly think for themselves but whom circumstances have rendered deferential and meek. When Europe colonised Africa, its administrators, soldiers and missionaries stereotypically took on the role of the Teacher archetype to 'educate' the African 'Student'. The goal of Europe's archetypal Teacher in Africa was to instil a mindset of Superiorism, which enshrined Europe's values as the pinnacle of civilisation and denigrated African cultures and knowledge systems.

The academic challenges that the continent faces are connected to a psychological infrastructure that is connected to the historical subjugation of African minds. Societal problems such as inequality, poverty, exploitation, imperialism, violence and war are all entangled with the fundamental issue of dualistic education.

Dismayingly, the pedagogy designed to reshape the African worldview, aligning it with European ideals and practices while dismissing African scholarly traditions, is still evident today. Across the continent, some of its most desired schools promise their students and their parents, a 'strictly British education' (or French, American, etc.). The topics taught in these schools carry a clear Western emphasis; English and French are prioritised over local languages, flutes over percussion; Islam and Christianity over indigenous spiritual systems. These colonist educational curricula may now be sprinkled with nuggets of African cultural heritage but the emphasis on British (or French, American, etc.) education shows the continued entrenchment in the Teacher/Student dualism.

But in a curious twist of events, the Self has reversed a crucial element. Rather than the lead the dance, the archetypal Self now wishes to be instructed. In the latest iteration of the Teacher/Student dualism in the social imaginary, the Self has unexpectedly taken the role of the Student. The Other is thus necessarily the Teacher, for in the dualist waltz, the Self is always dancing in the direction that the Other is not. The Other is always the antithesis of the Self. If the Self is sanctified, then the Other is barbaric. If the Self is rational, then the Other is emotional. If the Self perceives itself as advanced, it projects an image of the primitive onto the Other. And if the Self is the Teacher, then the Other is necessarily the Student. Whatever the shape, the Self leads the dance.

In these times, the Self is rescinding the Teacher role to increasingly assume the role of the Student, and specifically the doe-eyed and enthusiastic Student -prepared to studiously educate themselves about their malevolence and culpability in the world. Where the Self once was unwilling to listen to the Other's point of view, the Self has now fashioned itself so that it desires to be educated precisely about the preoccupations and concerns of the Other. It wants to be taught how to be conscientious of its role in creating an unjust world, and how to fight against those injustices. This Self wants to understand the preoccupations and concerns of the Other.

This is a positive development in many ways, but there is an aspect of the Self-as-Student archetype that is off-kilter. Insofar as Students go, this Student does not 'only' want to learn but also to atone. The problem is that atonement is the act of the one with power, and this minor detail renders the Self's studentship contradictory. The even bigger problem is what the contradiction reveals: the Self still wants to impart morals and values, even while assuming the Student role. To conceal this desire, the Self-as-Student must justify being the Student and the simultaneous subject of atonement. It needs a device that can seamlessly bring studentship and atonement together without a sense of compromise. This device is 'allyship'.

Allyship, the *idée fixe* of our times, comes in as the perfect vehicle to synthesise the dialectical relationship of student and wrongdoer. It allows the Self-as-Student to be trained and educated about diversity, equity, inclusion, privilege, biases, and so on, while simultaneously making amends for past wrongdoings. It is a secularised rendering of the biblical idea that, if only one confesses their sins, then God too will respond with faith and righteousness. Replace the wish for forgiveness with the idea of 'being educated', and the Student becomes akin to the Bible's King Saul, whose pleas for forgiveness from God were eventually self-deceiving attempts to avoid facing his fears of insufficiency in the eyes of the Almighty. Allyship offers a pathway for those in positions of historical power to both educate themselves and maintain a position of relevance and atone for Superiorism.

Are Liberals Really the Problem?

Before I further address the allyship worldview, a few words on white liberals, or the adjacent 'contemporary left', who are the most likely to consider themselves 'allies'. It may seem that I am suggesting that this group is the primary opponent of progress for Africans, or black and brown people around the world, for that matter.

This isn't the case; white liberals have, in many instances, been the leading opponents of those who both directly and obliquely deny the humanity of non-whites. This point is significant to make in times when racially motivated, ultra-conservative sentiment is on the rise. That my criticism of allyship could also be seen as a critique of liberal-left patterns of behaviour rather than those of conservatives or, for that matter, the far right, is to do with the adjacency of white liberalism to the questions that are of concern to African feminists. Issues and tropes that are related to whiteness – such as the 'white saviour', globalisation, human rights, privilege, entitlement, enlightenment and universalism, to give a few examples – are bound with liberalism, as well as with colonialism and patriarchy. Unfortunately.

In the same way that African feminism must develop a critique of the distinctive ways that male-dominant behavioural patterns shape Africa because such masculinist ideals are in close proximity – and contention – to the African feminist cause, it is also essential for an African feminist political philosophy to scrutinise the adjacent ideological underpinnings of white liberalism and how these set the foundation of the world in which African feminists live. Moreover, to the extent that we are talking about actual white people who are liberals rather than liberal ideology, they constitute a group with a thoroughgoing and longstanding relationship with the continent. They are charity workers, expatriates, repatriates, journalists, philanthropists, Africanist scholars, the sons and daughters of administrators, colonialists and 'pseudo-humanists', about whom Aimé Césaire said: 'This is the great thing that I hold against pseudo-humanism: that for too long it has diminished the rights of man, that is the concept of those rights has been – and still is – narrow and fragmentary, incomplete and biased and, all things considered, sordidly racist.'[6]

On the other hand, white people who harbour blatantly racist views about black Africans don't typically have much to do with the continent except in roles such as religious proselytisers, tourists, in the military or security services, or as businesspeople. Members of groups such as these certainly shape the outcomes of politics and business in Africa, and warrant analysis and criticism where it is due. But they are not as directly entangled in shaping the continent's perception in the social imaginary, precisely because they don't believe that Africa has anything of philosophical value to offer in the first place. The Africa they interact with is the dark, backward, regressive and exotic place crafted in the social imaginary of previous centuries, and they see no need to upgrade that story. Arguably, when it comes to narratives that shape our perceptions, there is also a lesser need for Africans to expend substantial amounts of intellectual energy countering blatant biases, therefore. But for those, usually liberal, Westerners who entertain the idea that Africa – like other parts of the world – is at the very least a place in evolution, Africa plays a *more* significant role in the shaping of the world. I emphasise the word 'more', as it is not the case that Africa plays an essential role in this context either. But to the extent that liberal Westerners engage with Africa as a shaper of knowledge and ideas, understanding the underpinning power dynamics is essential.

How Can I Be a Better Ally?

Before its renovation into a social justice term, 'ally' was – and still is – used to describe the forming of treaties, leagues, confederations and the military affairs of nation states. For example, NATO states are allies; during the Second World War, the United States, Britain, France, Canada and China were allies; the Church and the State can be allies.

As a term connoting solidarity, whether with the feminist movements, the racial justice movements, the LGBTQI movements, the anti-war movements, the immigrant rights, anti-poverty, or pro-justice movements, 'ally' still imports some of its political-military sensibility especially because it prevents the kind of intimate engagement with the cause it is allied with.

What 'the Other' needs, frankly, is not 'allies' but bona fide feminists, anti-racists, anti-poverty activists, etc. Of course, the reason that this does/will not happen is that, per definition, an ally's goal is not to end patriarchy, racism, homophobia, poverty, or other social ills but rather to support those wishing to end patriarchy, racism, homophobia, poverty, or other social ills. Much like *noblesse oblige* – the duty to behave responsibly that 'justifies' aristocratic privilege – an ally's biggest concern is their role as an ally.

As such, the ally informs a modern reiteration of the Teacher and Student, or Self and Other dualisms even though it now positions itself more humbly in the passenger seat, as Student, so that it can atone for past crimes.

I do not mean to completely dismiss efforts to support social justice causes or to say that one cannot teach people how to change for the better. A part of the constituted Self genuinely yearns for virtue and knowledge. Some of the most conscientious people I have met and learned from consider themselves to be allies. I also don't believe that *individuals* should pay for the sins of their ancestors. Whether we are born into privilege or disadvantage is beyond anyone's control. What should be of general concern, however, are the power dynamics that are repeated by dualistic thinking. If the reverse Student and Teacher are still the result of dualistic thought, they are merely a reinvention of the wheel of power. An actual act of solidarity is to *see* the power dynamics that create oppression, violence and confusion, and act from that insight.

That the reversed archetypal roles of Teacher and Student are replicas of the same long-held power dynamics becomes apparent when one refuses to embody them. For instance, it is now common for people to try to prompt a deeper conversation with me – and I presume that this is the experience of other black women – with the innocent-seeming but loaded question: 'How can I be a better ally?', or a variation thereof.

'How can I be a better ally?' is the prompt that lets me know that someone is offering me the 'opportunity' to be the Teacher (or in contemporary parlance, 'the educator'), to enlighten a 'naive and unassuming' white person about their biases and myopias. In such an instance, it is expected that I not only automatically accept the offer to educate but relish doing so. After all, why would anyone who belongs to a marginalised group not take advantage of the sudden vulnerability of the oppressor? Why would any person of colour not take pleasure in educating privileged white elites about their biases? Why would I not want to be the archetypal, powerful Teacher?

Well, perhaps because I have other preoccupations. Or, because I am tired of dancing the dualist waltz and I'm flowing with a different rhythm altogether. Maybe I don't want to exhaust my limited energy to this 'Ally Fever'.

What those infected by Ally Fever don't seem to understand is that in offering me the opportunity to assume the role of Teacher, they are also inviting me to revisit the pain and suffering that racialised oppression has caused, and worse, to then also relieve them of shame and guilt. Black people's automatic impulse to educate white people – for instance through the wide-spread diversity, equality and inclusion (DEI) initiatives that have sprung up since the 2020 Black Lives Matter protests – troubles me, not because teaching people how to be better individuals in the world is wrong, but because there is a difference between being an educator who teaches out of a place of freedom and being an educator who still operates within the dualist pairing of Teacher and Student. This reverse Teacher role prevents the minoritised person(s) from doing the same thing that the Self has always prevented the Other from doing – introspecting and having the agency of an inner world. If my racial identity confers upon me a greater understanding of race than a white person's, then it is not an expertise which I wish to reduce to an administrative methodology. When I awkwardly refrain from responding to the question: 'How can I be a better ally?', and thus from assuming the role of Teacher, then allyship reverts to its combative etymological origins – which essentially is a dissatisfaction with my performance of race, which essentially is a return to racism.

But now I am contradicting myself. I started this chapter by describing how teachers are chosen, and how that is a beautiful practice. Why, then, won't I apply the same graciousness to 'allies' choosing me as a teacher? Because it is not me whom they are appointing. It is my skin colour, my gender, my heritage.

In the reversed Teacher position, the Other may access more institutional, economic and symbolical power than history ever permitted. They may educate 'allies' on their biases and blind spots in initiatives, workshops, courses, YouTube tutorials, podcasts, you name it. To be clear, I'm all for minoritised groups profiting from this industry, and I don't believe it is cynical to do so. But we shouldn't deceive ourselves concerning the dominant dualistic thought pattern. The Other continues the trademark behaviour of the Other, namely: to pander to the Self. In his essay 'Black lives matter, But to whom?', Bayo Akomolafe asks us to consider how calls for DEI, or similar notions like 'Black excellence', made him feel some discomfort, like 'wanting a front row seat on the *Titanic*. Or seeking an equal piece of a carcinogenic pie.'[7]

Even after the ally does the workshops, after they memorise the toolkits, and after they've learned, like well-behaved children, what questions are offensive, problematic or triggering, then what? The ally does not eventually grow in rank to become a captain ally or an ally emerita. There is no 'peak' ally. What would seem the most logical outcome is that the ally becomes someone who dissents to the Othering of the Other. And for that, the ally must understand and reject the dualist nature of the Teacher/Student, Educator/Ally roles and explore a non-dualist way of knowing.

5.

The Ghost of Whiteness

If a decent society has been a possibility for at least a very long time, the real problem becomes to explain why humanity did not or perhaps would not want one.

— Zygmunt Bauman[1]

It is that curious feeling you have, as an African, that the psychological explanations for what is happening to you are to be found elsewhere, not around you or in yourself.

— Kopano Ratele[2]

The Negro in America is a kind of madness that manifests itself in white people.

— James Baldwin quoting Walter Hines Page[3]

Far safer, of a midnight meeting
External ghost,
Than an interior confronting
That whiter host.

— Emily Dickinson[4]

I was six years old the first time that I saw a ghost. The sighting happened the day that my best friend Veronica's home help, Gloria, kidnapped me. Veronica and I were just returning from our swimming lesson to her house when Gloria ran to the car shouting 'Mimi! Mimi!' (my nickname). Among the buzzing medley of characters that framed my life, Gloria was relatively central. Veronica and I played together almost daily, and on the occasions that we were at her house, Gloria often featured in our activities, either preventing our mischief from escalating to chaos, or by joining our rambunctious playtime herself by sharing one of the many stories she liked to remember. And so, when she shouted my name, I willingly ran into her arms. But Gloria had other plans, this time, than to play. She planned to kill me.

Unbeknownst to anyone, Gloria's unconcealed fondness for me had developed into an unhealthy obsession. She believed that if she sacrificed me and then became pregnant, I would be reborn as her child, rather than my mother's. She grabbed me and ran to the condo behind my friend's house, where she lived, and where she had prepared for the killing to take place. Despite the machete lying in the centre of the room, amidst other paraphernalia, Gloria proposed that I shouldn't be afraid. She assured me that we would soon be reunited as mother and child, as things were meant to be. Somehow, I summoned a future mature version of myself. One who, when I look back, understood more about the human psyche than six-year-old me actually did, and I began to negotiate with Gloria. I suggested that perhaps we could already be together, that maybe we could leave Lagos and travel to her hometown. Fortunately, this mediation bought just enough time for Veronica's driver to break down the door and rescue me.

Moments later, I was upstairs in the safe familiarity of Veronica's parents' room, staring out of their window. Gloria was now in the courtyard. Or rather, a phantasmal version of Gloria was in the courtyard panting apace like a caged animal. Her typically braided hair was gone, and her bald head was accompanied by an absence, also, of her teeth. Even her clothes had disappeared. All there was left of what appeared to me as her ghost, was a naked and fevered spectacle of a woman speaking in tongues, and her agitated, haunted scream.

I later reasoned that the head tie she wore when she snatched me probably masked her shaved head, and that she could have painted her teeth black, or have removed false teeth that she'd worn all along.

Who knows? The adults that now were in the compound trying to calm her including my parents, would later share that they were equally confounded by her metamorphosis. I am sure that there was some kind of logical explanation to her transformed appearance, but the image of her as an anguished ghost prancing around my friend's courtyard is forever imprinted on my mind. The Gloria incident was, to my parents' dismay, far from the only near-death event I encountered in my life. But this experience is the one, I believe, that has provided fodder for my fascination with ghosts.

Ghosts, I should start by saying, are not spirits. Spirits are entities that have positively completed their mission in this realm and transitioned to what we might call the astral, liminal, or ancestral domain. Conversely, ghosts are restless and vengeful entities that are tethered to the tangible world because they have 'unfinished business' to do. Ghosts, in this context, are resentful, while spirits are at peace. The Ghost in this chapter – the Ghost of Whiteness – is not a spirit; it is distinctly a ghost.

Ghosts, in the above sense, are frequent visitors in literary and philosophical works, such as Toni Morrison's *Beloved*, Jacques Derrida's notion of 'hauntology', Octavia Butler's *Kindred*, and more recently, Naomi Klein's *Doppelganger*, among many others. I'm hardly the first writer to use the metaphor of ghosts to discuss traumas of racism, and what I so far have referred to as Superiorism. However, with a few exceptions, such as the doppelganger gestalt in Klein's book, the spectral figures in literary narratives commonly represent the baggage of historical injustices imposed on *marginalised* communities in a predominantly white society. The ghost 'Beloved' in Morrison's book of the same title, for example, embodies the pain and violence experienced by black women in antebellum America.

The ghost in this chapter diverges from this norm. Instead of embodying the despair or vengeance of the *Other*, this ghost enshrines the anxieties and neuroses of *white* identity.

—

Biologically, what is referred to as whiteness arose approximately 8,000 years ago in human populations that had settled in Europe. To enhance vitamin D synthesis in conditions with little sunlight, the ancestors who migrated to Europe's cold climates adapted by developing pale and amelanated skin.

The application of the term 'white' to this process of evolutionary adaptation is sociopolitically motivated to make a spurious association between the development of pale skin and supremacy. The word 'white' does not describe any biological fact, rather it encapsulates this arbitrary and misappropriated association between evolution, biology, migration, geography and power.

The Ghost of Whiteness is, therefore, also a construct, and does not equate to any inherent qualities of a particular group of people. Consider a culinary analogy: when sugar, flour, eggs and milk are combined and cooked, the result is a pancake. Yet, none of these ingredients constitute a pancake in themselves, just as a person with pale and amelanated skin does not inherently represent whiteness. If you were eating a pancake and said: '*Mm*, this pancake is delicious,' you would mean the pancake and not the eggs. Similarly, when we speak of whiteness and say something along the lines of: 'Whiteness perpetuates injustice', the whiteness in question should be understood as a combination of factors rather than any single race-specific trait.

Insofar that the attributes of Superiorism and the phenotypical traits of Europe's descendants do converge, it is a convergence with a sense of grandiosity so large that it has become an ideological system that manifests as various forms of bigotry – racial, ethnic, nationalistic, socioeconomic, and so on. This institutionalised system that conflates evolutionary phenotype with supremacist power, aka racism, has been substantially analysed and debunked. We've identified and critiqued institutionalised racism in detail, from its inception to the dehumanisation of enslaved people, to scientific racism, to human zoos, to apartheid, to genocide, to discrimination. Yet, despite all the insight, racism continues to shape society in significant ways. I'm inclined to believe we've hit a wall. Illuminating the many modes of racism and how they corrode the social fabric is no longer the enquiry of deep transformation. The more pressing query is the one encapsulated in the Zygmunt Bauman epigraph above, pondering why, despite the apparent ability to do so, humanity has not chosen to establish a 'decent society'. What causes racism to persist even when its supporting anatomy is dissected and discredited?

What interests me here, therefore, is not racism per se. The Ghost of Whiteness is not a semblance of the relationship between biological factors and racialised fantasies of grandiosity. It is not directly a phantom of racism's wickedness, but rather, more complicatedly, it is a psychological emblem of the discordant world that Superiorism creates. The function of the Ghost of Whiteness is not to heal, process or avenge events of the past, as other metaphorical ghosts might do; rather, it prevails to guard the structures of the past by reinventing them in ways that fit the present. The Ghost of Whiteness symbolises the internal conflict to renounce the tenets of Superiorism and the impulse to maintain them. It is a ghost that houses contrasting desires and emotions: shame against smugness, conscience wrestling with power, humility in contention with resentment. The Ghost of Whiteness is both a doula for the death and for the rebirth of white supremacy. It is a residue of systemic deception and a world order that is both in agreement and at odds with its own framing story. Like a radio antenna that picks up the fears and anxieties of the collective mood, the Ghost of Whiteness broadcasts confusion and crisis until it becomes the dominant frequency, burrowing into the listener's memory like a subliminal earworm.

Of course, the significance of the spectre is predominantly engendered by those socialised within a framework that conditions them to be 'white'. We are living through an age where there is both a widespread recognition of injustices that stem from white supremacy and, simultaneously, a persistent and privileged clinging to the epistemic and material structures that have resulted from it. The false ascription between Superiorism and whiteness, which was once a source of pride, now meets the growing dissatisfaction of those to whom the label 'white' applies. Whiteness rings a discomfort in the psychic consciousness like tinnitus. This paradox looms over society, manifesting as a powerful force to simultaneously condemn and uphold. Individuals and groups conditioned as white are those who principally, albeit not solely, feel trapped in this tug-of-war between competing urges to both banish and upkeep the Ghost of Whiteness. As Toni Morrison said, there is something appealing about 'the safety of ghost company'.[5]

Even as they resist the Ghost of Whiteness, people are drawn to it. They are consumed by it. They adopt a paranoid and libidinal practice towards it, monitoring others – who is racist? Are you? You *are*? The scrutiny extends also to people of colour, with a perverse longing for these individuals to express anger at the ghost. The anger of the Other serves as a twisted reassurance to those most haunted by the Ghost of Whiteness, allowing them to deflect and project the deep- seated trauma of racial delusions onto others, rather than confronting it within. The ghost is whiteness telling itself a story of overcoming whiteness where the Other, as ever, is its prop.

A scene in the 2007 Paul Thomas Anderson film *There Will Be Blood* helps further capture the driving force of this scheming ghost. Set in the early twentieth-century American oil boom, the film is about the rise of a ruthless oilman named Daniel Plainview, and his crooked ways of pursuing wealth and power. Plainview forms a fraught relationship with a young, devoted and charismatic preacher named Eli Sunday. What the men have in common is that, despite their different fields, they are both driven by greed and corruption, and through these motivations they both manage to alter the course of an entire community. In one of the film's most powerful scenes, Eli Sunday performs an exorcism on an older woman, claiming to expel an evil ghost responsible for her arthritis. He begins the ritual with a gentle and tender demeanour, softly coaxing: 'Get out of here, ghost … get out…'. But his whispers eventually escalate into unhinged outcries: 'GET OUT OF HERE, GHOST, GET OUT!' Seized by the performance, the church members submit – not to the authority of the priest but to that of the ghost.[6]

If we interpret the ghost in *There Will Be Blood* as an allegory for whiteness – a plausible reading given America's history – then it becomes clear that the ghost Eli Sunday conjures is not solely a representation of the old woman's arthritis, but rather it exemplifies something even worse and more painful: the creaking bones of evil and depravity. The focus of the congregation is the old woman's arthritis. But Sunday's ritual deflects from the deeper, more convoluted ills troubling the fictional 'Little Boston' community – their simultaneous thrill and guilt with enslavement, occupation, violence.

In a similar vein, our contemporary rituals against the material effects of historical injustices are only effective if they address the knottier, metaphysical and ontological entanglements lurking beneath the machinery of Superiorism. When we fail to address social justice in deeply explorative and self-enquiring ways, then the Ghost of Whiteness is empowered by misdirected attempts to repress it, and it eats away at whatever potentially positive forces emerge, leaving deterioration and confusion in its wake. It takes language that propagates for diversification, representation, decolonisation, decarbonisation, you name it, and converts it onto an ever-spinning conveyor belt of crises, which are then tackled with meaningless and watered-down incentives, policies and performative rituals at the same institutions that cause crises. It finds nooks and crannies in the social imaginary where it implants new exertions of power and renewed methods of relevance. It swallows progressive ideas like tender morsels of meat, regurgitating them as gibberish. It speaks of anti-racism but doesn't contextualise it, making it seem as though racism fell out of the sky. It reduces the deep and structured analyses of decolonisation into a series of token gestures. It aggregates the sentiment that whiteness has no roots, no history, no customs, no traditions – and therefore it is the default, it is neutral and is the very canvas to draw humanity upon. It is anti-context. Anti-specificity. It sustains its presence – somewhere between existence and cessation – because it has transformed its warped narratives into tangible substance, and from that substance, it has derived crisis, and from crises, power, all while divorcing itself from its motivations. The Ghost of Whiteness would rather burn up the whole planet than admit it is implicated and gets a kick out of doing so. Its refusal to confess to this innermost impulse is the state of denial in whose deep roar we all find ourselves, with seemingly no portals of escape.

The Ghost of Whiteness enters people's dreams, affects their relationships, confuses their minds and echoes in their thoughts. It has rendered everyone a performer in its theatre. It is everywhere: in the media, in discourse, in art, activism, philanthropy, education, family dynamics. No doubt, it lurks in this text, too. The Ghost of Whiteness is like the immortal jellyfish that uses cellular transdifferentiation to regenerate its deteriorating cells into polyps and restarts the process of life all over again. It hovers over history, repetitively mutating and avoiding death.

Nowhere is the Ghost of Whiteness in such a state of neurosis as in America, due to its position of political and cultural power, and no country's ghosts have metastasised into other countries like America's. In places as far and wide as Colombia and India and Ethiopia, American neuroses are so ubiquitous one scarcely notices them anymore. Yet it is also in such places that the ghost meets its true exorcist – not the priest, the businessman, or the policy-maker; not even the activist, the scholar, or the writer; but the sangoma. Sangomas are traditional healers in Southern Africa who know that confronting the essence of a ghost is essential for its release. Sangomas know that ghosts are restless, vengeful entities that refuse to leave because their very purpose is to create confusion. They know that there is nothing more arrogant, in the ghost's opinion, than the idea that people could engage in a civic project to foster peaceful co-existence between humans and the rest of the natural world. They are not afraid of the ghost's fangs, roars, or its wrath. Because they are experts on fear, they approach the darkness, they step into the abyss, they hold vigil, and they look the ghost in the eye. And they don't only say: 'Get out of here, ghost...' but rather: 'Get out of me, ghost.'

'Get out of me.' This might be the simple prescription of a sangoma, to exorcise the Ghost of Whiteness. Firstly, recognise that whiteness and white skin are distinct, and then grasp that to be white without embodying whiteness means abandoning Superiorism – the ghost's wellspring. It's that simple.

But simplicity is indeed not simple to achieve, especially in a world that encourages confusion and division through dualistic thought. We might heed the words of Bayo Akomolafe, one of the sangomas of our world: 'Maybe there are other genres of the human [...] many creaturely actions in a fragile ongoing world', he says.[7]

6.

The Human Illusion (and the Post-Pandemic Awakening to It)

You're just pushing that line that the lives you care about are worth more than others and you can gtfo with that shit.
— Instagram user, 2023[1]

Most eras end imperceptibly – and most eras also end abruptly. It seems a paradox, yet history supports it. Suddenly, long-held cultural symbols, social patterns and value systems are redefined. This is how Christianity spread across the world, how secularism arose in the West and how feminism changed gender norms globally. It is how economic empires fell and rose, how world wars started, and how dominant ideologies shifted the core of societies with them.

Paradigm shifts may appear sudden, but they are often the culmination of years of going against the stream. It took centuries and the approval of scientists like Galileo Galilei and Isaac Newton before Copernicus's discovery – that our planet was not orbited by celestial bodies other than the moon – became so incontestable even to the religious institutions that for so long resisted it, that it revolutionised scientific knowledge. Similarly, Pan-Africanism (the ideology that aims to foster solidarity between African heritage people in the continent and its diaspora) dates back at least to radicals like W. E. B. Du Bois and Amy Ashwood Garvey, who championed its principles in the early twentieth century. But it was the independence movements of 1960s Africa that finally institutionalised Pan-Africanism into the fabric of African society.

Equally, the invention of the birth control pill in the mid-twentieth century transformed women's lives, but its invention owed a lot to decades of feminist activism, including from the suffragist movement, of which the pill's key developer and financier philanthropist Katharine Dexter McCormick, was part.

Neither are paradigmatic shifts straightforwardly progressive by default; rather they can be erratic and anachronistic. For example, the spread of Christianity in Africa and the eventual capitulation to a monotheistic God, when viewed across the span of history, was a result of colonisation, yes. But it was also the spread of a belief system that already existed in the continent. Pluralistic devotional systems which had dominated Africa historically were already being rejected prior to the imposition of foreign cultural value systems.

Thomas Kuhn, the physicist known for introducing the concept of paradigm shifts in his classic work, *The Structure of Scientific Revolutions*, posited that paradigms shift when challenges or as he called them, anomalies, to common beliefs accumulate, and over time transform the fundamental framework, to the point of eventual replacement. According to Kuhn, these anomalies, or new perspectives to unresolved questions, recur cyclically until they reform accepted beliefs. This entire cyclical process is what Kuhn termed a 'paradigm shift'.

Although Kuhn's paradigm shifts concerned science, they have transcended their origins to also describe sociocultural transformations. Today, we find ourselves at such an inflection point where foundational structures are being undone by 'anomalies' and where our societal deliberations are shifting in an almost palpable way. 'The old is dying and the new cannot be born,' Antonio Gramsci famously said about the interregnum between fascism and a new culture in 1930s Italy. His words echo in our own time.

What exactly is dying, and conversely what is struggling to be born? Anti-establishment types on the left might argue that it is the West, or capitalism, or the patriarchy, that is crumbling. Their counterparts on the right might say that tradition, meaning, stable political institutions are facing extinction. Some believe that the emerging world is a diverse, feminist and queer one; others warn of a confused, deconstructed post-reality future scenario. 'A deep truth is a truth whose opposite is also a deep truth,' the scientist Niels Bohr is to have said. We may not agree on what is ending or beginning, but we all sense 'the shift' – *something* is undeniably breaking apart while something else is breaking through.

My thesis in this chapter is that the thing breaking apart and the thing that is struggling to be born are one and the same: the human.

I don't mean the human as a biological member of *Homo sapiens*: the one that is distinguished from other primates by, for instance, their capacity for speech, brain size, reasoning, processing, posture, etc., and evolving from this distinction according to our environments. Considering our growing number on this planet, that fellow is hardly breaking apart or eroding.

What is losing ground, is the narrative of the human; the story of who we are. As with all narratives, the human narrative has a beginning, a middle and an end. We are probably living in the beginning era of its dissolution, and struggling with it, as are all the institutions built upon the narrative – our legal, educational, political structures – that it once sustained.

To fully grasp the origins of the human narrative that we are now seeing collapse, we must go back to the moment it began – a time when new worlds were 'discovered' and the concept of the human began to be constructed to fit this age. If I were to pick one symbolic moment for the invention of the human, it is on the shores of the Caribbean in

1492, where the Genoese explorer Christopher Columbus arrived. His so-called 'discovery' of the region and its Arawak people, set in motion a rendering of the human that lauded Europe and violently erased groups of indigenous people. There were over a million Arawak when Columbus arrived in what became Hispaniola. By 1550, they had been reduced to a mere 500.[2] Columbus himself, long dead by then, may have felt little concern. As he callously wrote in his captain's log: 'they would make fine servants ... with fifty men we could subjugate them all and make them do whatever we want'.[3] This moment marked not just the violent erasure of a people but the beginning of Superiorism, a narrative that would control and *dehumanise* entire populations in the centuries to come. Europe's entrance into the Americas was not only the beginning of globalised exploitation and imperialism, but it was also the initiation into a particular understanding of the human that defines the modern world.

A lesser known of Columbus's 'discoveries' starts us off on this journey of understanding the beginning of the human, namely: his encounter with a unique fruit, the pineapple, which he introduced to Europe when returning from Hispaniola.

In today's modern global capitalist system, pineapples are transported to the West at a market size estimated at almost $30 billion.[4] But in early modern Europe (from around the sixteenth to the eighteenth century) the pineapple was such a rare treat that only the continent's elites could afford it. A craze for the exotic fruit swept through Europe. Businesses emerged where people could rent a pineapple for a day, in a similar (tacky) way that someone might rent a limousine today. Pineapples symbolised abundance and prestige, both which, at this point in Europe's biography, were becoming symbolic of the connection between the shift of resources and wealth from 'Places of Colour' to Europe. The pineapple symbolised Superiorism ascending the heights of glory.

Pineapples are also a good example in response to the question posed at the end of Chapter 2: what does Superiorism mutate into when challenged? While indigenous communities of tropical regions, where pineapples grow locally, may notice that the fruit is no longer as plentiful as it once was, the symbolic pineapple still speaks to the swap of abundance *to* Europe, and scarcity *from* Europe, to regions where such a notion as scarcity may not have previously existed. Today, in shops and markets in European, and by extension North American, Canadian, Australian, and other Western globalised cities, the privileged classes can visit shops such as Whole Foods or Planet Organic and purchase products like 'Pineapple Yuzu Sparkling Matcha', or a 'Fermentary Pineapple & Turmeric Kraut'. Pineapples are still a status symbol – if for proportionally lesser amounts than our sixteenth-century ancestors paid.

What's more complicated, and demonstrative, of modern-day Superiorism is that it is slyer. The Western brands that sell products which include pineapples or other exotic ingredients (matcha, turmeric…), are often contributing the shifting of values – towards something 'greener', more diverse, healthier, and so on – even while remaining entangled in global production methods and market logics that bolster Superiorism, as well as in narratives of the Self and the Other in the social imaginary that shape market logics.

The aim here is not to point fingers; I too am a consumer of 'conscious' products. Rather, the aim is to show one of the many ways that Superiorism mutates to maintain its position as the dominant narrative. I cannot help but think of the famous Bertolt Brecht piece where he writes about belonging to 'the haves', but refuses to ignore the fact that others died so he could drink water.[5]

1492 is also a connotative starting point of the conception of the human according to the hierarchical parameters of Superiorism.

Columbus's mission (as with other similar missions) required a justification, and the 'category of the human' fitted the task perfectly. The problem however, was that the category didn't exist – it had yet to be invented. Or perhaps I should say that it had to be borrowed, in this instance from the Greek philosopher, Aristotle.

Appropriating Aristotle

When it comes to defining the human, Aristotle's views have tenably had more impact than any other single individual on the concept. In the making of the modern world, Aristotle's views of human nature have become deeply integrated across time and place, migrating from Europe to Africa, Asia, and beyond. From the ways that we interpret the human being's role in the family, politics, state, religion, philosophy and the sciences, Aristotle's ideas fill up a large volume of the pool of collective knowledge. In fact, he conjured many of these domains and areas of study in the first place. This book, too, is inescapably Aristotelian – metaphysics, after all, was his invention.

What made humans human, and differentiated humans from animals and plants was, according to Aristotle, our capacity to reason and rationalise. In his Lyceum in Athens, he followed an unusually scientific approach (for the time) to prove his thesis. He systematically categorised animals into species, laid down the principles of deductive reasoning and built the foundations of empirical observation. Unlike Plato, his teacher, Aristotle was not strictly preoccupied with abstract forms (archetypes) and ideas. He focused on material reality as the source of answers, and his methodology remains the bible of the modern mind.

Aristotle contended that the purpose of human existence was to achieve the state of flourishing, or *eudaimonia* as he called it. And who on Earth doesn't want to flourish? Certainly, in our times, we are still under this spell of Aristotelean conjuring. We may call it happiness, optimisation, well-being, or indeed flourishing, instead of *eudaimonia*, but the underlying premise is the same – even if these qualities weren't then embedded in a massive capitalist industry.[6] Nonetheless, because Aristotle believed that the faculties of reason and rationality led to *eudaimonia*, he also saw these as the very defining features of the human.

That we can reason and rationalise our ways through the problems and puzzles of life is by all accounts one of the most vital tools that our species has, but it is not the only way of understanding who we are or orchestrating human flourishing. There are sources of knowledge that are not rational per se, but that give profound meaning and purpose. Meditation, for example. Widely recognised as a source of knowledge about the individual and the collective consciousness, meditation is a form of knowledge where rationalising is counterproductive. Meditating is, in a sense, to pause analysis, logical thinking and problem-solving.

Or take dreaming, another example of 'non-rational' knowledge, which offers unpredictable and non-linear insights. To give a personal example, during lockdown I had nightmares with a recurring theme that seemed connected to climate change. In one dream, a sudden hailstorm erupted on a sunny summer beach. Eerily, no one seemed to care; children continued to play, adults read and chatted, and so on. In another dream, a beautiful park I once visited in Hong Kong was turned into ashes. Jarred, I googled 'climate dreams' and landed on a page titled the very same thing, 'Climate Dreams', where a psychologist had found such an increase in the nature of such dreams that they had started collating them. That numerous individuals were simultaneously having 'climate dreams' reminded me that there are different ways of knowing. We cannot simply discard such a phenomenon where patterns emerge in the collective dream-world as irrelevant to the broader discussion of what it means to be human. There's something in the unconscious that goes beyond what we can methodically explain.

And then there's poetry, a realm where, to borrow from Audre Lorde, we 'give name to the nameless so it can be thought'.[7] I dare anyone to attentively read a poem that they love and not feel time stop, however fleetingly. Although distinctive, the ability to rationalise is not the definitive trait of the human mind.

Even the mind of a very rational person (perhaps the public intellectual and advocate of the computational theory of mind, Steven Pinker?) would inevitably be messier and more nuanced, if observed in granular detail. Imagine if we could be in Imaginary Steven Pinker's mind for only ten minutes. Even this undeniably logical mind would bounce from rational thoughts to random deliberations, to embodied sensations to emotions. Say that Imaginary Steven Pinker has a meeting at two o'clock and calculates that since it takes one hour to reach his destination, he must leave at one o'clock – a rational estimation. Imaginary Steven Pinker may start preparing for his departure when he suddenly bangs his toe against his piano and, without rationalising the matter, finds himself experiencing the embodied sensation of pain. This sensation, in return, leads Imaginary Steven Pinker to recall an intimate conversation regarding pain with a family member, and the memory evokes an emotional state of affection. In the middle of this thought, Imaginary Steven Pinker intuitively senses that time is speeding by, and rationality takes over again as he rushes into the shower to prepare for his appointment.

In only ten minutes, the life of Imaginary Steven Pinker produces a more complex (and beautiful) rendering of reality's kaleidoscopic and complicated nature than the reductive dualism between the Rational and the Emotional, so dominant in the world, could ever conjure. Staunch rationalists might argue that Imaginary Steven Pinker could at any moment within this ten-minute sequence choose to focus instead of letting his mind ruminate, and that the ability to choose makes rationality the dominant quality to observe. They may insist that critiques against rationalism (such as this) themselves necessarily employ our rational faculty. Or they may counter that rationalists don't oppose emotions or the imagination as such ('Real Steven Pinker' is himself hopelessly fond of hypothetical examples). But my point is not simply that we are multifaceted beings, it is certainly not that rational thinking is bad. What I am saying is that the likelihood that Imaginary Steven Pinker doesn't control his mind in every waking moment, shows how other qualities of mind are as distinctive as rationality to the human experience – and thus to intrinsic human value. And the issue with Superiorism is that it denies this truth.

It is not only that there are other sources of knowledge than rationality, but that the ways we think about this human capacity is itself so limited. We typically associate rationality with empirical knowledge, but we could equally think of rationality as the tool that we use precisely to enrich our affective and intuitive embodiment.

When we talk about the human, we are not only discussing a species that is logical and cerebral; we are also talking about a species which dreams, desires and feels. An animal that collectively behaves in ways that are complex and mysterious to the point, oftentimes, of seeming irrational. Human behaviour often transcends logical explanation and, sometimes, this whimsical, undisciplined or orgiastic side of our nature – rather than the sensible, detached, coherent one – is precisely what makes for *eudaimonia*. With a more expansive view of rationality, we could create institutions that use faculties of reason and logic to help people lose – rather than exert – control. One of the tragedies of history is that one of the most unique and versatile of human traits – rationality – has been convoluted into a measure and a metric that supports a passionless Superiorist value system.

Excluding people is, however, precisely the second problem of Aristotle's legacy. His systematic distinctions drew him towards hierarchies, not only between humans and non-humans but also between humans themselves. In his worldview, some groups of humans were not as capable at reasoning, which, as mentioned, he saw as the central function of being human. In other words, if the principles of rationality and reason defined the human, but not all humans could abide by those principles, then not all humans were, well, human. The slave, he wrote, 'participates in reason only to the extent of perceiving it, but does not have it'.[8] And 'the deliberative faculty in a woman', he added, 'is non-authoritative'.[9] A number of scholars, including feminists like Martha Nussbaum[10] and Cynthia Freeland[11] have pointed out that Aristotle wasn't suggesting that women don't have the ability to reason at all, but rather that they could not reason about *politics*. There is something cherry-picking about this argument. If women cannot apply reason in the political domain, then they do not really have reason, because it is a limited type.

All this is nevertheless a simplification of Aristotle's irrefutably impressive contribution to knowledge. The account of his work that I am giving here certainly does not paint the full picture. However, the point here is not Aristotle himself, but rather the impact of his work as it concerns the human. Aristotle's writings are central to the foundations of Western thought, and Western thought today is the foundational structure of dominant and conventional global knowledge. His ideas steered us to the worship of materialism and empiricism (a dogmatic worship known as 'scientism') and to the hierarchical organisation of human nature, human value and human privilege by gender, class, race, and other distinctions. The combination of these two factors makes for a particularly toxic way of organising society that is at once seemingly impossible and utterly imperative to escape.

Aristotle himself may never have imagined that the hierarchies he had observed would continue to shape thought for centuries to come – only with a much wider and more disturbing reach than they had in the Athens of his time.

His views on the human did not have a big impact during his lifetime. It took centuries before his texts were resurfaced from a mouldy cellar, and figures like the Christian theologian Thomas Aquinas and Islamic philosopher Ibn Rushd popularised them – simultaneously importing Aristotle's view of the rational human to both Christianity and Islam. Aquinas interwove Aristotle's thesis about the human into Christianity with the pervasive argument that rationality was a gift from God. Aristotle argued that only humans (or certain humans) possessed an immortal, rational soul (*anima rationalis*) that endured beyond physical death and was distinct from our life-sustaining soul (*anima vegetativa*) or sensory soul (*anima sensitiva*). Aquinas, following his guru, argued in his most famous work, *Summa Theologica*, that the source of the human soul and its faculty of reason was what he called *spiritus seminis* – in essence, the gassy substance that gives sperm its foamy texture.

Ibn Rushd played a similar role in synthesising Aristotle's argument about reason as the main function of the human with Islam by arguing, controversially for his time, that true philosophy and true religion could not contradict one another, as both ultimately lead to the same truth.

In short, following the footsteps of their teacher Aristotle, in the genealogy of defining the human both Aquinas and Ibn Rushd, and many others to follow, conflated human value with the capacity for rationality and understood this capacity as one not equally distributed.

It was the Middle Ages, after all, and Europe and Christendom were forming in tandem. Centuries after his death, Aristotle had unwittingly provided the perfect narrative for the idea that would emerge from the amalgamation: Superiorism.

The patterns of equating the human with rationality, and rationality with a specific group, would become even more pronounced over time. In the Early Modern Period, the French philosopher René Descartes famously equated human existence with cognition, and even further down the line, during the aptly named Age of Reason, Immanuel Kant, similarly defined humanity based on its membership of the 'community of reasonable beings'. According to these influential theories, to be human was to be rational and the attribution of rationality was always limited and always selective. Women did not possess Descartes- revered cognition skills. Nor did they, or the people of Africa – as the continent had by now been baptised – belong to Kant's 'reasonable beings' community. The human was, by now, distinctly European and conclusively male.

Once the human was defined as male and white, he became predominantly shaped around two central discourses. The first, popularly traced to the philosopher Thomas Hobbes with his influential work *Leviathan*, famously described life in its natural state as 'solitary, poor, nasty, brutish, and short'.[12] To whatever extent the human was a peaceful and good species, Hobbes believed that it was because of his fear of death, rather than because he innately was good. Immortality inclines men to peace, he said, and an almighty authority that demands peace and order – a Leviathan – is, therefore, needed for humans to protect themselves from harm.

The French philosopher Jean-Jaques Rousseau, with his 'noble savage' discourse on the human, diverged from the Hobbesian view.[13] He argued instead that the human is innately disposed towards freedom, equality and *amour de soi* (self-love). 'The first man breathes nothing but peace and liberty; he wishes only to live and remain idle,' as Rousseau argued in A *Discourse on Inequality*.[14]

Adding their voices to the debate centuries later, the anthropologist David Graeber and the archaeologist David Wengrow jointly, and rightly, argued in 2021 that the question about whether humans are innately good or evil, peaceful, or violent, is ultimately redundant because 'noble' and 'savage' are artificial constructs contingent on a worldview that can only understand itself through such binary distinctions in the first place. As they succinctly put it: '"Noble" savages are ultimately just as boring as savage ones; more to the point, neither actually exists.'[15]

We have thought about the human as something binary, as the Hobbes vs Rousseau debate suggests. We have claimed to be the masters of the universe (or the imagined sandbox), and consequently sought to control the bodies of ourselves and others, time, land, nature, etc. We have made a false distinction between humans and Nature.

But ours is a time when Nature is making it clear that it is not separate from the human, that human actions are Nature's actions, and vice versa, and that we are in an entangled manifestation in which we ultimately all suffer or flourish together. The flaws in the Aristotelian definition of the human are demonstrably being revealed as anomalies shaking the paradigm, as Kuhn might say. Society is undergoing a profound re-evaluation with the human at its centre. The beginning of the human is ostensibly, then, also its end.

The Three Waves of Decolonisation

I am not suggesting that we are the first generation to ponder what it means to be human. Ancestors in all corners of the world have approached this question, if in different ways – through mythology, religion, science and philosophy, producing diverse but often overlapping responses. In *The Dawn of Everything*, Graeber and

Wengrow make a case for what they refer to as the 'indigenous critique', referring to how, from the seventeenth century onwards, 'Native intellectuals' such as the Wendit statesman Kandiaronk critically opposed and argued against the political structures emerging from the Enlightenment, and made political solid arguments that countered it.[16]

Also, if we take seriously the contributions of feminism and decolonisation to the shaping of the world, as we should, then it becomes clear that both movements, at their core, have always been articulations against the conceptualisation of the human as the Vitruvian man (Leonardo Da Vinci's painting representing a European male as embodying the rational order of the universe). The philosopher Donna Haraway describes the process of presenting a distinctly male, European and white perspective as objective and universal – 'the god trick': a 'conquering gaze from nowhere' that claims 'the power to see and not be seen'.[17]

The decolonisation movement is one of the strongest articulations of resistance against the god trick. I will divide decolonisation into the Three Waves to help understand how this movement is even vaster than people think both in terms of temporal and epistemic scope.

—

The start of the First Wave of Decolonisation could be attributed to a voodoo ceremony in Bois-Caïman, Haiti, in 1791, where the descendant of runaway slaves, a maroon priest named Dutty Boukman, gave the following speech to rouse enslaved Africans to revolt:

> ... This God who made the sun, who brings us light from above, who raises the sea, and who makes the storm rumble. That God is there, do you understand? Hiding in a cloud, He watches us, he sees all that the whites do! The God of the whites pushes them to crime, but he wants us to do good deeds. But the God who is so good orders us to vengeance. He will direct our hands

*and give us help. Throw away the image of the God of the whites
who thirsts for our tears. Listen to the liberty that speaks in all
our hearts.*[18]

There are debates about the veracity of Boukman's speech, but
historians agree that some sort of ceremony took place, likely on 21
August 1791, and that following the ceremony enslaved Africans
staged an uprising, destroying parishes and demolishing thousands
of sugar plantations and coffee plantations.[19] For the next thirteen
years, until 1804, they fought until Haiti was theirs, liberated from
colonial rule.

Although not all directly linked to the Haitian revolution, a ripple
of anti-colonial struggles followed worldwide during this period.
There was the Battle of Carabobo for Venezuelan independence
versus Spain in 1821; the Java War against the Dutch in Indonesia
from 1825; the Muslim slave rebellion known as the Malé Revolt
against the Portuguese colony in the Empire of Brazil in 1835; the
Matale Rebellion in Sri Lanka led by peasants in 1848; resistance
against French rule in the Wassoulou Empire (freed by Samory Touré
in 1882); the resistance against the British during the 1897 Benin
Expedition; and the 1900 Ashanti War led by Queen Yaa Ashantewa
versus the British.[20]

From a political perspective, these uprisings and wars were about
reclaiming sovereignty and power, but from a broader view, all
decolonisation is also simultaneously and inevitably a dissenting
response to the human as it was invented to serve the Superiorist agenda.

The First Wave was not 'wholly' successful; decolonisation is
a process. The Second Wave of Decolonisation, from the mid-
nineteenth century, was equally a response to the definition of the
human that Superiorism entailed. The Scramble for Africa had,
at this point, treated the continent as putty for European countries
to mould as they wished; the Enlightenment had affirmed the
inferiority of the black race through pseudo-science, and racial
segregation and the denial of political rights to colonised people in

their own lands was widespread. These combined events normalised the dehumanisation of the Other. They justified the day-to-day exploitation and oppression of the colonised; brutal practices such as detentions without trial, mass executions and genocides, forced resettlements and extreme torture were deployed to maintain the hierarchical system that now governed much of the world. Superiorism was so unabashed and shameless during this era, that resistance against it was of an equally potent nature. The Second Wave of Decolonisation was marked by the political, military and cultural overthrow of European colonial power.

The shapers of the Second Wave were politicised and resentful. They were soldiers such as Barack Obama's grandfather, Hussein Onyango Obama, who had been conscripted into the Second World War and who returned to East Africa with a decolonial consciousness. They were artists such as James Barnor, Chinua Achebe and Iba N'Diaye, who conjured creative critiques of colonialism with their lenses, pens and brushes. They were freedom fighters, political activists and intellectuals who fuelled movements such as the 1955 Bandung Conference in Indonesia and the 1956 Conference of Negro-African Writers in Paris. They were a force that formed a band of hope and unity amidst despair and exploitation. They were a generation who found community in grievance. They were black and proud, and in fact, more human than the white world could bear.

—

The Third Wave of Decolonisation, which we are amid, gained momentum in 2015 when Chumani Maxwele, a University of Cape Town student, threw excrement on a Cecil Rhodes statue, sparking the 'Rhodes Must Fall' movement. The movement soon expanded globally, and prompted calls to 'decolonise' various sectors, including curricula, mental health, design, nature and museums. In contrast to the first and second waves of decolonisation, the Third Wave focuses attention on restructuring institutions of culture and education. With its emphasis on academic institutions and cultural public spaces, it has addressed issues such as the importance of representation and the trauma of historical injustices. Identity politics and epistemic injustice have also been central themes to the Third Wave of Decolonisation. A central aim of the Third Wave being to challenge and transform prevailing narratives and imaginaries, I perceive this book, and my previous writing too, as part of the ongoing discussion.

As I have presented them, these periodisations are sweeping and incomplete. There remain numerous unanswered questions. What are the connections between the resistance movements of the first, second and third waves? What was the nature of colonial power in these periods? When exactly does each period or 'Wave' take place?

Like the Three Waves of Feminism, from which I derive them, the Three Waves of Decolonisation are overlapping and cannot be neatly organised. For example, a text like *Decolonising the Mind* by Ngugi wa Thiong'o is central to both the second and third waves. It is also not my intention to imply that there was no resistance to the colonising tactics of Superiorism before the eighteenth century, or in between what I loosely attribute to the three waves. There were decolonisation attempts prior to these examples, such as the Bayano Wars versus Spanish colonists in 1550s Panama; or the Irish versus the English in Ireland, and the Anglo–Powhatan wars, both in the seventeenth century. My dividing of colonisation into three waves starting with Boukman's speech and the decolonisation struggles that followed it, is as they took place in a concentrated period of time. This period also has a specific relation to events in Africa.

The Three Waves of Decolonisation are helpful in contextualising the history of resistance and developing an understanding of the human condition in the twenty-first century. These designations also show that, while the momentum of the first and second waves of decolonisation have hardly left any trace in the public memory of Europe, outside of Europe's navel-gazing borders, their impact has been tremendous. As the political scientist Samuel Huntington said:

'The West won the world not by the superiority of its ideas or values or religion (to which few members of other civilisations were converted) but rather by its superiority in applying organised violence. Westerners often forget this fact; non-Westerners never do.'[21]

Similarly, the Argentine professor Walter Mignolo says: 'You cannot be modern without being colonial, and if you are on the colonial side of the spectrum, you have to transact with modernity – you cannot ignore it.'[22] To Mignolo, coloniality is the logic of hegemony that is inherent to modernity. According to Mignolo, it permeates four social domains: the economic (control of finance, land, etc.); the political (control of authority, etc.); the civic (control of gender, sexuality, etc.); and the epistemic (control of knowledge and subjectivity).

There is a fifth domain I would like to add to Mignolo's colonial matrix: the temporal. The temporal domain is where coloniality controls the understanding and organisation of time, including history, the perception of past, present and future, and the way societies plan for and anticipate future challenges and opportunities. Think, for example, of how Europe's history is centred in the chronologies that shape global narratives. For this reason, when it comes to African history, colonialism has become the defining axis. Earlier, I addressed how the rendition of African history into Precolonial, Colonial and Postcolonial periods implies that Africa had no history before Western colonisation.

What might be an era of technological innovation for one society is, for another, an era of loss, violence and destruction. The temporal domain involves the rhythms of life and work, such as cycles of production and consumption, leisure time, working hours, life stages, and the pacing of everyday life. It affects how societies remember their past, experience the present and imagine their future; influencing decision-making, governance and cultural continuity. The 'colonised subject' (to borrow from Frantz Fanon) is thus deprived of the agency that time provides, whether that is automatically belonging to the narrative timeline of human history, or to possessing the comfort of the present moment. They are not the person, group or entity to which time is devoted and, as such, the colonised subject is not actually human because to hold a stake in the wider world, a sense of uninterruptedness is necessary. That sense of abiding continuity is instead the privilege of those whose humanity is assured.

The Post-Pandemic Awakening

In 2022, the Africa Studies Association of Africa hosted a conference titled 'Africa and the Human: Old Questions, New Imaginaries', which took place in Cape Town. The gathering asked: 'What does it mean to be human today in Africa, African in the world today, and what can Africa contribute to thinking the human?' I found the concept note written by the organisers, Professor Divine Fuh and Professor Akosua Adomako Ampofo, riveting. They emphasised that 'the question of the human is urgent and essential to tackle, especially at this moment of global existential crises provoked by the Covid-19 pandemic', and that 'Africa currently has an opportunity to re-produce the world and provide new terms of reference and recognition for the future of humanity'.[23]

Indeed, on both grounds, no event has pushed the question about the human to the fore as the announcement of a global pandemic on 11 March 2020. When the director general of the World Health Organization, Dr Tedros Adhanom Ghebreyesus, said on that day that: 'In the days and weeks ahead, we expect to see the number of cases, the number of deaths, and the number of affected countries climb even higher … We have therefore made the assessment that Covid-19 can be characterised as a pandemic,' his statement marked a turning point (or an anomaly) in the history of the human, almost instantaneously bringing to question our very understanding of what the notion means in the first place.

Every crisis arising from the pandemic, whether related to the environment, warfare, poverty, social unrest, or health threats, was exacerbated by the prevailing understanding of what it means to be human. For one, observing non-human life flourishing during lockdown prompted a profound question: if we are indeed human, what kind of species are we that we must be isolated for other species to thrive? The pandemic revealed that the non-human was indefensibly exploited by the human. As global engagement with the question of what a human response to a pandemic should be, a Pandora's box of other questions opened. Questions that had predominantly been the concern of marginalised groups prior to the pandemic came to the fore for everyone. What is a human response to the climate emergency? To inequality and corruption? And to racism, sexism, homophobia, transphobia, islamophobia, anti-Semitism, ableism, classism, religious discrimination and the silencing of indigenous people – Superiorism – of any stripe?

The demographic disparities that emerged in Covid-19 infection rates and the impact of lockdown measures seemed to say something deeply troubling about the state of the human. In the UK, as elsewhere, black, and South Asian individuals were roughly twice as likely to succumb to Covid-19 compared to their white counterparts. People with disabilities found themselves dehumanised by herd immunity policies that ignored the precarity of their communities, and governments treated the elderly more inhumanely than ever imaginable. Meanwhile, women around the world shouldered an increased burden of childcare and housework, while domestic violence and unemployment disproportionately affected them. Those we began to call 'essential workers' were not provided with adequate sick leave or job security when they contracted Covid-19. Precarious economies struggled under the weight of lockdowns, pushing over half a billion people into extreme poverty. Yet when pharmaceutical companies like Pfizer and Moderna rolled out vaccines, they were hoarded by wealthy governments for the benefit of their people alone, creating a sort of 'vaccine apartheid' as though the virus could care about manmade borders.

Western perceptions of Africa have hardly ever been kind. Still, the pandemic brought to the fore all the murky and offensive ways that

Africa is a spectre in the Western mind, in a manner that I hadn't encountered quite so forcefully in years. For example, when South African doctors detected the Omicron variant of the virus in 2021, African nations – despite Africa being the continent least affected by the virus – were subject to unreasonable travel bans that Europe imposed in patronising and dictatorial ways, and without forewarning, leading to the plummeting of currencies and the reactivation of colonial trauma. Even though it was Europe that introduced Covid-19 to Africa, and not the other way around, and although African nations managed the crisis efficiently in comparison by immediately implementing strategies such as contact-tracing and the closing of borders, long before Western nations took the same strategies seriously, old egregious tropes of Africa and its people as incapable, primitive, and therefore inferior, resurfaced during the pandemic. The long-held perceptions that negate the humanity of African people were still in wide circulation.

As people were forced to retreat in quarantine and could not do much else than observe, they collectively noticed aspects of human value that had long been concealed in plain sight. There was a heightened focus on social welfare systems, healthcare infrastructures, workers' rights, homelessness, environmental concerns, and other questions that previously had been insufficiently discussed by those who weren't directly affected. Money that should have prevented ecocide, strengthened healthcare and lowered unemployment had instead boosted corporate interests. In short, inconsistencies, inequalities and abuses of power became so visible and treacherous that even those who usually would pay no heed to them couldn't ignore what was glaringly there. As Naomi Klein writes in her astonishing book *Doppelganger*: 'Covid was different. It scrambled my personal world, as it did all of our worlds … I woke up every morning exhausted and stared at my various screens in a stultified daze. For the first time, this was not someone else's shock.'[24]

We were forced to grapple with questions about who we are, and why, and whether we might prefer to be something different. Furthermore, it became clearer to growing numbers of people during the pandemic, that human experience is too easily reduced to data, statistics and infographics about flattening the curves, etc. The political shifts that we see as facts, data, stats and analysis also have an emotive and relational side, and when this side of human experience is ignored, it emerges as a shadow. As Klein says about the chaos of doppelganger culture, it is a maze of, 'racial and ethnic projections and fascist doubles and the studiously denied shadows that are all coming to the surface at once'.[25]

Into this pandemic atmosphere of heightened anxiety and tension, coupled with the increased consciousness and awakening concern of injustice, came the news of the grotesque murder of George Floyd in May 2020. Right there on every screen was the final evidence that the human was profoundly relative. It was painfully clear that dominant American, and by extension, globalised Western power, did not value the humanity of black people equally to that of white people.

The widespread Black Lives Matter protests against racial injustice that took place in the days and months that followed were not only demonstrations against George Floyd's murder, or even racial injustice. I contend that they were also the beginnings of the mass resistance against a logic that insists on a hierarchy between humans, as well as of humans over other species: Superiorism.

Our post-pandemic society is not the first to unequivocally question and reconfigure past definitions of the human. The pandemic, lockdown and protests prompted conversations about the human that were previously mainly held by anticolonialists and/or feminists, as well as by specialised scholars shaping fields like posthumanism and transhumanism (two very different fields), and by other small, specialised groups of philosophers and scientists concerned with a broader take on the characteristics of human nature. More recently, even high-level international gatherings like the Davos 2024 economic forum and climate conferences such as COP28, featured discussions about 'Navigating the Future of Human – AI Partnership' and 'The responsibility of being human' respectively, demonstrating the buzz that exists around definitions of the human today. More people than ever are questioning classical conceptions of the human to question. In return, this questioning is reshaping our ethical principles, political ideologies and the dynamics of our relationships with one another and the world. It is the key reason we find ourselves amidst an era of shifting paradigms.

According to Kuhn, for a theory to become a paradigm, it doesn't need to explain all facts; it just needs to seem more encompassing than its predecessors and alternatives. As Kuhn remarked: 'Paradigms gain their status because they are more successful than their competitors in solving a few problems that the group of practitioners has come to recognise as acute.'[26] The pandemic is akin to such an occurrence, which Kuhn refers to as a 'crisis point', when the problems in the dominant paradigm are so acute and problematic that they cannot be ignored.

The boundary between the 'before' and 'after' of the human is not straightforward, however. From our present vantage point, it may seem like the pandemic was the catalyst of the shift we are seeing now, but it was not the pandemic itself that caused a paradigm shift. The actual cause of the change was the realisation that the notion of the human, as it broadly has been understood, is an illusion. What the pandemic did was to expose and, consequently, begin to unknot the fundamental lie that has been keeping the systems of the world spinning, namely, the God trick.

Events that have since unfolded have continued to carry the rejection of this logic. The massive protests against the genocide in Gaza are also a struggle against the hypocritical stance that Superiorism generates, that certain lives are more valuable than others. Furthermore, they have raised the question of how the West can champion human rights when it clearly does not assign the same value to all humans?

I do not intend to reduce one of the most deplorable atrocities in human history into a textbook example for my argument. Nor is this book the place to expand on the Gaza atrocity. The actor Angelina Jolie's comments, made in a December 2023 interview on Islam Channel, are instructive to my point. Jolie captured the mood of the growing rejection of Superiorist logic when she said:

In my head, there was some idea of the good guys ... and that there was going to be these human rights goals laid out ... I really thought that was what the United Nations was about ... But to watch and understand more and more, how it's just simply not the world. The world is not – these are human rights. It is these are human rights, sometimes, for these people, maybe sometimes for these people, never for these people. It's food aid – six per cent for these people; fifty per cent for these people. It's justice for these people, but not for these people; accountability for this crime but not that crime if there's business interest, and this is truly the ugly state of much of the world that we are just becoming more and more aware of.[27]

Or as the Instagram user in the first epigraph of this chapter says – a comment which was also in response to the genocide – 'You're just pushing that line that the lives you care about are worth more than others and you can gtfo with that shit.'[28]

Structures of oppression have pertained for so long because the prop that propels them has remained intact, namely: the human. They have stayed intact because people took the Aristotelian descriptions of the human to be unquestionably true and neutral even when all the sociopolitical institutions that have shaped their lives suggest otherwise. They fought for human rights, humanism, the humanities, human status and human progress, not realising that the innocent-seeming word 'human' was the prop that upheld the height and might of Superiorism.

Even the most radical ideas have missed this insight – when thinkers such as W. E. B. Du Bois or James Baldwin probed racial dynamics, they stayed within the defined narrative of the human by insisting that the black person was as 'human' as the white person. They fought to be on equal footing as humans when the embedded bias in the concept of 'humans' made them unequal.

Du Bois and Baldwin stayed with the narrative of the human because their times demanded it, of course, and not because they weren't aware of its limitations. It was blatant: black peoples were denied what white peoples were encouraged to do, such as vote. As James Baldwin said: 'Our passion for categorisation, for life neatly fitted into pegs, has led to unforeseen, paradoxical distress, confusion, a breakdown of meaning. Those categories meant to define and control the world for us have boomeranged us into chaos, in which limbo we whirl, clutching the straws of our definitions.'[29]

But now, people are no longer pleading to be 'as human as'. Instead, they're challenging and questioning whether being 'human' was ever worth desiring in the first place. The idea of the human was based on erroneous postulations about human nature, and the more exposed these false postulations become, the larger the claustrophobic gap between the human as narrative and the human as experience grows. The gap seems to be a trap now. People now want a way out of 'The Human Illusion'.

II

FEMINISM

7.

Spider Mentality

The male wolf spider (Lycosidae) is considerably smaller than the female, and he risks getting eaten by her. So to protect himself, he captures some appropriate prey – a fly, mosquito, or small butterfly – wraps it carefully in his silk, and presents the package to his companion with a deference visibly mitigated by fear. He then backs off and waits to see if the strategy will work. If the female succumbs to her usual gluttony, the male can finally cozy up and couple with Madame Wolf, risk-free, while she munches down her little gift. You do your thing, and I'll do mine, she seems to say.

— Louise Bourgeois, through Jean Frémon[1]

I was two months old when I moved to Lagos. Ahead of this move, the doting nurses at the Finnish hospital where I was born counselled my mother that she should prevent people from carrying me when we returned to Nigeria, lest I become contaminated by tropical diseases. And so, the first thing my mum did when we arrived at Lagos's Murtala Muhammed International Airport was hand me over to the aunties, uncles and family friends who awaited us there. Had she not wanted her child to be 'contaminated' by tropical people (oops, diseases), my mother reasoned, then she would not have had an African child.

As I grew older, I did indeed perceive myself as a child of Africa. My other identities were constantly in flux. I was not straightforwardly Finnish, Nigerian, Yoruba, Muslim, Protestant, white, or black. Despite my European heritage, I certainly could not emphatically claim to be white, or even European. And although I felt more 'black' than 'white', the word 'black' was not as widely used then as it is now, at least not in Nigeria. The only feature about my identity that I held as a constant was that I came from a part of the world known as 'Africa', and that whatever was true about this part of the world was also, therefore, true about me.

What was 'true' about Africa back then, and remains true, was that Africa represented the opposite of whatever the West purportedly stood for. If the West was modern, then Africa was not. If the West was developed, then Africa was underdeveloped. These sentiments stemmed from a dualist Western mindset intoxicated by Superiorism, but there was a similar, if more flattering, binary pattern within Africa too, to forge an identity pitted against the West. That pattern of thought suggested, for instance, that if the West was greedy, then Africa was generous. If the West was individualist, then Africa was communitarian. This way of defining African identity gave rise to a sociopolitical disposition (that I refer to in Chapter 11 as 'Populist Anti-Western Nativism', or PAWN), where rather than of its own accord, African identity forms around arguments that contrast it with the West – the arguments subsequently being doubly exploited by both imperialist and populist agendas. I will outline PAWN in more detail later, suffice to say for now that it is a problematic disposition not least because by forming African identity in opposition to Western values, people consequently also oppose societal features that are *deemed to be* Western, such as homosexuality, individual rights, vegetarianism, mental health advocacy, and most centrally here, feminism.

Nevertheless, growing up there were also positive implications of 'PAWN'. If the West was greedy and exploitative, then Africa was charitable and big-hearted. If the West was unwelcoming, then

Africa was convivial. It was nice to identify with positive attributes of this nature.

It was the 1980s, and the first generation to have escaped colonial rule had matured into power. Towering figures like Fela Kuti, Nelson Mandela, Chinua Achebe, Muammar Gaddafi and Wole Soyinka energised the times with the spirit of transition, dissent and nation-building, albeit in different ways. If it shocks you that I include Muammar 'Villain' Gaddafi in my list above, then consider your reaction as an invitation to query the ways that 'good' and 'evil' are not only binary, but also often both geographically and temporally arbitrary and relative – and I say this as no fan of the man.

The matching cultural narrative about 'Africanness' – the term first used by the Tanzanian president, Julius Nyerere, in 1963 to describe 'A feeling of mutual involvement, which pervades all the political and cultural life of the continent'[2] – came to represent this counter-Western ontology of shared values, attitudes and cultural ethics. 'Africanness' had a double purpose. It was a way of describing the characteristics of Africa, for example, that '*Africa* is a place where people are mutually involved', as Nyerere puts it. It was simultaneously also a way of describing the condition of being African, that '*Africans* are people who are mutually involved.' It was, in other words, simultaneously a qualifier and a state of being, a description and a premise. 'The suffix-*ness*,' as linguists Frank Anshen and Mark Aronoff argue, 'abstracts the adjective so that it speaks to the quality of the adjective and state of the associated noun.'[3] In Africa's case, the 'quality' defined by Africanness suggests states of mutual involvement, and the 'state' of Africanness described mutually involved qualities.

The conceptual vehicles that drove this 'ontology of Africanness' across the continent's interior and diaspora were slogans and notions such as 'African Unity' and *ubuntu*. These concepts inculcated the belief that Africans (unlike Westerners) looked after the elderly, venerated their ancestors, fought for the oppressed, regarded one another respectfully, and kept the spirit of human interrelation alive.

Such were the framing stories of African identity, and I too believed them. Assiduously.

Had I not also turned out to be a feminist, the harmony between my female identity and my Africanness would have remained intact. I would have continued to comport myself with the unscathed sense that to be African was to be on the side of justice and concordance. I would have viewed African culture as uncompromisingly egalitarian. I would have single-handedly blamed inequality and oppression in the continent on colonisation and exploitation. As a result, I would advocate that women's empowerment was contingent on a return to some 'true' African ethics that championed mutuality and entitled women with power.

As it was, my feminist character complicated the matter. It opened my mind to what my eyes could already see. Women in African milieus were not *only* oppressed by the Western world's Superiorism. If you happened to be a woman, Africanness – that 'feeling of mutual involvement, which pervades all the political and cultural life of the continent' – was in fact not so 'mutually involved'. My commitment to a feminist life meant I could no longer ignore this fact.

Yes, I was a proud African woman with a strong sense of belonging. I felt a strong sense of community and revelled in the spirit of Africanness. But I also became weary of my environment. The culture around me was neocolonial and traditional-patriarchal. People accepted things that they deep down inside found oppressive simply because they were 'tradition'. We were expected to conform – to colonial legacies, indigenous family codes, religious norms and a 'politics of respectability', coined by Professor Evelyn Brooks Higginbotham to describe how polite manners, cleanliness (of person and property), and sexual purity particularly imposed on black women.[4] These elements of African culture made me feel imprisoned. I became increasingly convinced that 'Africanness', as it was conceptualised, was part of the problem for African women. To be African, according to these conceptualisations, was to be male.

My happiest coming-of-age memories involved feelings of defiance. My freedom came from books, from being in nature and from my imagination. It came from observing my mother, whose rebellious spirit I admired. She was a white woman from Finland, which suggests that I inherited a Westernised feminism from her. That wouldn't be entirely false. Western feminism – to the extent such a monolith exists – has shaped my life in significant ways. Undeniably, the second and third waves of feminism and their focus on independence, sexual autonomy and a specific kind of irreverence to moral codes, play a key role in how I view the world. Incidentally, however, my mother was the first person to introduce me to the canon of black and African feminist literature, which she herself was an avid reader of. Furthermore, what was conformist about Nigerian society to me was what freed my mother from the conformity of Finnish society. Through her, I saw that conformity was cultural and relative. She left Finland for Nigeria because she felt suffocated by its pettiness and prejudices. She rebelled against conventions, and I learned that I could, too, even if the nature of the conventions differed.

Sometimes, I wonder what my life would be like had I not taken this commitment to feminism seriously. Had I not found in feminism a way to understand and be in the world, how would I think? In what way would I live? What would my relationships look like? What would my sense of identity be in relation to being a woman?

The thought experiment sends shudders down my spine. Without feminist intervention, I'm afraid that I would have become a museum of twenty-first-century female compromise. The power that we give to male rule, male entitlement, and deeply anti-woman cultural stories in the continent and diaspora (and the world at large, for that matter) would be too big to individually go beyond and transcend without the fortification of the compendium of women-centred knowledge and healing that feminism is, and I would have been forced to conform.

To conform is to negotiate one's deepest beliefs and desires, to accept passivity to power, and to adapt to the status quo. To be coerced to conform is to be oppressed. Such conformity to patriarchal values that restrict your life by convention and politics is even more than a negotiation; it is a denial of the self. The joys of living are impossible when you squeeze yourself into a worldview that constricts and etiolates you. I discovered that the more I tried to create harmony between my inner desires and external social patterns, the more I shrivelled and shrunk.

So I rejected the script of my environment through my choices. Choice gets a bad rap in feminist discourse today, but it's one of the most important words in the dictionary that shouldn't be disregarded because it was co-opted by neoliberal market forces. Bad choices have a ripple effect that can last a lifetime if not generations. 'Choice feminism' is tied to consumerism and capitalism, but 'choice discourse' ought to be resuscitated from the discursive neoliberal rubble. Choice goes beyond consumer patterns; it is fundamentally about existence.

Rather than excite me, the thought of wifehood and motherhood, for example, were destinies that I actively chose against. I was not opposed to these roles in principle, but I could not disentangle their implications from patriarchal dominance. As Simone de Beauvoir said: 'I'm not against mothers, I am against the ideology which expects every woman to have children, and I'm against the circumstances under which mothers have to have their children.'[5]

So tied are marriage and motherhood to social acceptance in Africa, that when Safina Namukwaya, a seventy-year-old Ugandan woman, gave birth to twins in 2023, she told journalists that the reason she wanted to have children was because her co-villagers mocked her for being childless.[6] Namukwaya's news was rightly received with joy, both by her community and certainly on social media, where tens of thousands of people left comments such as 'God's miracles' on the many posts about this unique story. But I couldn't help but feel sad about the reason Namukwaya gave for her desire to become a mother. Would she still have had babies if her community had not shamed her for being childless at *seventy*? Or did she have to put her body through such hard labour to finally be accepted and feel a sense of belonging in her community? As I scrolled and scrolled comments on the post, despite myself, it dawned on me that most people approved of the news, because 'In Africa, every woman, she desires to have a baby in her lifetime, even when she is not mocked, that's a prayer for every family to have a baby.'[7] Hers is only one story but it is indicative of a cultural disposition that shapes the continent.

I don't mean to suggest that a woman must always know *what* to choose. Life is messy and complicated precisely because choice exists. There are always features of life requiring varying degrees of negotiation. From what you eat for dinner, to what you read and which political views you hold, choices must be made. Furthermore, when it comes to the defining choices in life, I am not even sure that we truly make them independently. I did not make a deliberate choice to become a feminist; the journey chose me. It was never an option to exist in this world as a woman, and not be a feminist. Rather, it was a disposition I held from as far back as I can remember even before I made the articulation. Choice is both the problem and the redemption. The more important thing is to detect one's likes and dislikes and attune them into one's life through trial and error. As the West African proverb teaches: 'You learn to cut down trees by cutting them down.'

Whatever choices I *have* made and risks I have taken pale in comparison to those made by countless women on the continent who attempt to make independent choices about their bodies, minds and souls, and consequently may become subject to ostracisation, persecution and imprisonment. I spend considerable time in Nigeria, but the hidden mores that govern society are less of a threat (and a provocation) for a woman living and writing in the West, like me. Africa has become inevitably more distant and nostalgic to me, a place that I both grieve and memorialise through the lens of my specific desires and fears as a nonconforming woman. My life remains marked by a piercing yearning for Africa, even when I am there.

If feminism gave me the gift of independent and individual choices, it took away the comfort of belonging. It created a rupture between notions of Africanness that were my source of pride, and my commitment to freedom. The same paradoxes, tensions and frictions between Africanness and feminism that this book explores have shaped my life too.

Freedom always involves prioritising the need for truth over consensus. Nonconformity is not defying rules for the sake of defying rules. That would be contrarianism. Rather, it is defying rules because they have ceased to be true to you, and to abide by regulations whose agenda you've seen through therein becomes not merely unappealing, but counterintuitive. It becomes too much of a negotiation with your sense of self. The silver lining is that at this point, adapting becomes uncomfortable and comfort is, reversely, sought in dissent and forging your own path.

Nonconformity is not an alien concept to Africa. It is ingrained into stories and myths of the continent, such as the famous rebel Anansi, in the Ashanti folktale 'Anansi the Spider', who is celebrated for a sometimes female, and sometimes male, singular-minded wit. No matter Anansi's opponent – tigers, elephants, Nature itself – Anansi's ungovernable and insolent character outsmarts them.

Widely celebrated in Africa and the diaspora, the ancestors who first told the story of Anansi, and through whom it spread as far into the world as any viral story might today, seem to have known something about spiders that scientists would only confirm much later – that spiders are indeed nonconformists. Unlike most insects, spiders do not live in eusocial societies, which are characterised by complex social structures and a division of labour. Insects who live in such eusocial societies (like bees, ants and termites), typically live in a hierarchical world divided into clans, where individuals have specific roles like 'worker', 'soldier', 'drone', or 'queen'. Bees forage for food, for example, which they bring back to the community. Soldier ants defend the colony, and drones' primary role is to mate with the queen. Spiders, however, do not engage in cooperative behaviours, which is the observation that ancestral African storytellers seem to have made when they envisioned the stubborn and charming Anansi.

Which is not to say that spiders are uncaring. As I wrote this chapter, a spider serendipitously began constructing a web outside my window. When I arrived at my desk in the mornings she was already there, shining and bobbing around the three huge, spiderling eggs that she guarded like they were the keys to heaven. Week after week, I watched her glide up, down and sideways, spinning her silk web, and catching prey and predators in her spinnerets. She seemed so singularly dedicated, I thought of the deep joy and meaning that motherhood can bring women, especially when a woman embodies motherhood on her own terms, as 'my' spider so naturally seemed to do.

By 'Spider Feminism' I mean embodying such Anansi-style traits. To refuse to conform but out of a sentiment of care toward what matters. To live an expressive life in a world carved out by and for men. To weave a life so intimately of one's own that the mind unlearns external manipulation. To live as detached from patriarchy as you can live while necessarily living *in* patriarchy. To build, to guard, to take space. To not let social pressure shrink you. To not match your life to society, but from your centre. When you make mistakes, to get up and start again, like the spider. Be there for others, take care of the communities you are a part of, but march to the beat of your own drum.

Conformity is not a flaw, I should say. Humans are not only conformists out of fear or pressure but also for survival. We are not only like spiders, but are also like bees, ants and termites, who need to 'swarm' to protect themselves from invasions. Humans, too, need smooth and efficient societal cooperation to fight against the many vulnerabilities surrounding us. In 1955, in one of the earliest studies of conformity, the Polish-American psychologist Solomon Asch proved the significant urge for social conformity in humans through his 'lines' test, where individuals yielded to social pressure and misidentified what they had previously identified as accurate. Decades later, psychologist Bibb Latané developed 'social impact theory', which went as far as to argue that conformity was analogous to a physical force such as magnetism.[8]

Social conformity enables predictability in an ever-changing world. Without any norms, we would lose a sense of meaning, and without meaning, we would annihilate society, which is not what I am calling for.

What I *am* in favour of is the elimination of norms that decipher the human need for meaning in the worst possible way: those that compel us to pursue acceptance from forces that aim to destroy us. Those that exert power, control and domination, yet claim – with pathos and fervour – to strive for harmony.

8.

Harmony Feminism

Unlearning being patriarchal women is a difficult and daunting task. So many women catch a glimpse of the possibilities of crafting new identities for themselves that are based on a sense of freedom from the control of males. But often, at some point during their lifetime, they revert to being 'good and decent' women, and sometimes it seems that they are relieved at having returned to the fold of patriarchal 'solace' and the rewards of being acceptable.

— Patricia McFadden[1]

If the rhythm of the tam-tam changes, the dance step must adapt to it.

— Kossi Proverb

Harmoniousness, the dictionary tells us, is marked by the quality of agreement. The desire for harmony, whether in personal relationships or the social order, has shaped human cultures and beliefs across eras and regions. In Ashanti mythology, the symbol for harmonious cooperation is called *Nteasee*, the Akan word for 'understanding'. In the Chinese Dao system, when Yin and Yang are in balance, there is peace in the world. The Sanskrit *Om* similarly reflects unity, and, in Greek mythology, Harmonia was worshipped as the god of cosmic balance.

Across place and time, socially and individually, people have sought for life's journey to have this irresistible harmonious quality. Like music, they want to live with others in a eurythmic symphony of percussion and horns. They may not achieve this state of unison, but the desire for harmony is ostensibly what makes a society in the first instance. Whether we think of societies in the broadest sense, as the world, or as nation states, or even more narrowly as local communities, the creation of sociopolitical, cultural and economic tools that aim at social congruence is central. In a modern state, a citizen partakes in the political processes of their society; they work and pay taxes, and maybe feel a sense of pride in belonging to where they find themselves. In ancient times, gods fulfilled a similar purpose of a shared destiny. Monarchies, republics, feudal societies, and even anarchies, all need consensus to function, which is why many of the most loved symbols and images in the social imaginary speak to society's attempts to produce harmony.

Yet neither humans nor their gods have ever achieved harmonious co-existence. The cantankerous spirits of Discord and Chaos have always kept people on their toes. In ancient Greece, snubbed by a wedding invitation, Harmonia's counterpart, Eris, started the Trojan War. The Goddess Hathor in ancient Egypt had to be sedated to prevent a killing spree. Oya, the Yoruba goddess of transformation, whose ominous name translated means 'She Tore', hid small thunders of lightning underneath her tongue so that her followers could use her words as lethal weapons against others. Political and social institutions have not fared better than divine entities in creating harmony between groups of people. Everywhere, the dream of a harmonious society remains precisely a dream.

Seen in the context of Africa, harmony has a unique character. Imperialism and colonialism not only crushed African soil, but also African people's self-image, ushering a chronic sense of discord, rather than harmony, in the continent's collective consciousness.

Since independence, the word 'Africa' has served as a verbal altar of pride and healing; contention and confusion; sorrow and shame. As Ryan Coogler, director of the Marvel film *Black Panther*, said about his struggles with African ancestry: 'I came to understand that Africa was the birthplace of human life … but the images I saw about Africa often filled me with a sense of shame.'[2]

Coogler's film became the highest grossing superhero film of all time. It is the only superhero film to date to win an Academy Award. This triumph has everything to do with how well the film embodies a sense of dissonance that underpins Africa's self-image: the dignity and pride contrasted with the shame and pain; the conviviality set against the despair; the metaphysics of consensus and mutuality between humans and other species as opposed to the disregard of political virtue. As Coogler said, the film was inspired by 'cultural references that are very real and very alive in Africa'.[3]

From Burkina Faso to Brazil to Black Britain, Africa's descendants have always brought cultural practices, such as art, music, ritual and stories, to bear the spirit of harmony as a suture for the painful memories of slavery and colonialism. As a result, harmoniousness became desired to such an extent that it assumed the quality of Scripture, a counter- hegemonic script to adhere to religiously.

One of the cultural references that has come to popularly symbolise harmony on a continent-wide and diasporic scale is the famous *ubuntu* dictum from Zululand that says: 'I am because you are.'

But what then for African feminism? If feminism at core is a disruptive force, and if the quality of harmony – for myriad reasons – underpins Africa's cultural aspirations, then where exactly does that leave African feminism? 'I am because you are' may be the aspiration, but much of African culture and identity rests upon this proclamation: 'He is because She is not.'

Ubuntu is a complex philosophy shaped by a multiplicity of debates and interpretations, and its meanings are complex and vast. The worldview that *ubuntu* espouses involves leading figures of philosophy, spirituality and criticism, such as the renowned philosopher John S. Mbiti, the charismatic bishop Desmond Tutu and the revolutionary Steve Biko, who have played important roles in popularising *ubuntu*. There is more to *ubuntu* than the slogan it is famously derived from: *Umuntu ngumuntu ngabanye bantu*, which roughly, and profoundly, means: 'A person is a person through other people.'[4]

In African and diasporic cultural discourses, *ubuntu* has emerged as a contending framework for Africanness. From the African Union to Pan-Africanist initiatives, to development work in the continent, to a vast array of scholarship and literature, *ubuntu* is a common, if not dominant, reference point of social organisation in Africa. Here, too, it predominantly assumes a distilled meaning where the slogan 'I am because you are', or versions of it, has come to mean something superficially to do with respect, interconnectedness, and harmony, but lacks the depth to effectuate its promise. Yet when truly practised, as is done especially in the Southern African regions from where the philosophy is derived, if at varying degrees of diligence, *ubuntu* truly nurtures a quality of interrelation and mutuality.

As a philosophy, *ubuntu* is as rich and layered as the teachings of Zen or Yoga. But like Zen or Yoga, mainstream *ubuntu* is simplified and decontextualised, both inside and outside of the continent. Across the Western world, *ubuntu* is invoked in an almost identical way that Westerners recourse to the word *kumbaya*, which admittedly follows a similar line but means something different – namely, to ignore differences and get along. Nevertheless, numerous projects whose aim it is to 'get along', therefore, well-intentionally connect their goals to the popular African ethical framework, *ubuntu*. Ethics, of course, are rarely straightforward, and nor are they in this instance.

Harmony is a metaphysical quality that cannot be empirically measured, but as I write this, armed conflicts occur in over thirty-five countries across the continent. Thousands of people have been killed and millions displaced by the ongoing armed conflict in Sudan between the Sudanese Armed Forces (SAF) and the government military force, Rapid Support Forces (RSF); the country's museums and universities have been looted and destroyed, and half the country's children require humanitarian assistance. Yet, the African Union, which often references *ubuntu* in its initiatives and policies, has hardly put the crisis on the top agenda. Across Africa there is a deep and debilitating inequality between the wealthy and the poor; the governed and the governing; and, of course, between women and men, with some of the highest statistics of rape and violence in the world. I'm afraid that Africa is not a harmonious continent.

Yet in the context of the African social imagination, the dream of harmony is so charged that no matter how disharmonious African societies are, the narrative overshadows reality. But without acknowledging the shadow, we cannot transcend disharmony. As Carl Jung, who popularised the notion of 'shadows' within the collective psyche, said: 'The shadow is the sum of all those unpleasant qualities we like to hide,' which, if left repressed from consciousness, 'forms an unconscious snag, blocking the most well-meant attempts.'[5]

To attempt to escape the shadow has the consequence of amplifying whatever is being evaded. It is reminiscent of the 'good guy' whose hidden sexism prevents him from the deep connections he yearns to have with women; or the 'people-pleaser' who hates the people whose approval they seek and ends up distancing rather than pleasing them; or the gay person who, for personal and/or political reasons, represses their desires and comes to fear his own mind. The same psychological effects are true for a society on a cumulative scale. The most well-meaning of attempts to build a harmonious society backfire when society's collective unconscious is unallowably repressed. As Jung continues: 'Mere suppression of the shadow is as little of a remedy as beheading would be for a headache.'[6]

The shadow of Africa is part of the immense beauty of the continent. By shadow, I don't mean the material suffering or structural problems. Rather, I mean the psycho-spiritual shadow: the grievances, the insecurities, the anxieties, the fury, the self-loathing. These are collective emotions that are masked, occasionally by hubris and denial, producing the inability to take responsibility, and therein realise the true voice and alignment. A shadow, after all, must be acknowledged in order to be healed. And this is key: a shadow can be healed. A shadow is not an impasse. True darkness is the absence of a shadow.

There is a fair portion of validity to the assertion that Africans are a harmonious people, however, we should not imbue Africa with a material harmony that it does not have, neither should the layered qualities of harmoniousness that Africanness does indeed possess be denied. I'm often stirred by the grace and bonhomie one witnesses among Africans. A magnanimity and generosity of spirit is, indeed, almost palpable in Africa and the diaspora. You can see this conscientiousness in small gestures of courteousness such as the 'black nod' – which it may surprise some readers to learn is even more common in Africa than in the diaspora and is, thus, not simply a greeting that two alienated black people may extend to one another in a white environment. Despite its size, Lagos is, for instance, a city where it is still commonplace to greet strangers, regardless of their class or background, when passing them by – and in fact it is socially rude not to: 'The African understanding of greeting is the affirmation of our spirit and interconnectedness,' the South African philosopher John Eliastam argues, adding that it is 'not uncommon to hear Africans referring to someone who does not greet as *ga se motho,* (s/he is not human).'[7]

Foreigners who spend a substantial amount of time in Africa also often share how warm and friendly people are, and how their time on the continent helps them to develop a humanistic outlook. In global rankings of charitable donations, three African countries (Kenya, Sierra Leone and Zambia) are listed in the top ten for having the highest scores and participation in giving across the world.[8] This large- heartedness is remarkable considering that these countries are also ranked among the world's poorest.

Still, there might be other reasons for the harmonious quality of kinship that can be found across the continent and diaspora and that is alluded to by philosophies such as mainstream *ubuntu.* The deep sense of solidarity that comes with having been harmed by an external force for so long, as Africa has with its pained relationship to the West, is one likely reason for African conviviality. That Africa historically consisted of city-states and kingdoms, may be another reason for its close-knit character.

Seen in the context of the divisions that wreak havoc in the continent, the insistence on a practised spirit of harmony seems a pyrrhic detachment from reality. It appears that African societies proclaim harmoniousness, while in fact being pathologically disharmonious. How do we reconcile this? Certainly not by avoiding the shadow. This focus opens crucial issues about social harmony for feminism. Can feminism be confronting *and* co-operative? Can women be liberated *and* accordant? Or do feminists have to choose between harmony and freedom?

I imagine that many African feminists would assert that feminism cannot be harmonious and nonconforming at once. They would argue that the nature of feminism is, by contrast, disruptive. Radical, paradigmatic shifts of the social order are what motivates feminism, and feminism is nothing if it is not subversive and if it does not disturb the peace.

Yet I want to trouble this stance somewhat, because the feminist movement itself tells a more complex story. Rather than pull the plug on patriarchal institutions and subvert them, feminists have often affected change through pragmatic strategies, such as the power of argument, appeal to emotion and common-sense negotiations. The relatively few concerted feminist strategies that break with the status quo – separatism, political lesbianism, matriarchal communities, etc. – stand out precisely for being outliers. In the 1990s the Nigerian feminist Obioma Nnaemeka called for an approach to feminism that she named 'Nego-feminism', a coinage which stems from 'feminism of negotiation'. Her theory was based on the argument that unfavourable conditions ought to be challenged through negotiation, a concept which Nnaemeka argued lay at the heart of African cultures. Therefore, Nnaemeka also proposed, Nego-feminism had a double-meaning. It was also a contraction of 'no ego feminism', which she contrasted to Western feminism's imperialism and arrogance.

Similarly, Nigerian feminist Molara Ogundipe-Leslie coined what she referred to as 'Stiwanism', an acronym for 'Social Transformation Including Women in Africa'. The central purpose of Stiwanism was a pragmatic one – to involve more women and men in feminist work without having to deflect energies from repetitively responding to charges of imitating Western feminism.[9]

In the next chapter, I'll address some key contentions between African and Western feminism, but here I want to emphasise another strand of what I shall describe as 'Harmony Feminism', feminism that appeals to consensus. This strand is not specifically 'African' but rather it is a global one, namely: Liberal Feminism. The liberal feminist movement, arguably the most widely known of feminist schools of thought, has largely been a branch that has progressed through pragmatic and negotiating strategies. Liberal Feminism has not changed politics through the radical uprooting of society, but rather through attempts to harmonise social institutions. It has changed policies through advocacy, unequal power structures through quotas, gender roles through educational incentives, and tradition through appeals to rationality and science.

I am a supporter of all feminism. That is, I acknowledge and largely appreciate all strands of feminism that adhere to its core principles, rooted in anti-patriarchal ideology, while recognising variations in their implementation. Hence, I find myself unable to align with movements like 'Reformist Feminism' and 'Conservative Feminism'. These ideologies, instead of embracing an explicit anti-patriarchal stance, often propagate the notion that women's genuine empowerment stems from conforming to and acquiescing within traditional patriarchal structures.

But despite its association with certain problematic Enlightenment ideals and my misgivings about those associations, I preserve support for Liberal Feminism. Similarly, I extend my support to other 'problematic' feminist ideologies, such as Cultural Feminism, which may exhibit essentialist tendencies, or religious feminisms like Islamic or Christian Feminism, despite their entanglement within persistently patriarchal belief systems. None of these feminist schools directly shape my primary intellectual or psychological endeavours. Nonetheless, in a world rife with harmful ideologies, even these 'flawed' feminisms are contributing to social change in important ways, in my perspective.

Also, you could argue that it doesn't matter which tactics feminists use. So long as the outcome improves women's lives, the tactic is secondary.

For these reasons, even while raising concerns about it, I also appreciate that what I will henceforth refer to as 'Harmony Feminism' is a form of feminism characterised by an emphasis on achieving progress through the cultivation of harmony, rather than through disruptive means. Harmony Feminism is a methodology centred around the pursuit of concordance. It prioritises the inclusion of women into cultural narratives through tactics such as representation or gender-inclusive history that incorporates women's perspectives, achievements and struggles into the historical record.

Two Icons

Transformation can emerge from both negotiation and disturbing the peace. Two of Africa's most iconic figures of women's liberation, the South African revolutionary and politician Winnie Madikizela-Mandela, and the South African artist and activist Miriam Makeba, speak to the sensibilities that I am addressing here. The first African to ever win a Grammy Award, Miriam Makeba was a darling of liberal international audiences who lauded her for her talent, glamour and sharp tongue. In a talk she gave at the United Nations, she pleaded in her typically reserved but determined manner: 'I ask you and all the world leaders: would you act differently? Would you keep silent and do nothing if you were in our place? Would you not resist if you were allowed no rights in your own country because the colour of your skin is different to that of the rulers, and if you were punished for even asking for equality?'[10]

Winnie Madikizela-Mandela, on the other hand, never asked for freedom. Believing in the right of black South Africans to defend themselves, including, controversially, ultimately, with unflinching violence, Madikizela-Mandela was imprisoned, violated against, abused, shouted at, forced into isolation, judged and reprimanded, but stood her ground.

Both women were committed to the African feminist causes of women's emancipation and African liberation. Still, Madikizela-Mandela adopted a direct, troublemaking attitude. At the same time, Makeba's more reconciliatory approach granted her the saintly moniker 'Mama Africa', and her signature 'Pata Pata' song symbolises the harmonious quality that she so powerfully conveyed. Despite their differences, both Makeba and Madikizela-Mandela were deeply committed to justice and left an indelible mark not only on the history of Africa but also on the world. Both women fought for the rights of African women but with different demeanours.

To the extent Makeba was a feminist (a claim, which to my knowledge, she never publicly made), you could say that she was a Harmony Feminist. Madikizela-Mandela, on the other hand, could be described as what the scholar Sara Ahmed calls a 'feminist killjoy', the feminist who disrupts the perceived social harmony in the context of gender and patriarchy with her uncomfortable truths. The feminist killjoy refuses to participate in social norms and traditions that are sexist or uphold systemic inequalities, by contrast, making them uncomfortable for others too. The term 'killjoy' is used somewhat ironically, however, as the feminist killjoy is not about diminishing joy but rather about questioning and dismantling the structures that limit the full expression of agency.[11]

In previous chapters, I discussed my opposition to dualistic thinking, and I should therefore clarify that the Harmony Feminist and the feminist killjoy are not straightforwardly contrasting, and neither are Makeba and Madikizela-Mandela. Makeba, too, was a feminist killjoy. She was a renegade who married five different men (at separate times) in a culture where people expect women (but not men) to be infinitely loyal to just one partner. On stage, she evoked the femme fatale to an extent that makes the erotic power of Beyoncé's alter-ego 'Sasha Fierce' seem as innocent as a lotus flower. Makeba was an unusual but striking blend: a gentle and maternal woman with a huge appetite for life, and an unscrupulously independent woman with a tender soul.

On the other hand, Winnie spent many years portraying herself as the 'mother of the nation', and the doting wife of her imprisoned husband, Nelson Mandela, until she famously didn't. She too had two starkly contrasting images. She was 'Mandela's wife', a woman who made heavy sacrifices for the struggle against apartheid, and yet she was possibly one of the most 'un-wifely' political icons that the twentieth century produced.

So, if I am invoking a binary 'Malcolm X vs Martin Luther King' type of contrast about Winnie and Makeba, it is because I am speaking about them as icons, and the images that their personalities implanted in the social imaginary, rather than as the far more complex women that they were in reality. In this regard, I contend that Miriam 'Mama Africa' Makeba's image is a harmonious one that evokes feelings of unproblematic love and pride in Africans and Westerners alike; whereas Winnie Madikizela-Mandela image represents a presence towards which people harbour both fear and awe.

As already stated, my aim in this chapter has not been to make a judgement about Harmony Feminism, as I accept that, under the right circumstances, this form of feminism can effect desirable change. At its core, Harmony Feminism champions the preservation of a kind of moral beauty and mutual understanding within society, for harmony is undoubtedly a soothing quality. Harmony is arguably a balance between chaos and nothingness. Entropy is avoided by harmony, and at its most potent, the effect of harmoniousness is blissfully felt through the senses. Eliastam argues that harmonious relations within a community amount to good health, whereas ill-health is the experience of disharmony in one's relations with the community. When someone responds: 'Re gona/teng' ('We are here'), they affirm good health. But from an ethical view, Re gona means that harmony prevails in communal relations, and there is good health therefore.[12]

Yet, Harmony Feminism contains elements to be watchful of. When the pursuit of harmony becomes gospel, when an individual's flow threatens a society's accordance, and a society's coherence comes at the cost of an individual's well-being, then harmony becomes counter-harmonious. When feminism loses its bearing as a movement that is in opposition to conformity, then it risks homeostasis and becoming part of the oppressive pattern.

There is no rulebook for feminism. Feminism is a multi-faceted space of activism, resistance, theory, storytelling, play and imagination. It is in constant and fluid movement. In my view it is permissible, even desirable, to mix the many schools of feminism according to one's individual and shared situations. There are occasions when, either by impulse or intention, we call upon our feminist killjoy persona, and there are scenarios where Harmony Feminism works. To be a feminist does not mean to constantly be on alert and ready to call out sexism at every turn.

Yes, feminism is polemical at its core; it predicates an ideological position that is 'against' something else – patriarchy. But feminism is also a place of vision and lived practice – trial and error. With time and commitment, feminism becomes second nature, and although it never becomes 'easy', as the epigraph by Patricia McFadden in this chapter implies, freedom from 'the control of males' is indeed a complete possibility in one's personal space at least.

The idea that African women ought to have the same rights and privileges as African men – indeed as all men – is a premise that remains contentious across the continent. Deeply ingrained social, political, and cultural values and codes push back against the idea of gender equality. Discussions that concern the independence of African women are met by an adversarial cultural logic that is profoundly anti- feminist because feminism is seen as disruptive of social harmony. But feminism, at its core, is an anti-authoritarian philosophy. And even if an authority *insists on harmony*, it is still an authority.

Can feminism be African? is an intentionally peace-disturbing question. It prods both into what it means to be African and what it means to be feminist: two forms of identity that are contentious in themselves, let alone when brought together. However, my aim is not to disturb the peace for the sake of disturbing the peace. It is to engage with the provocations that feminism raises concerning Africa, or we will continue to be avalanched by patriarchal backlash and pushback from all corners. It is to harmoniously be a feminist killjoy. (This is glib, but it's worth considering.)

I started this chapter with the image of music. But even in music it is true that harmony and conformity are not necessarily the same. Instruments clash when, in fact, they are creating something new. Notes stray off, but that makes the song unforgettable. The atonal guitar lends character to the performance, and combinations of seemingly discordant musical genres can capture your intrigue.

African feminism is a melody of this atypical nature. It has the perilous task of rattling and shaking our false self-assumptions regarding harmoniousness, and illuminating the shadows underneath which some of the worst evils of patriarchal rule lurk. As an African feminist, you barter – the comfort of belonging, your sources of pride, your nostalgia. You can no longer praise Africa, its ancestors and its history without reservation. The once unwavering love you once poured upon your African identity becomes more complicated and haunting. But it also becomes more unwavering for this reason. You love Africa with – and not despite – its disharmony. To the extent that African identity is constructed on fantasies of harmony, you are now a conscientious objector, the one who cares enough to disapprove.

9.

Andro-Africanism

Have an imagination that is plain stubborn, that can invent new gods and banish ineffectual ones.
— Yvonne Vera[1]

We have to free half of the human race, the women, so that they can help to free the other half.
— Emmeline Pankhurst[2]

Let us begin at the end of the launch of the intergovernmental 'Organization of African Unity' (OAU) in Addis Ababa in 1963, and with the closing remarks presented by the Ugandan envoy, H. E. Milton Obote. 'Allow me, Your Majesty,' Obote remarked, 'also on behalf of my colleagues to express their thanks to the Secretary General of the Conference, the Secretary, the interpreters, all the officials and aids who have made our work easy and very interesting, and to the Ethiopian people who cheered us and kept us happy day and night.'[3]

The inclusion of the words 'and night' in Obote's remarks was a wink to his co-presenters – presenters who included none other than the towering figures Léopold Sédar Senghor, Kwame Nkrumah, Julius Nyerere, Sekou Touré, Haile Selassie and Tafawa Balewa. To Western readers, these names may not say much. But to Africans, they denominate larger-than-life figures, freedom fighters and luminaries who threw the colonialists from Africa's driving seat and steered the wheels of the continent towards independence.

Obote's 'and night' was an inside joke referring to the fact that the all-male leaders of Africa's thirty-two newly independent nations had not only been cared for by their official hosts but also, in the wee hours, by Addis Ababa's most exclusive sex workers. As Professor Bereket Habte Selassie, who participated in the inauguration as Ethiopia's chief lawyer, writes: 'The government had coached and admonished the women to behave like proud Africans and devotees of African Unity and to be ready to perform their services in pursuit of that noble ideal.'[4] We cannot be sure, even if it seems unlikely, that it was the government's 'coaching' that specifically perfected the sex workers' services to such an extent that Chief Madame Aseghedech Alamiro, their manager, would be awarded medals by His Majesty King Haile Selassie. What is more believable, however, is the argument that their services were so satisfactory that they provided a key reason that the OAU, which later morphed into the African Union (AU), became an Addis-based-affair.

The African Union is, notably, the largest existing institution rooted in Pan-Africanism. Pan-Africanism is certainly the ideological movement that has impacted Africa more than any other. The doctrine rose to the world with the first Pan-African conference in 1919, and by the fifth series of the gatherings, in 1945, it was an established school of political thought, set to shape the course of human history.

Twentieth-century Pan-Africanism is primarily associated with heroical avatars of black identity, such as W. E. B. Du Bois, Marcus Garvey and George Padmore. However, perhaps the most central figure of Pan-Africanism that we in the twenty-first century refer to is Ghana's first president, Kwame Nkrumah. As historian Toyin Falola argues: 'Modern Pan-Africanism evolved with Kwame Nkrumah in 1957 as Ghana gained independence and he emerged as the country's prime minister. His political vision of Pan-Africanism quickly became the forefront of Pan-Africanism in Africa.'[5] This perspective of Nkrumah's had a lasting impact on the continent. According to historian C. L. R. James: 'He raised the status of Africa and Africans to a pitch higher than it had ever reached before.'[6]

Nkrumah's position can be summarised by the slogan 'African Unity', which he defined as: 'A political kingdom which can only be gained by political means', and which became a matter of contention at the Addis Ababa launch of the OAU. At the event, Nkrumah's Tanzanian counterpart, Julius Nyerere – who, as said, coined the notion of Africanness – provocatively proclaimed: 'There is not going to be a God who will bring about African Unity, by merely willing unity and saying let there be unity.'[7]

These words aggravated Nkrumah, to whom they indeed were directed. With his 1968 socialist theory of *Ujamaa*, Nyerere propagated what is referred to as a 'gradualist', slower-paced and more pragmatic approach to African Unity than Nkrumah did. Aware of his iconoclastic status, Nkrumah threatened to leave the event due to Nyerere's provoking remarks. But he was eventually persuaded (by Guinea's first president, Sekou Touré) to stay, with the ultimatum that African Unity be established there and then, or 'we who are sitting here today shall tomorrow be the victims and martyrs of neocolonialism'.[8] At large, Nkrumah turned out to be right. Yet, as the men moulded and shaped Africa's future day – and night – there was another system of oppression and another type of 'martyr', whose absence remained unacknowledged: African women.

The point of sharing the Addis Ababa story is not to make any judgement about sex work but rather to argue that, aside from the geographical, historical, cultural, etc., dimensions of Africa that I referred to in the first chapter, another response to the question of what is Africa? is a man. To be African is to be male. 'Andro-Africanism' is a concept that I coin here to describe this conflation of masculine identity with African identity. It is one that implants androcentric ideals into the very notion of Africanness.

In my book *Sensuous Knowledge*, I conceptualised a term that is comparable to Andro-Africanism – 'Europatriarchy' – to help describe a worldview that is simultaneously Eurocentric and patriarchal.

This was not so much to critique the biases of what I refer to as 'Europatriarchal Knowledge', as it is evident that any biased way of knowing is incomplete, by definition. Instead, I wanted to understand the characteristics of Europatriarchal Knowledge and how they create harm far beyond the borders and delineations of Europe. I argued that these characteristics leaned upon a worship of rationality whereby any societal feature which cannot be rationally explained – for example: freedom, love, the future or intuition – is diminished and forced into a framework of rigid logic or neglected. Inevitably, this pattern of behaviour leads to a robotic disposition befitting of the controlling tactics of combined Eurocentric and patriarchal beliefs. I have continued many of these threads in this book as well.

My definition of Andro-Africanism is cut from a similar cloth. Again, my aim is not simply to critique male dominance in Africa, or the multitude of issues arising from it. It is evident to any thinking person today that male dominance is an impediment not only to socioeconomic and political progress but also to ethical development and wisdom. No society can thrive if one half of its members psychologically and systemically controls the other half. To the extent that I focus on 'the oppressor' in my work, the aim is to illuminate their actions towards my real focus – 'the oppressed' – so that we can free ourselves from systemic deceptions and have the capacity to flourish (*eudaemonia*!). My motivation in pointing at the ways that men have woven masculinity into the foundational architecture of what Africanness means is so that women can see the construct more clearly, and consequently reject definitions of Africanness that alienate and Other us.

The term 'androcentrism' was coined by the sociologist Lester Ward in 1903 to describe the viewpoint that: 'the male sex is primary and the female secondary in the organic scheme, that all things centre, as it were, about the male, and that the female, though necessary in carrying out the scheme, is only the means of continuing the life of the globe, but is otherwise an unimportant accessory, and incidental factor in the general result'.[9] In short, the male is at the centre, and the female is at the periphery. Africa is no different to other continents in the world, where whatever autonomic space the society offers the individual, it is less if one is female. Unfortunately, we do not know of a time in modern history when women of a racial/ethnic/class group were not disadvantaged in comparison to men of the same racial/ethnic/class group. We know of times (including this current one) when women of one race, ethnicity and/or class may have social advantages over men of another race, ethnicity and/or class. We pay attention to the ways that patriarchy – that is, the psychological and political system that values the male higher than the female – uses law, tradition, force, ritual, customs, education, language, labour, etc.. to keep women governed by men in both public and private life. African feminism sees that African men and women could have mutually beneficial, transformative and progressive relationships in the private and public spheres if our relationships were non-patriarchal and egalitarian. The problem, is that this prospect is impossible with Andro-Africanism. Africanness is not neutral, it is in fact shaped from the androcentric thresholds of male experience.

If we were to adopt a woman-centred and feminist perspective on Africanness, the notion would undoubtedly assume different qualities. If women had more say in the discourse on Africanness, a quality like *healing*, to give one example, might be central in shaping the discourse. *Imagination* is another quality that African women might feature as a prominent one. I also suspect that if women were the shapers of Africanness, the notion would be infused with *insouciance*, or what in Nigeria is referred to as *shakara*.

Shakara is a term that implies a kind of ostentatious behaviour, used to signify confidence and to indicate that one does not assign more importance to others than they deserve. A conceivably gendered term, when it comes to women, *shakara* has an erotic power. Women who engage in *shakara* behaviour may do so through their fashion choices, demeanour and social interactions. They carry themselves with poise and self-assurance, demand to be treated with respect, and are selective about who they associate with. A woman with a *shakara* mindset is simultaneously disobedient, powerful, serious, troublesome, wise, playful, tough, authentic and erotic – in the Audre Lorde-ian sense of the erotic as a source of power that both includes and transcends sexual passion.

'Female freedom always means sexual freedom' (as Toni Morrison said[10]) and importing *shakara* into gender politics implicates the relationship between the erotic, power and liberation. A *shakara* mindset is to not let biased political narratives – none at all, not men who sit mightily on power, not respectability politics about appropriate or normative behaviour, not white supremacist fantasies about racial hierarchies, not religions that dictate that women should submit to men, not ideas that negate the life-giving act of mothering, not media that obsesses with depicting women weakly, not even the inevitability of ageing, let alone the mortifying mythification surrounding it – compromise a woman's appetite for life. If women shaped Africanness on the institutionalised level that men do, then healing, imagination, insouciance and *shakara*, among other things, of course, would be directly or indirectly implicated. And that would change the continent's internal and external relations.

Instead, male-dominant shapers of Africanness have tended to follow a Pan-Africanist school of thought, where male authority and female passivity are celebrated, except in the domestic space. Male authorities have depreciated – if not shown contempt – for nonconforming women who embody elements such as healing, imagination and *shakara*, while inscribing ideas about masculine prowess and entitlement as a kind of natural law, among other bellicose claims, into African identity. For instance, writing about polygamy in his autobiography, Kwame Nkrumah said: 'However unconventional and unsatisfactory this way of life may appear to those who are confirmed monogamists, and without in any way trying to defend my own sex, it is a frequently accepted fact that man is naturally polygamous.'[11] This may or may not be the case, but who is to say that the female sex is not also 'naturally' polygamous. Women in ancient Africa also had multiple male lovers, and many African cultures codified this practice.[12] Women could equally draw from the past for supporting arguments to any given desire.

The theme continues in Chinua Achebe's *Things Fall Apart*, one of the most seminal books that has shaped Africanness. The novel's protagonist, Okonkwo, represents Andro-Africanism in his prime. Okonkwo is a strong and chauvinistic man who is determined not to become like his lazy father, Unoka. As he succeeds in this mission and rises to become a warrior and leader in the Igbo community of Umuofia, located in what is now Nigeria, he takes three wives. When British colonialism and Christianity encroach upon Umuofia, some members of the clan convert to Christianity including, to Okonkwo's ire, his son Nwoye. In an uprising, a church is destroyed and Okonkwo is arrested. Upon his release, Okonkwo kills a British administrator, assuming his clansmen will support him. However, the clansmen do not, and Okonkwo forsakes his cause to protect traditional society and takes his own life. *Things Fall Apart* is a portrayal of Andro-Africanism.

Alongside the weighty political conferences, stories and manifestos, Andro-Africanism solidified in ideologically driven cultural festivals, such as the 'Rumble in the Jungle', where Muhammed Ali and George Forman fought in Zaire (Congo), under the $10 million sponsorship of the country's endemically narcissistic and corrupt leader, Mobutu Sese Seko. The world's most-watched live television broadcast at the time, 'Rumble in the Jungle' helped Mobutu, who some years before had served as the chair of the OAU, in his self-imaging campaign as 'King and Messiah of African Unity'.

As the Afrobeat originator Fela Kuti, another inspiring figure who was also staunchly Andro-Africanist, once said: 'To call me a sexist … for me, it's still not a negative name. If I'm a sexist, it's a gift.'[13] (And if Fela's words sound shocking, then I'm sorry to inform you that it is vanilla misogyny compared to the sexism in the contemporary succession of Afrobeat – Afrobeats with an 's' – with numerous artists profiting from the codified cultural exclusion of women in what it means to be African: Andro-Africanism.) In the political scene, a disgraceful perspective of the role of women was expressed by former Nigerian president Muhammadu Buhari when he, in a meeting with German chancellor Angela Merkel in 2016, uttered the words: 'I don't know exactly what party my wife belongs to. Actually, she belongs in the kitchen, the living room and the other rooms in my house.'[14]

It is not my intention to mitigate the important achievements of Africa's founding fathers. They were individuals driven by an unwavering passion for African liberation. Kwame Nkrumah is one of the greatest revolutionaries to have lived. *Things Fall Apart* is a masterpiece. Fela Kuti was of another dimension, and one of the ancestors by whom I am the most inspired. Sure, there have been numerous disasters – Buhari is one such case – but there are also good men in their midst, some exceptionally so. Thomas Sankara, the revolutionary president of Burkina Faso, and Amílcar Cabral, the anti- colonial leader of Guinea-Bissau and Cape Verde, for example, were exemplary in their attention to gendered oppression, among other bars they raised during the period when Andro-Africanism was inculcated.

Furthermore, the Andro-Africanist worldview is not necessarily malicious; it is, in many instances, just a consequence of not knowing better and/or being drunk on entitlement. The 1960s were, after all, a period of possibility for Africa's leading male elite. The times were, for this demographic, characterised by access to real transformative power and potency, frothing with the spirit of independence, modernity and brotherhood. The male elite hosted and attended conferences, roundtables and summits that would shape Africa – Empirical Africa and Metaphysical Africa – its political institutions and social imaginaries. They were made to seem flawless.

But obscured in the iconoclastic myths left behind were scandalous elements. Nkrumah had populist Big Man tendencies, despite Guadeloupean writer Marysa Condé's spicy assertion that he was 'vegetating in mediocrity'.[15] For all its strengths, Pan-Africanism brought a spew of machismo and essentialism to African identity.

It is important to challenge the miseducation, not the people subjected to it. It was no accident that the early Pan-Africans held thoroughly patriarchal views. They had been conquered by a foreign patriarchy that made it clear that their masculinity was a threat. The transatlantic slave trade had capitalised on their bodies and minds.

They, therefore, believed that to decolonise, Africa must nationalise, and nationalism and patriarchy go hand in hand.

In one of the best books of the twentieth century, *Black Macho and the Myth of the Superwoman*, author Michele Wallace defined, within the context of America, a type of black man who was both the fantasy and the nightmare of white men: a man who could 'combine the ghetto cunning, cool, and unrestrained sexuality of black survival with the unchecked authority, control, and wealth of white power'. This man was the 'Black Macho' – the hypersexualised man whose quest for black liberation equated with his retaliatory assertion of manhood. As Wallace writes: 'Out of his sense of urgency came a struggle called the Black Movement, which was nothing more nor less than the black man's struggle to attain his presumably lost "manhood".'[16]

If black liberation in America produced the Black Macho, then Pan-Africanism on the continent delivered Andro-Africanism – a parallel phenomenon envisioned through Big Man politics, strongman literature, male-centred history, art, music and social narrative. Just as the Black Macho grew out of the Black Movement, Andro-Africanism bloomed during the struggles for African independence. They grew out of the same intertwined and hybrid space, where a love for 'the people' and a desire for male supremacy, sad to say, interbred.

The black community wasn't open to hearing feminist truths about the harm that patriarchy does. Wallace's book received ferocious criticism; she was vilified, scoffed at, ridiculed and attacked. The historian Gerda Lerner said: 'Perhaps the greatest challenge to thinking women is the challenge to move from the desire for safety and approval to the most "unfeminine" quality of all – that of *intellectual arrogance*, the supreme hubris which asserts to itself the right to reorder the world. The hubris of the god makers, the hubris of the male-system builders.'[17]

Yes. Wallace wrote *Black Macho* with the 'intellectual arrogance' (also, *shakara*) that Lerner speaks of. So do I in this book. When it comes to intellectually 'reordering the world', *shakara* should be the disposition of more women (the epilogue of this book will expand on *shakara*). After all, what else is feminism but 'reordering the world' and how else do we do this if not with a healthy amount of *Fuck-yous* in our temper? The task of feminism is to understand how patriarchy subjugates women so that women can challenge the severe problem that, as a female, you don't possess the same rights as men: you are disadvantaged in the most critical aspects of livelihood; your religion is at war with you; you don't have access to equal education or land ownership; the medical system is not tailored to your female anatomy, and is often spun against it; walking down the street isn't safe, as you are at the risk of being violently abused simply because of your gender; and your history is unwritten and thwarted. How do you address all this if you don't believe you are entitled to change the system?

Without the interventions of the Andro-Africanist fraternity securing Pan-Africanism we would be worse off today. The problem is that the 'we' in this instance is not a straightforward 'we' (is it ever?). African men would indeed be worse off if not for the visions painted onto the African canvas by the Pan-African heroes of the independence era. Still, when it comes to African women, it is not a hundred per cent clear that things would altogether be worse without the boom of Pan-Africanism in the 1960s and 1970s – a controversial remark, I know.

Of course, African women are better off living in independent African nations than in colonised ones – this is not an invitation to pursue the imperialist logic that African women need saving from African men, especially not by any analogous patriarchal system from the West. It is undoubtedly not a convoluted tribute to colonial rule. What the continent's women would have benefited from would have been feminist post-independence politics. The fact is that the poor rankings of the quality of life for African women – the abuse, violence, misogyny, rape, dismissal and harm – is caused equally by Andro-Africanism as it is by Superiorism and neocolonialism.

The type of African man that emerged from Pan-Africanism's heyday had no time for women, except 'at night'.

To him, feminism was unnecessary in the same way that it is redundant to eat vitamins if you follow a healthy diet. He was convinced that he loves and respects African women. He honours their strength, determination and resilience. He 'celebrates' them, especially his amazing mother, glorious grandmother, extraordinary great- grandmother and his most fantastic great-great grandmother. African women didn't need feminism; they simply needed to return to their maternal, if not their matriarchal, roots. Thus, canonical books such as *Decolonising the Mind* and Nkrumah's *Consciencism* said nothing about the feminist roots of the continent. Quite the contrary, they contributed to the backlash.

Long before this era, in times when African civilisations were organically taking shape, women indeed had access to spiritual and political power – although it is questionable if they lived in matriarchies in the sense of the term that means a social system in which women hold primary power and leadership roles, particularly in political, economic and social spheres. The appeal in the matriarchy myth is to silence feminist calls for change, since if we once upon a time lived in matriarchies, then we are supposed to imagine that we one day might return to them automatically, as a law of nature.

Myths are powerful tools to help us shape our identities; they can be psychologically empowering and balancing, and I hate to be unsentimental about them. Like many women, I love to read about societies in which women historically had more power than is typical today. Furthermore, there are truths to most myths. It is true that African women were goddesses, healers and shamans. They were powerful traders and queens. They also fought side by side with men (and without them, for that matter) during the independence struggles for autonomy from colonialists. But the truth of the matter is that from the 1960s onwards – that is the period that has been seminal in shaping Africanness as we think of it today – the contributions of women were forgotten, and it was not until 2012 that a woman, Nkosazana Dlamini-Zuma, took her seat as the chairperson of the African Union. Although men have typically agreed that Africanness is a difficult concept to define, they have nevertheless not only defined it, but they have also done so in ways that compromise women's minds, bodies and contributions to society.

What are the consequences of defining Africanness through an androcentric lens? How does the presumed neutrality of male perspectives about African identity impact women's lives?

Also, what kind of institutions would Pan-Africanism have built if women had equally been its architects? What would the continent's 'Founding Mothers' make, for example, of a notion like honour – a typically masculine emotion? How would women encode Africanness into spiritual, cultural, social and political life? To give an example, capitalism depends on the patriarchs, the essential men who decide what to spend money on (or not spend it on). After all, those with political responsibility also have economic responsibility, and those with financial responsibility also steer the culture. What response to capitalism would engender a 'Gyno-African' (female-centred African) identity rather than an Andro-African one? What would our African women ancestors say about Africanness? What would Africanness look like if the ideas of women such as Adelaide Casely-Hayford, the Sierra Leonian educator; or Wangari Maathai, Kenyan ecofeminist and Nobel laureate; or Albertina Sisulu, the Pan-African activist; or Nana Yaa Asantewaa, Ghanaian chief of army; or Funmilayo Ransome-Kuti, Nigerian activist and political figure; or Winnie Madikizela-Mandela, South African anti-apartheid activist and politician; or Miriam Makeba, South African artist and Pan-Africanist; or Charlotte Maxeke, South African revolutionary; or Queen Nzinga of Angola; or Sophie Bosede Oluwole, Nigerian feminist philosopher, had had the same impact as those men at the helm in shaping our shared identity.

We cannot know because men's ideas, thoughts, arguments, values, beliefs, attitudes and preoccupations with Africa dominate our aesthetic, political and cultural thoughts. How would women have shaped states that now push rigid heterosexist ideas as the norm? How would they unlink sexual dominance from sexual pleasure? And prevent women's bodies from bearing the wounds of history, and of foreign intrusion and prolonged national struggles? How would they address the psychological and physical suffering that women endure after violation?

These hypothetical questions and could-have-beens are not indulgent thought experiments. It is necessary to take women's understandings and experiences into account when it comes to Africanness, because there is a way of thinking about gender that predicates the continent's identity, and the area of identity is one that is unconscionably male. Thinking about women's experiences brings clarity to specific issues concerning entitlement and masculinity. 'Entitlement,' philosopher Kate Manne writes in her book *Entitled*, 'is not a dirty word: entitlements can be genuine, valid, justified.' Yet entitlement has 'most often referred to some people's undue sense of what they deserve or are owed by others'. Men, she argues, believe they deserve 'Masculine goods', which according to Manne are: 'power, authority, and claims to knowledge'. On the other hand: 'Women are expected to give traditionally feminine goods (such as sex, nurturing, and reproductive labour).'[18] Defined as by the above, the word 'entitlement' is befitting the Andro-African. It is not that women are not 'African'. It is that Africa is not one of our 'Feminine goods' to shape.

African women come from a continent which imperialist powers have subjected to centuries of various kinds of assaults, from slavery to colonialism, to unfair trade agreements and capitalist interests, to religious change. These historical experiences have a different impact on women and men. The marginalisation of Africa in the global economy has gender implications. So, for instance, Africa is a continent where most farmers are women, and yet it is also a continent where female farmers are disadvantaged by lack of access to land ownership because women are not entitled to own lands or manage money. The Nigerian senate, for instance, has repeatedly denied a bill that advocates the right of rural women 'to have access to agricultural credit and loans, marketing facilities, appropriate technology and equal treatment in land and agrarian reform', with claims that the bill is 'antagonistic to African traditions'.[19] If African traditions only enable men to own land, then it seems that women are not fully African. Within the construct of the Other, African women are the Other's Other.

The material, the metaphysical, the sociopolitical and the psychological dimensions of Africa all have an androcentric leaning. Women are not equal makers of the African project. 'Until the lions produce their own historians, the story of the hunt will glorify only the hunter,' says a classical African proverb. 'The lion' in this proverb is the African people, and 'the hunter' is imperialism. Also, the lion is an African woman, and the hunter is Andro-Africanism.

While writing this book, I watched a video recorded in Burkina Faso. It featured a large group of women of mixed ages all wearing red wrappers around their waists, hands, necks and heads. Only their breasts were bare. They had gathered outside a male authority's quarters to express their dissatisfaction with him. They sang a plaintive protest against androcentrism, even if they did not call it that. Their wailing was mournful and lingering, like a melodious jeremiad, with layers of lament – weeping, chanting, screaming, bellowing, howling. Against the background of their chorus there was whistling, singing and the faint beat of a drum. The fusion of these sounds produced an eerie but beautiful piece de resistance. It was like a hymn of *shakara*. These women did not care what the men thought about them. They were unaffected by judgements about their nudity, or taking up space. Their focus was on their needs. They were entitled.

Africa was never truly matriarchal, but its women are and were undoubtedly powerful. Rather than merely 'celebrate' African women, as Andro-Africanism often claims to do, women should be listened to, and our opinions and experiences should be centered in the defining of Africanness.

10.

Homegrown Feminism

The case is for an uncompromising politics for the substantive power of African women – all African women – no ifs, no buts.

– Simidele Dosekun

On the day that the publication of this book was announced, I received an email from a scholar proclaiming that the UK title of my book was misleading because 'feminism existed in Africa long before in Europe'. Given this book's provocative title, I welcomed, understood and anticipated such responses. In fact, in the early aughts, I wrote what still is one of the most popular posts on my *MsAfropolitan* blog: 'Feminism has always existed in Africa'. As the title of the post implies, I made an almost identical argument to the scholar whose email I received.

However, both the frustrated scholar and I were wrong. Feminism has not always existed in Africa, and it did not exist in Africa before it did in Europe. The word 'feminism' was coined in France in 1895, and the international movement that it came to represent around the turn of the twentieth century was, nevertheless, predominantly inflfluenced by developments in Europe and the United States. Conversely, it wasn't until the 1970s that a group of African women began to directly refer to feminism as a sociopolitical movement with explicit anti-patriarchal goals, and it was first in the 1980s that a significant and cohesive group of women, identifying themselves as African feminists, emerged.[1]

These pioneering feminists, who established the movement of women's emancipation known as feminism in the continent, are the originators of the topic that this chapter is concerned with: 'Homegrown Feminism'.

Homegrown Feminism is a notion that carries a dual meaning. On the one hand, by Homegrown Feminism, I mean a unique African feminist movement that has developed of its own accord and which is tailored to the continent's specific cultural, social and historical contexts. This aspect of Homegrown Feminism acknowledges the authenticity and specificity of African feminism, recognising it as a *sui generis* movement born in the 1970s from the lived experiences and struggles of African women. In this empowering sense of the conceptualisation, Homegrown Feminism is interdependent with, rather than invented by, feminism in the West or elsewhere.

On the other hand, I employ the phrase 'Homegrown Feminism' in a less empowering way. The second meaning of the concept somewhat derisively describes the tendency to position feminism in Africa as something inherently and naturally 'homegrown', in a bid to appeal to the claims of the cultural intelligentsia that feminism is an alien concept unsuitable for the African context. Their argument is that only if feminism existed in historical Africa can it exist in Africa today. And the reasoning of the scholar who emailed me, as well as my blogpost are, when looked at closely, seeking to mollify such absurd anti-feminist arguments.

One of the gifts of living a long enough time is that you begin to accept and even rejoice in your ability to contradict yourself. With time and experience you learn that the opposite of integrity is not self-contradiction, but rather the lack of effort to live according to your own philosophy. You realise, furthermore, that if your philosophy is anything outside of the status quo, then living your philosophy means that your likes and dislikes stretch into the old world that formed you, and the new world that you seek to create. This way of being in the world inevitably invites contradiction and paradox. Yet life also bestows on us the opportunity to change our minds about things that we once held as certainties. The changing of one's mind is a gift;

for once you change your view on something you were previously convinced about, the possibility of expanding your view on other matters emerges as well.

This is a roundabout way of saying that I don't feel qualms in admitting that I was wrong about the premise in that blogpost. In fact, I credit the writing of this book in large part to this pivotal shift in my understanding of the African feminist cause. Once I began questioning the claim that feminism had always existed in Africa, and variations of it, I could start exploring my previous motivations in making such a claim. What I began to ask myself were questions such as: 'Why does feminism need always to have existed in Africa?'; 'So, what if it hadn't?'; 'Whose political agendas did my claim of an enduring African feminism support?'; and 'If the actual genealogy of feminism in Africa clashes with these assertions, then why are feminists making them?' Can we only be feminists if our ancestors were feminists?

What I do regret, however, is responding to the most counterproductive backlash against the feminist movement in Africa since its inception – namely, the claim that feminism is unAfrican – with a stance that I now realise only strengthens its reach. The debate over whether feminism is unAfrican has been thoroughly addressed and refuted by numerous African feminists, including Molara Ogundipe-Leslie, Amina Mama, Mamphela Ramphele, Fatou Sow, and countless others, so I won't delve into those arguments here other than to pose a few follow-up questions to the people who typically make these claims: is it African to deny women equal rights to land, inheritance, divorce, decision-making and education? Is it African to prohibit women from being in control of their bodies? Is it African to cut girls' intimate areas? Is it African to force women into polygamy, or to pay a bride price? Is it African to kill women accused of being witches, or those who wear certain types of clothes, or those who are queer? Yes, regretfully, the answer is yes.

And precisely because there is a *homegrown* oppression is why there is a need for Homegrown Feminism, in the first, empowering sense described above. The complication is that for this empowering version of Homegrown Feminism to be effective, the second, derisive version – where we seek to prove that feminism is African by claiming that it goes further back in time than it does – needs to be laid to rest.

Protofeminism and the Legacy Trap

Throughout the ages, in every part of the world, women have struggled against exclusion. They have fought to control their bodies, fought for positions of power, and fought against male-dominant traditions and laws. Home to some of the world's oldest patriarchal civilisations, Africa is no different. The continent has numerous records of women's resistance, such as the Dahomey Amazons of present-day Benin, who formed history's most formidable female army. Or historical figures like Nzinga of Angola and Mnkabayi of Zululand, royal women who leveraged their power to fend off invaders. Other strong female icons of African history include: the nineteenth-century educator Adelaide Casely-Hayford, mentioned earlier, who dedicated her life to girls' education in a time when it was seen as controversial for both women and Africans to be educated; and Charlotte Maxeke, who, as early as the 1920s, spoke of the interplay of class, gender and race – the concept now known as intersectionality. Additionally, incredible female activists like Léonie Abo, Andrée Blouin and Josina Machel have shaped decolonisation struggles across Congo, Mozambique, Guinea, Algeria, Angola and Kenya, to name a few places where women fought for independence in fierce and rebellious ways.

Yet for the sake of clarity – and clarity is precisely the point in this chapter – the above are not examples of feminism. Rather, this form of historical resistance to male oppression and domination is known as 'protofeminism', a global phenomenon that describes ideas or individuals that advocated for women's rights before the formal establishment of the feminist movement in the late nineteenth and early twentieth centuries. In Europe, figures like the fifteenth-century

Italian writer Christine de Pizan, who had a critical stance of how misogyny undermined women's roles, was a protofeminist. In the Middle East, the radical Iranian scholar Qurrat al-'Ayn, who in the 1840s sparked controversy by advocating for gender equality and choosing not to wear a veil, was also a protofeminist. If women who prior to the creation of the feminist movement resisted male control in other parts of the world, such Italy and Iran, are generally referred to as protofeminists, then why in Africa's case do we conflate protofeminism and feminism?

The answer is that the uncritical integration of protofeminism into feminism in Africa is largely due to the backlash, and to what we can call the 'legacy trap', where rather than disproving the orthodoxy of patriarchy in Africa – and, more importantly, how to end it – our feminist focus is turned to proving that feminism is a part of our African legacy.

Take, for instance, a 1982 article that introduces 'Women in Nigeria', one of the first feminist organizations in the continent. Its authors describe how 'the long history of women's resistance, activism and associations in Nigeria' proved that feminism was not simply an imitation of a Western discourse, 'as divisive opponents like to charge', but rather that feminism was 'indigenous' to the continent.[2] This is an example of the backlash distracting important feminist work. Such a landmark publication should not have needed to prove that Nigerian feminism had a long history, or to have argued that Africa had always been feminist. It would have been more appropriate to focus on the fact that Africa is feminist now, rather than the past

Other instances of mixed messages due to the 'legacy trap' include an interview with Flora Nwapa, the celebrated Nigerian author who, when once asked whether she agreed with the statements of the important Pan-African leaders Léopold Sédar Senghor and Ali Mazrui that 'African women have always been liberated', responded enthusiastically, referring to her hometown: 'Yes! In Ugwuta, women have certain rights that women elsewhere, in other parts of the country, do not have.' Notwithstanding that the question was a typical legacy-trap question, the examples that Nwapa consequently gave tell a different story than what she had initially asserted. 'In Ugwuta,' Nwapa said:

> a woman can break the kola nut where men are. If she is old, or if she has achieved much or if she has paid the bride price for a male relation and that member of the family is there, she can break the kola nut. And everybody would eat the kola nut. But in certain parts of Igboland, a woman is not even shown a kola nut, not to talk about breaking it.[3]

This statement does not, of course, demonstrate that a woman has power, at least not in the sense that feminists fight for power and equal value given to womanhood in society, but rather that a woman is powerful only when she is 'permitted', for various reasons, to behave like a man.

Similarly, the Nigerian author Chimamanda Ngozi Adichie is proud of cultural legacies in a way that intersects with the legacy trap. Adichie often contextualises her heritage in a feminist framing. For instance, when her community bestowed on her the title *Odeluwa* – 'the one who writes for the world' – she wrote in an Instagram post that she was: 'The first woman in my hometown to be made a chief, and it makes me happy to know that more women will follow.' Adichie continued: 'Culture does not make people, people make culture … Ours must become a culture that celebrates achievement, whether it comes from a man or a woman.'[4]

Now, there is quite a big difference between Adichie's and Nwapa's praise of their cultural heritage, which perhaps speaks to the progress of time. Adichie's stance is unquestionably feminist, and it does focus on women – unlike Nwapa's response, which inadvertently centres men. However, although the *Odeluwa* title is a beautiful and meaningful gesture, there is still that inevitable tension created by rejoicing women receiving titles that are respected primarily because of their association with maleness and patriarchal traditions.

My remark is not a swipe directed at Adichie – or Nwapa, for that matter – whose expression always carries that spike of feminist fervour that I am deeply inspired by. Besides, I too have been caught in the jaws of the legacy trap on several occasions (and will no doubt be caught again), including my aforementioned blogpost.

I too am proud – to be African, to be Nigerian, to be Yoruba. Pride about cultural legacies can be a warm and joyous feeling to be cherished. But these days I am more mindful of the agendas that inform my pride – which, incidentally, is not insurmountably challenging when you shift the grounding of your feminist lineage from African protofeminism to African feminism. As the visionary writer and feminist Patricia McFadden, says: 'Gendered nationalism has been the bane of radical thought and activism everywhere on the continent.'[5] Yet, this split – between national and ethnic pride on the one hand, and the painfully sexist legacies that are perpetuated by your culture, on the other – is one that I probably will never fully reconcile nor transcend. It's a branch breaking off a tree and even if it's re-rooted, the throb of the phantom limb persists.

While writing this book, people have frequently asked me: 'Are you writing about strong women in African history?' And because I had already separated protofeminism from actual feminism, I began to see what had been obscured by the commitment to protofeminism, namely: the ordinary women in African history. All the powerful and legendary superhuman women who accomplished extraordinary deeds against great odds had done wonders for women's feelings of empowerment and strength. But they had overshadowed the broader narrative of African women's history, which is primarily composed of stories different to those women in positions of majesty and power.

The experiences of our mothers, grandmothers and great-grandmothers are generally more aligned with acceptance of a patriarchal gender order than active resistance against it, let alone victory over it. Our female ancestors, as many of our contemporaries, did not battle against male dominance; they accepted it. For every larger-than-life Queen Nzinga or the Amazons, there are thousands of women who either wilfully or coercively accepted male domination. The legacy trap deflects from this important truth. The focus on situating African feminism in Africa's ancient past comes at the cost of developing the movement's arguments, theories and visions that can compete with patriarchal logic today, for the average African woman. As Patricia McFadden puts it: 'For the majority of African women, however, life has remained basically what it has always been: precarious, vulnerable, and unjust.'[6] Like women in every part of the world, African women need the feminist struggle because it is the movement that has the highest success rate in freeing women from the crippling weight of patriarchy. Feminist history should not only be about celebrating women's past accomplishments, but about becoming frustrated with the institutionalised deprivation of women's freedom and agency throughout history. Positioning African women as larger-than-life heroines of survival, obscures that we are people with desires, fears, hopes and griefs, and ideas about the world.

On the surface, the legacy trap seems empowering. Referring to various examples of protofeminists from past centuries – queen mothers, influential tradeswomen, members of female armies, warrior goddesses, near-mythical figures capable of extraordinary feats – as evidence of a long feminist history on the continent gives a sense of harmoniousness, validation and rootedness. But that is exactly what makes it a trap. The aim of the legacy trap is to assuage the claims that feminism is unAfrican by proving that it is part of the continent's history. In other words, the legacy trap is a negotiation with Andro-Africanism. It is the attempt to fit feminism into a traditionalist, nationalist and masculinist agenda with essentialist views about what is 'purely' African. This is why the legacy trap is accompanied by a host of other deceiving claims – that homosexuality, too, is unAfrican; that Africa was once matriarchal; that there was no gender distinction in historical Africa; that motherhood gave women access to equal power – each having no grounding.

The legacy trap uses reverse psychology to, on the one hand, agree that African culture can be authoritarian (as it denies women their feminist fight for freedom), and on the other postulate that women should glorify the same culture (that denies them freedom) because it has apparently always suffered from this problem. Recognising the trap allows us to critically analyse and escape its flawed logic and imagine genuine freedom and equality for women from all walks of life in contemporary African societies.

The legacy trap is not unique to Africa. For instance, in the wake of Queen Elizabeth II's death, leading feminists across the UK lauded her as the 'ultimate feminist icon of the 20th century'. The queen was eulogised in ways that made her appear a benevolent matriarch and a role model for female empowerment. This response was ensnared in the legacy trap too. In truth, we hardly know anything about the queen's character; she essentially made silence a virtue by refusing to share any parts of her personality, her views, feelings, or beliefs. And while voicelessness may have served her, allowing her to maintain authority among her people, it makes Elizabeth II's alignment with the feminist cause conjectural.

'What would happen if one woman told the truth about her life?' the poet Muriel Rukeyser once asked in a tribute to the artist Kathe Kollwitz. Her answer: 'The world would split open.'[7] Feminists have fought precisely for women to have a voice, to split the world open and – driven by a deep sense of self-expression, full of fire, passion, resistance, bravado and love – tell their stories. They have paid a heavy price for this. African feminists such as Stella Nyanzi, Mona Eltahaway and Simamkele Dlakavu have been punished for daring to speak out, and yet they have spoken. As Audre Lorde says: 'Your silence will not protect you.'[8]

Queen Elizabeth's silence did, nonetheless, protect her. Not only that, it also protected the patriarchal and imperialist institution she was head of. Few institutions in modern British history have suppressed women's voices quite as much as 'The Firm'. Even in the contemporary era, female royals sacrifice their voices – from Lady Diana to Kate Middleton, to Meghan Markle, who had to give up her passport, website and email access when she became a member of the royal family. It's the age-old story of female censure. 'For if she begins to tell the truth, the figure in the looking glass shrinks,' as Virginia Woolf wrote.[9]

I do understand the desire for female iconography and symbolic representation, whether in Africa, Europe or elsewhere. Women are so deprived of status and power in comparison to men that there's an impulse to project feminist dreams onto visible women. Feminist critiques of other women always risk a kind of 'feminist policing', which I don't wish to add to. Feminism isn't a police officer but a map that helps women navigate around a man's world. But there are specific issues which are always true of the feminist struggle, one of which is voice. And it's easy to mistake power for voice.

It is hardly the case that any society automatically empowers women with a voice. Even in the Western world, which has achieved the highest 'measurable' records of gender equality, and where women typically have more political and social freedom than elsewhere, patriarchy remains mockingly victorious across the board of societal institutions. Every day in Germany, 'a man tries to kill his partner or ex-partner,' a 2020 femicide report showed and, 'every third day an attempt is successful.'[10] A revivalism of old, patriarchal and conservative values and a backlash against women's rights is spreading across the West. Sexist ways of thinking remain deeply ingrained as the 'Me Too' scandals, to give just one example, have revealed. Yet the West hides its ingrained patriarchal values under the cloak of modernity with claims that the region is post-feminist. If the backlash against feminism in Africa argues that feminism is not necessary due to Africa's historically empowering past, then the backlash to feminism in the West rests on the false argument that modernity has led to equality. There is something unique, however, that happens in an African context. Not only is your ideology questioned, as feminism is everywhere, but it is questioned on the merit of origin. Nobody asks if a European or American feminist can be feminist because she is American. But if you're African and feminist then you experience variations of that question all the time.

There are factors other than the backlash for the merging of African protofeminism and African feminism. There are critical counter-hegemonic motivations for turning our attention to women in African history, such as the negative stereotyping of African women in the

Western cultural media, as well as the prejudices African women face in the feminist movement at large. In a world that often seeks to undermine black women, we have rightly carved out affirming stories of matriarchs, queens and warriors. It is understandable – due to the Othering and alienation of African heritage women in the West – that black women around the world have emphasised lineages of strong and brave foremothers, and I too celebrate that with all my being.

Also, frankly, the history of powerful women in Africa is interesting. It is fascinating to learn about the empowered status that female monarchs held in historical Africa; the important political figures who ruled autonomously, at least over 'women's' issues. There is no denying that these historical events are central to African feminism. It might be a cliché to say that our grandmothers were amazing. But mine certainly was – I dedicated a chunk of my most watched online talk on TedX to her. I am sure that it is true for most readers with African grandmothers (with any grandmothers, really) that they are among the most inspiring people in a woman's life. Were they feminist, though?

The Founding Mothers of African Feminism

Perhaps the most despairing consequence that the conflation of protofeminism with contemporary feminism is that it prevents clarity on the genealogies of feminism in Africa. Applying the feminist label anachronistically creates confusion around the timings and patterns of feminist resistance in the continent. And this undermines the achievements of the actual pioneers of African feminism. The work of feminists like Awa Thiam, Obioma Nnaemeka, Mariama Bâ, Molara Ogundipe-Leslie, Altine Mohammed, Bene Madunagu, Amina Mama, Nakanyike B. Musisi, Ama Ata Aidoo, Ayesha Imam, Micere Mugo, Filomina Steady, Fatima Mernissi, Ifi Amadiume, Sylvia Tamale, Akosua Adomako Ampofo and Carole Boyce Davies, to provide a very incomplete list of the feminists who initiated the movement in the continent, is compromised when we entangle protofeminism with the contemporary school of thought. While protofeminist activities empowered women, they were not a political movement or philosophy. Feminism, on the other hand, is a political movement and a political philosophy – the only one to focus on women. And it is the pioneering women such as those mentioned above who first resisted patriarchy directly as feminists, who politically, socially and culturally, are the original African feminists. I don't say this to simply acknowledge or celebrate the crucial and inspiring work that these women undertook; they themselves might dispute the need for such an acknowledgement and prefer to focus on the struggle rather than whom to attribute it to, or any other line of thought that I am proposing here regarding Homegrown Feminism. But, chronology is political, and African feminism does not need to have ancient roots in history to be valid today.

By contrast, the African feminist movement has been trailblazing. In addition to the numerous feminist writers, artists and activists in all parts of the continent and diaspora who are tirelessly speaking about women's situations, often at significant personal risk, there are also organizations such as Femnet (based in Kenya); Baobab, and Win (Nigeria); the Ghana-based African Feminist Initiative; and platforms such as the Feminist Initiative in Nigeria (which in 2020 galvanised the most extensive national protests the country had seen since independence). These are examples of organizations that have produced some of the most radical feminist work that I have encountered anywhere in the world – and feminist advocacy has taken me across Europe, the US, Asia, Caribbean and Latin America. There are campaigns and manifestos, such as the lodestar document, the 'Maputo Protocol', which shines globally as a pioneering feminist text ratified by nation states; and South Africa's dynamic #PatriarchyMustFall campaign, which catalysed movements that rippled across the continent and the world. In addition, there are the continent's feminist writers and poets, such as Chimamanda Ngozi Adichie, Yvonne Vera, Tsitsi Dangaremba, Pumla Dineo Gqola, Jessica Horn, Wana Udobang, Hakima Abbas, Abosede Ipadeola, Nana Sekyiamah, Maha

Marouan and Warsan Shire, to name only a tiny few. And we also have the artists and creatives: Zanele Muholi, Angelique Kiddo, Aderonke Adeola, Laetitia Ky, Peju Alatise, Zaynab Fasiki, Ethel Tawe…, etc. Africa's contemporary feminist movement may be relatively young, but it is remarkably revolutionary. We don't need to dutifully refer to protofeminism in historical Africa to justify feminism today.

The confusion around the timings and patterns of feminist resistance in the continent is used in the service of political agendas that oppose feminism. The more confusion there is about the movement, the easier it is to dismiss and derail it. We need clarity about African feminism, and African feminism needs to produce lucidity and transparency about its history.

I often get pushback when I position 'clarity' as a feminist goal. My sense is that the resistance stems from the association of the term with the much-criticised Age of Enlightenment. However, clarity is not exclusive to the Enlightenment, or to the elite white male thinkers who applied it in distinct ways: making exact and persuasive assessments, discernments, calculations, and the like. We should not equate 'clarity' with 'rationality'. If anything, rationality can obscure the kind of clarity I am speaking of by turning reality into a puzzle that can be solved when reality is more quantum-esque and koan-like, in other words, something that makes us both puzzled and illuminated at once.

By clarity, I'm invoking an embodied sense of lucidity and a holistic interpretation of the patterns and structures in which we form our lived experiences. I mean an understanding of reality where everything is everywhere, and everywhere is everything: where humans, ants, rivers and stars are one; where I begin a sentence and it is finished by the grass and spider webs; where conversations are portals to dance with the collective mind and to see things we have labelled 'politics', 'news', 'art', 'Africa' anew. To see something *clearly* is to see it in its complexity. And this type of kaleidoscopic clarity allows us to see beyond surface- level understandings, and to also perceive the coy and prismatic ways in which patriarchy consciously and unconsciously affects individuals and societies.

In essence, the strength of feminism lies not just in its ability to critique and oppose patriarchy, but in its capacity to bring such dynamic clarity to the complex and often hidden dynamics of patriarchal rule, thereby empowering women from within.

This reclaiming is especially important today as we face a backlash against feminism, cultivated through traditionalism, populism and quasi-progressive posturing. Whereas in the 1980s and 1990s, you could relatively easily identify the backlash against feminism, in today's environment of co-opting social causes and women's empowerment-speak, alongside new technologies and an internet culture that facilitate the spreading of false information and conspiracies, more clear thinking – clear in the non-uniform way that I am describing – is required. If today's African feminists have an urgent task, it is to demystify the ways that conservative, patriarchal values have crept into progressive black and African movements. In our topsy-turvy world, this task needs the ability to traverse specified spheres of knowledge.

I should say, in closing here, that it is complicated to say that any feminism is 'homegrown' as such. Feminism is a movement that has always been international and belongs to no one group. While feminism may have started in the Western world, it was never strictly a white women's movement. The character of feminism was international from its inception. Rising feminist movements influenced early feminists in the West in other parts of the world. They organised mainly around the theme of voting at international women's congresses. Consequently, in the first few decades of the twentieth century, women in countries as wide-ranging as Finland, Sri Lanka and Ecuador gained suffrage.

African women participated in these international conversations of early feminism (even if they did not refer to themselves as feminists). Women like Constance Cummings John, an educationist from Sierra Leone; the Ghanaian activist Mabel Dove Danquah; or activists Adelaide Casely-Hayford and Charlotte Maxeke; and Funmilayo Ransome-Kuti whom I have already referred to. They were some of the African women who contributed to the growing international feminist arena in the first half of the 1900s. Ransome-Kuti, for example, was, among other things, the vice-president of the Paris-founded Women's International Democratic Federation. All feminism has, from its very beginning, been a call-and-response international affair. As the historian Lucy Delap writes: 'Historians of feminism must take care not to erase the local specificity of struggles and activism, however, it would be a mistake to simply look at all these debates and movements in isolation; they often share key ideas or drew inspiration from each other's struggles.'[11]

Yet, with access to influential institutions, Western, white and economically privileged feminists are typically the most vocal and prominent in the global movement. Consequently, other groups of feminists of different racial, ethnic or class backgrounds are commonly seen as fighting to be included in this 'Big Feminism' of sorts. Yet what would feminism be without anti-abolitionism, peace advocacy, the second and third waves, intersectionality, the focus on global issues like colonisation and resource extraction that impact women's lives everywhere? These are all essential feminist discourses that were generated from the margins. Homegrown Feminism has a third meaning in this regard: to dispel the myth that any feminism can exist in isolation. That Western feminists have been the most vocal and prominent in the movement does not mean that feminism belongs to them. The only feminism that is truly homegrown is the one that you plant and nurture within the shelter of your own being.

III

BEING

11.

Individuation

It is hard to defy the wisdom of the tribe, the wisdom that values the lives of members of the tribe above all others.
– Susan Sontag[1]

The path of life is not smooth, one is bruised by its sharp edges.
– Mariama Bâ[2]

One of my favourite paintings is the ethereal 1960 painting, *Flowers*, by the South African artist Gladys Mgudlandlu. The painting depicts a lush arrangement of oversized daisies gushing from the earth. Each flower has a purplish aural essence that hovers around it, but one of the flowers in the painting's centre has expanded into a tree composed of six gigantic leaves. Correspondingly, the purple aura of this outsized daisy stretches to the sky and beyond.

When I came across the painting it struck me, firstly, that like all Mgudlandlu's paintings, *Flowers* plays with paradox; it is simultaneously simple and deep; closely intimate and empyrean. Humans infrequently feature in her paintings, but their stories are ubiquitously interwoven into the landscapes from which they are absent. The daisy heads in *Flowers*, for instance, have dots on them that make them resemble a human face; in another painting in the series, the plants resemble female breasts. As is the case for her entire body of work, *Flowers* is embedded in an ongoing cultural commentary about Africa and identity. It is one of the best depictions of the sensitive relationship between the individual and their community in African art. In a tender and yet energetic way, *Flowers* shows how the beauty of community and the power of the individual are connected.

In this chapter, I will explore the relevance of the Jungian concept of 'individuation' for African feminist political philosophy. I begin by examining the rise of populism in Africa and its connection to the long-standing debate between individualism and communitarianism. I argue that for feminists, this debate often serves as a distraction from confronting patriarchy, and I make a case for individuation as a framework to transcend this limiting dualism. My motivation is twofold: to highlight how populist discourses can subtly undermine African feminist efforts, and to illuminate discussions that are overshadowed by these discourses. By integrating Jungian individuation with African feminism and Yoruba cosmology, I propose a novel approach to these challenges.

—

Today, the people of Africa, as everywhere, are becoming increasingly populist. One of the ways that populism manifests in the continent is through a divisive discourse about the community vs the individual, and more specifically through the position that Africa is communitarian unlike the West, where individualism prevails. In fact, populism in Africa rests on a definition of Africanness as a notion shaped, at large, in opposition to the West. This entails that whatever the categorical 'white man' represents, Africans should resent; and whatever the white man symbolises ought to be a symbol of resistance for Africans. I call this stance PAWN – Populist Anti-Western Nativism.

PAWN builds its worldview with no thorough ideological architecture of its own except its stance against the Western world. The defining characteristic of PAWN is that it takes the 'anti' in anti-Western literally to mean that whatever the West purportedly is 'pro',

Africa is against. And so, to give some examples: if the West is 'pro' homosexuality, trans-identity, animal rights, democracy, individualism, and, of course, feminism, Africa must be against these things. According to this circular reasoning, for something to be African, it cannot also be Western and that merely in declaring something as Western, it cannot then be African. This contrarian response to anything deemed to be Western is not only simplistic, but it also narrows Africanness to a limited range of possible ethics, attitudes and beliefs.

The appeal of PAWN to the body politic is the deft way that this perspective mobilises emotions such as anger, fear and grief as ways for the masses to understand and engage with complex sociopolitical narratives. This is what makes PAWN populist. What makes it nativist is the remedy that it provides as a solution to these valid emotions, namely: the anti-Western sentiment through which it simultaneously, and heuristically, offers Africa as a place that is absolved of ethical failure. The West is the wound; Africa is the balm. Africa, in terms of PAWN, is a place where morality and virtue appear seemingly of their own accord, by mere association with the continent.

PAWN is not new as such. As the author Richard Wright reflected about the Bandung Conference in 1955, where Asian and African countries met to promote economic and cultural cooperation and to oppose colonialism and neocolonialism: 'What had these nations in common? It seemed to me nothing, but what their past relationship to the Western world had made them feel.'[3] And James Baldwin reported on a similar gathering the following year, the First International Conference of Negro-African Writers and Artists that took place in Paris, where he wrote of the participants: 'People whose distrust of the West, however richly justified, also tends to make them dangerously blind and hasty.'[4]

Bolstered by the continuation of colonialist attitudes in the West's dealings with the continent, PAWN's anti-Western rhetoric remains justified. It is a narrative that is increasingly appealing to those Africans who yearn for decolonisation and liberation, which is, of course, most Africans. But the reckless myopia that Baldwin warns of is amplified by PAWN. Rather than liberate and decolonise, its misleading rhetoric represses a politics which is focused, pragmatic and conscientious, and instead advocates a reactionary political disposition. Africans have many valid reasons to oppose the West; PAWN, however, converts a legitimate opposition to Westernisation into a promotion of nativist, patriarchal and populist beliefs.

One example of a contemporary PAWN discourse is found in a popular and celebrated TEDx Talk by Cameroonian strategist Elma Akob: 'The Dangers of Western Feminism to Africa'. Akob uses the platform to share her denunciation of feminism on the grounds that feminism is individualistic and, therefore, 'not suited for the African narrative', which, by contrast is rooted in what Akob refers to as 'African community ideology'.[5]

Akob starts the talk by framing feminism as an identification that, 'every [Cameroonian] mother hopes to never hear her daughter say'. Although she describes how she herself at one stage embraced feminism, Akob now understands that the feminist movement is unsuitable to Africa because it does not promote, 'strong family values'; it does not 'accommodate tradition'; and 'women who choose to be housewives are seen as less'. Most importantly, Akob posits that feminism is not suited to African women because it is 'based on the concept of I', whereas 'African community ideology is based on "We"'.[6]

Akob's point that feminism is tied in some ways to individualism is not entirely incorrect. Early shapers of the movement, such as Mary Wollstonecraft, were indeed liberals, and consequently individualists and their worldviews still stamp significant sections of feminist work. For better or for worse, I might add. For all its imperfections, we have Liberal Feminism to indirectly thank for slogans and movements that African feminists also advocate, such as: 'My Body, My Choice', 'Me Too' and 'Equal Pay for Equal Work'. These slogans reflect legacies of individualism inherent in Liberal Feminism.

Akob is also right that the kind of individualism that is rampantly practised in the modern world is unappealing in Africa, where the notion of community is strongly valued. One of the reasons that many

Africans are suspicious of the feminist movement is because it exposes the tension between individualism and communitarianism, and I don't believe it is appropriate to brush these concerns aside. If there were another framework that had successfully freed masses of women from the patriarchy without importing any problematic neoliberal ideals alongside this liberation, then I would sign up. But there isn't one. I have yet to encounter women who have achieved freedom from systemic male oppression without the aid of feminism (directly or indirectly), except if they have 'only' achieved a sense of personal freedom, which of course is an individualist stance if ever there were one.

By contrast, communitarianism has unfortunately done little to free women in this regard. On the surface, the communitarian dream seems to be about humaneness, interrelatedness and compassion. Still, when looked at more deeply, the shadow of community ideology poses a fundamental threat to the liberation of women, queer, trans, and gender-nonconforming people. African communitarianism encourages values such as virtue, morality and good character, all subjective values that all too often coincide with a feverish respect for seniority – traditional rulers, politicians, family heads, chiefs, priests, imams, civil servants, you name it, all of whom typically are male.

Ultimately, Akob's talk is a demonstration of how FAWN is advanced through the binary juxtaposing of individualism and communitarianism, and how this kind of reductive intellectual pabulum colludes with populism and patriarchy. Ironically, like most PAWN advocates who claim that African cultures empowered African women until the West disempowered them through colonialism, Akob tacitly co-opts African feminist values (women's empowerment) and African feminist work (since it is African feminists who mainly have exposed the ways that colonialism disempowered African women), yet denounces feminism itself. This example further proves my point that feminism is the only successful movement for women's liberation on a collective scale, to such a great degree that even opponents of feminism use it to support their circular logic.

It is fair to say that populism is not altogether 'bad'. We need more, rather than less, mass mobilisation. But where populism typically fails is in critical thinking. Instead, it resorts to for-or-against thinking, simplified slogans, and soundbites, splitting the world into heroes and villains, while merging with conspiracist and superstitious tendencies, and entirely missing the point of freeing the people not only from the lies of power but also from the root cause of psychological oppression, namely: a mindset that centres the oppressor.

An unthinking discourse at best, PAWN masks a genuine interest to be progressive but wrongly equates progressivism wholly with anti-Westernism, as though Africa were a playground of inherent virtue and ethical conduct. At worst, PAWN is a perfect demonstration of what the German philosopher Friedrich Nietzsche referred to as 'ressentiment' – a weaponisation of morality whereby the Slave (archetype) derives their sense of power in punishing the Master with appeals to feigned morality. African progressives – in line with Nietzsche – have critiqued and warned of the risks of a reactionary attitude towards 'the oppressor'. Frantz Fanon, in *Black Skin, White Masks*, explores the psychological effects of colonisation and the internalisation of inferiority among the colonised. This, he argued, was evident in how oppressed individuals both adopted and resented the values of their oppressors, leading to a reactionary rather than revolutionary stance. The result was ressentiment, where the oppressed harbour a mix of envy, hatred and a desire for revenge against the oppressors. The character Beloved in Toni Morrison's novel of the same name is also an embodiment of ressentiment. Beloved's desire for retribution, while grounded in deep suffering, ultimately overwhelms both herself and her community. In terms of ressentiment, the novel suggests that addressing and reconciling with the past, rather than being consumed by ressentiment, is crucial for healing.

As a virtue, morality can nurture integrity, wisdom, and even love. As a weapon, as in the case of PAWN, I regret to say that morality has the adverse effect of concealing wounds of resentment, regret, fear, shame and secrecy from its sniper. Ressentiment needs the enemy because, without one, the volcano of difficult emotions within the victim would fulminate. And how do you live with a crackling, burning volcano inside you? Turning the enemy into the anchor onto which you unleash the anger is a far easier predicament.

But it is also costlier. It leaves a gap through which elites can manipulate the masses by feeding their thirst for simple narratives, which they can then take further advantage of. As Naomi Klein writes in *Doppelganger*: 'Being creatures of narrative, humans tend to be very uncomfortable with meaning vacuums – which is why those opportunistic players, the people I have termed "disaster capitalists", have been able to rush into the gap with their pre-existing wish lists and simplistic stories of good and evil.'[7]

I'm reminded of a pet budgie I had as a child, which I decided to free from its cage. It seemed reprehensible to deny a living creature its freedom. Yet a part of me was saddened at the bird's freedom as it took off, not even looking back once. I experienced what we might think of as 'the sorrow of the Master', in this instance, me! The experience taught me that the oppressor's fear is not necessarily to be overthrown but rather to be subject to indifference. The unexamined ressentiment that Fanon refers to because of PAWN (or a previous iteration of it) prevents oppressed groups from taking flight. True freedom would be to, like the bird, focus on the horizon of freedom and be indifferent to the reactionary cage of the oppressor's narrative.

To be clear, I am not advocating for indifference to oppression itself, but rather to the grip of power that maintains it. Like my pet bird's agency striking a pang of sorrow in me, Africa wields a veiled power over the West, too. The fear of losing 'Africa', of opening the cage and finding Africa soaring up and out across the vast blue skies, and not even once glancing back, is a fear that concealed in the Western mind. Africa may depend on the West, but the dependency is reciprocal.

PAWN and African feminism

With the growth of PAWN in the continent and diaspora, African feminism is called to challenge the patriarchal values that are imported through its narratives. PAWN reawakens the debate between individualism and communitarianism, which has been one of the main preoccupations of the African Mind at least since its encounter with Europe. It is a debate that we are called to revisit again and again, because it is one that intersects with African feminist subjectivity and holds a space for probing into the nature of the individual and collective self. Beyond the individualism and communitarianism debate lie questions of a deeper nature; it is a contention that is ultimately about desire: the desire to heal, to be authentic, to have roots and to have a story to embrace.

Individualism, simply put, is a political and philosophical perspective that prioritises the individual's social needs. It is a framework for Western politics and a school of thought that has an utterly negative connotation in convivial Africa, and often for the right reasons – individualist dogma is both the catalyst and perpetuator of social ills such as uncongeniality, greed and the anthropocentrism that bolsters the exploitation of the planet. In African cosmologies, Earth is seen as an Orisa (a deity) and shameless exploitation of the Earth is, therefore, undesirable. A Yoruba proverb says: 'Omo onile n te e jee jee, ajogi a te e basubasu.' ('The child of the owner of a piece of land walks gently on top of the soil, whereas a visitor just runs roughshod on it.'[8]) Individualism makes people believe they are independent 'visitors' on Earth rather than its offspring.

The years of the Covid-19 pandemic are one recent example that exposed the deep risks of rampant individualism that frames Western culture. Take for example how, while hoarding vaccines, Western powers used intellectual property protection to prevent impoverished countries from making their own vaccines. This exercise was a wicked demonstration of how individualist principles shape the global political order. Such behaviour diametrically contrasts the humanistic principles of African communitarian ethics, reflected, for example, in the Ghanaian Akan saying: 'Honam mu nni nhanoa' ('Humanity has no boundary').

In African contexts, the consequent tendency is, due to such Western conducts of behaviour, understandably to view individualism as categorically destructive, and communitarianism as wholly positive. Yet despite the pitfalls of individualism, the spirit of individualism is not altogether negative. The individual is also the seed of radical progressive change, and individualism can provide a more fertile ground for out-of-the-box thinking than communitarianism can.

Simultaneously, although communities encourage social cohesion, maintain healthy relationships, and are creative and generative, a community has no inherent moral value. Incels are also members of a community; neo-Nazis form communities, as do terrorists. For a community to have ethical virtues, it needs to consist of individuals with ethical virtues.

In other words, the line between individualism and communitarianism is not as straightforward as it may seem. Like all dualisms, the binary positioning of individualism as antagonistic to communitarianism allows little room for complexity and growth. Both individualism and communitarianism are more spanning than they are generally assumed to be.

The dualism also erases and abandons key elements of Africa's history. Individualism is not inherently Western, just as communitarianism is not exclusively African. The historian Cheikh Anta Diop, for example, has written about how traits that are typically associated with individualism, such as autonomy and agency, are stronger in Africa since, as he says, 'there always existed a reciprocal invasion of consciences and individual liberties' in the continent. Diop suggests, conversely, that the role of the individual in the West lacked such a sense of agency, and was historically, 'totally subordinate to the city'.[9]

Furthermore, Africa harbours many of the same individualist tendencies that it abominates. Africans may not have encoded trademarks of individualism, such as selfishness, egocentrism and nepotism, into a political philosophy, but these human traits are also part of the African psyche (since – surprise, surprise – Africans are human!). The belief that Africans would be absolved of human traits, however negative or positive, is problematic and, to my mind, an example of what the South African psychologist Kopano Ratele refers to as the 'Superhuman subhuman', where the African is assumed to not only have a different culture but to have a different psychology than other groups. As Ratele writes: 'Superman is not human. Superhuman is subhuman.'[10]

Individuation, a process which I shall now discuss, provides the kind of language that bridges the tension between individualism and communitarianism, a tension which has troubled African feminism since its inception. Individuation is a useful concept with which to explore the aims of an African feminist political philosophy because it offers a valuable framework for African feminists to navigate the complex, and often painful, space between cultural solidarity and critique. It allows us to embrace and honour African cultures without mitigating our critique of patriarchy nor our pursuit for autonomy and self-realisation as feminists. As individuation is a concept that connects to the interior realm, it also helps us to think about transformation in ways that aren't only empirical, but also invoke imagination, dreaming and affect; in short, inward reflection in the interest of outward transformation.

A Journey Towards Individuation

'Become who you are.' These are the words of the ancient Greek poet, Pindar. They are words which, despite their brevity, contain instructive layers of meaning. What does it mean to 'become who you are'? Does 'becoming who you are' imply something other to 'being who you are'? And what nature do these questions assume in our context of African feminism, PAWN and individuation? I'll attempt to answer these questions by sharing fundamental elements of my personal journey and process towards individuation.

At the beginning of my life, I depended on my parents for food and shelter. As I grew older, I increasingly had the will, but not the capacity, for autonomy. I recall how, as a child, I wanted to do things my way and be freed of the repressions of authority. To abide by rules, even when those rules were only daily routines such as waking in the morning and preparing for school, triggered an aversion in me. With adolescence, I began to separate myself from both familial and social authorities. I relished having more freedom of action. But my thoughts were not as independent as I imagined. I yearned for self-knowledge but didn't know enough to differentiate between internalised projections and my genuine desires. First, in early adulthood, I began to glean how critical decisions in my life – such as where, how and with whom I wanted to live, or not live, and the values that would support me in relating to this living – deeply corresponded to my hidden cravings. The desire to live a feminist life shaped my choices, which shaped my desires. And so, feminism reciprocally, and sometimes relentlessly, shaped my most intimate world – my dreams, my anxieties, my voice – in a manner that the conscious and unconscious parts of my personality could be integrated.

I imagine that what I have shared thus far is relatable to many feminists and dissenters of conformity. My personal journey was both complicated and enriched by an insight that embodying feminism brought about; namely that to 'become who I am', as Pindar instructs, I needed to become alone. Becoming who you are – or 'coming-to-be-of-the-self', as Jung, who coined individuation, described the phenomenon – I came to realise, means to become 'alone'.

By alone, I don't mean physically alone. I also don't mean 'lonely', a related but fundamentally different sentiment. By alone, I mean when even with people around you, some of whom you are deeply intimate with, and whom you love and appreciate, you are nevertheless viscerally aware, at your core, of being alone. As Jung described individuation, it begins 'with the individual, conscious of his isolation, cutting a new path through hitherto untrodden territory'.[11]

The paradox lies in that recognising and appreciating the fact of aloneness in life, you become better at honing loving, kind and honest relationships with others, as is necessary for people to do in an ethical and prosperous community. Whether it is friends, lovers, strangers, yourself, or humanity at large, approaching experience from the insight that one cannot escape the state of aloneness, makes you more present and consequently – ideally – kinder and more loving. For what is love but the absence of escapism, and what is escapism but the denial of aloneness? The insight of the inescapable nature of aloneness changed my position towards communities in drastic ways that threw me off balance. Once you are shaped by the reality of your aloneness, many defining features of community become counterintuitive. Community carries an all-too-strong a risk of group thinking, epistemic certainty and accepted norms, even when those norms are progressive. Communitarianism often discourages a mindset of aloneness and instead nurtures the sentiment of inseparability. Of course, everything in Nature is inseparable in some sense, but people who are nested deeply in communitarianism all too often tend to see inseparability as agreeability. This is why rather than yearn for community, I yearn, counterintuitively, to be in community with people who don't yearn to be a part of a community: those who don't want to conform to anything at all but qualities such as truth, love and friendship.

None of this is to make a case for individualism; I am neither an individualist nor a communitarian. Individuation is not individualism in different grammatical garb. If individualism is the centring of the autonomous self, then individuation, on the other hand, implies a specific kind of psychological-emotional-intellectual-spiritual maturation. If individualism implies *worshipping* the self, then individuation means knowing the self.

Of course, individualism may assist individuation because you cannot 'become yourself' if you don't have some determined sense of autonomy. But whereas the former creates a harmful separation from society, for individuation to develop, there needs to be a unity between an individual's external and inner worlds. As Jung said: 'Individuation does not shut one out from the world but gathers the world to oneself.'[12] Individuation is both distinct from individualism and incompatible with it.

Nor is individuation necessarily in confrontation with communitarianism. Individuation involves breaking away from group norms to form a unique identity, rather than from community itself. Individuation focuses on the individual, emphasising personal growth and independence, which can be perceived as antithetical in communitarian environments. However, the goal of individuation is to become a distinct, self-aware individual, and this can have important benefits for a community. Individuation and community might seem opposite; they are not mutually exclusive. Healthy communities often respect individual differences, and healthy individuals can contribute positively to their communities.

But we don't tend to think of community as a place to express individuality. This is why I have come to feel kinship with those who seek something more transcendental than community per se, something closer to a collective. The terms 'community' and 'collective' are often used interchangeably but there are key differences between them. Whereas community describes a sense of common identity and shared characteristics, a collective describes a group of people who are motivated to act together in pursuit of a social goal. There is an element of semantic nit-picking involved in distinguishing between communities and collectives as the terms are often used interchangeably and I do too in my day-to-day life. Yet, in the sense of the above definition, I am drawn to collectives, and apprehensive of communities.

My counterintuitive stance does not deny the value or the beauty of a community. The dream of community is a dream of healing. It is the desire for beauty and collective wisdom. These are dreams to uphold and nurture. And whether I like it or not, I am part of communities and I cherish them even while, due to my disposition, feeling detached from them.

The point is that there is a tension between becoming who you are, as Pindar instructed, and communitarianism To become who you are requires a healthy amount of solitude of the mind, soul and spirit. Even if a guide, friend, mentor, or collective, aids the process of becoming who you are, it is ultimately a journey that needs to be undertaken without the interventions of others.

The glinting of one's distinct individuality at an unconscious level and the transformation of one's conscious personality after that is the process of individuation that feminism embarked me on. I use the word 'process' because we are speaking of a 'becoming', rather than to present myself as having achieved individuation which, as Jung argued, is a very difficult, and very rare, thing to accomplish. The integration of the conscious and unconscious parts of my persona is something that I strive towards, and I therefore know the immense resolve that it requires. Yet if, irrespective of all authority and tradition, you become conscious enough of your distinctiveness to embody it, then you discover the jewel of individuation; a sense of collective existence manifest in your inner world.

Africa's cultures are not unfamiliar to this concept, which Jung referred to as 'individuation'. A similar process of becoming is integral to the cosmological underpinnings of many indigenous African cultures, where societal practices and institutions are constructed to aid individuals precisely to *become who they are*. For example, it is common for African names to hold an instructive meaning about who that individual is. My Yoruba name, Abiola, to give an example, means: 'Born to wealth'. (I regret that the African child does not always fulfil the destiny implied by the name; in any case, wealth is subjective, so touché.) Even in 'Westernised' urban African cities, naming ceremonies are still a serious matter. The ritual proceedings in naming ceremonies are still largely upheld, as indeed was the case at mine. To ensure that I could approach my *Ori* (which translates as 'head', but conveys something akin to 'destiny') I was fed a 'pinch' of water – because everything everlasting in life needs water to survive; palm oil – because it lubricates and facilitates a smooth flow in life; a kola nut – which is initially bitter but sweetens as it is chewed on, a reminder that some of the sweetest things in life are bitter at first; honey – for a balmy and 'golden' life; pepper – to ensure the right dose of toughness; salt – for a delectable experience; and dried fish – a reminder that, like fish, I must continue swimming when the waters get rough.

In a more traditional setting, my Ori would have been tied to a specific *orisha* – the divinities that govern life, as elements of Nature, and to whom an individual forges a close relationship through their life journey. To give some examples of orishas, there is the divinity Shango, that takes the form of thunder; the divinity that is embodied by the ocean, Yemoja; or by lightning, Oya. Or Eshu and Earth, both mentioned earlier. There are hundreds of orishas and each have their own unique and purposeful *telos* (the ultimate purpose of something). It was not until I received my orisha divination as an adult, that I began to understand the wise, deeply mysterious and simultaneously intuitive knowledge of these ancestral practices.

In African cultures, as in many indigenous cultures around the world, self-discovery was, and to a notable extent still is, encouraged from infancy. In fact, even before a baby's physical birth, parents would consult healers and mediums to advise them on the divine will of their child to be. In modern and individualist Western thought, such (individuating) tools are looked upon with disapproval or condescension. Individuals are generally encouraged to think of life as a blank page onto which *they* decide what their purpose is without external intervention. The formation of an identity is strongly shaped in adolescence, when teens eagerly explore and carve out their sense of self through clothes, music and hobbies.

This desperation was something that I experienced when I moved to Sweden from Nigeria as a teenager in the 1990s. At the time, I didn't have a favourite musical genre, or a pop band or literary genre I obsessed over. I had my obsessions, but they were a potpourri: for example, I adored Madonna (a love that came about independently, with some help from the marketing algorithms of that period); the Beatles (an inheritance from my mother); Millie Jackson (ditto); and Fela Kuti (impossible for the anti-authoritarian spirit I already possessed not to love); I watched Indian movies on repeat (Bollywood was a very popular industry in 1980s Nigeria). I also loved swimming, and swam almost every day. But none of these things seemed to be my identity, in itself. In my new environment in Malmö, I felt the need to integrate my favourite things (artists, hobbies, films) into my persona. I hung a poster of the boy band New Kids on the Block, on my wall. But I didn't really *feel* anything about the poster. I can't remember a single New Kids on the Block song by-heart today. I was just dutifully performing a search for identity that seemed to matter in my new environment.

I am not, again, creating a hierarchy or binary here. Of course, many African children have passions that they are obsessive about too. And there is also something healthy about this type of self-expression. Fan culture, and dedicated hobbies and fancies, promote feelings of belonging with like-minded groups, and in times that are saturated with output, are helpful to forming one's own tastes. There are many nuances and advantages to Western-influenced culture in this regard. Yet despite the diverging roads I have wandered since, I now realise that the path was always singular, and the Yoruba attitude towards destiny describes my experience more satisfyingly. Accompanying me, it now seems, there was always some force or drive, like the Ori, a kind of 'persona' that one 'chooses' before being born. Because such indigenous cosmologies are not individualistic, the persona I am speaking about is also not about the ego. As an individual becomes more conscious of their Ori, that is, as they individuate, the better they can contribute to their communities.

These are some of the reasons why I propose individuation as a useful tool in the African feminist kit. Individuation enables a perspective that protects the legacies of African cultures without fortifying the swamps of Superiorism, Andro-Africanism and PAWN. The aim of African feminist individuation is to both dissent and love, in fact, to dissent because it loves, and love because it dissents, and through this methodology usher transformation.

When Pindar said: 'Become who you are', he was asking us to take space, not as ready-made selves, but as selves in the making. In the context of African feminism, Pindar's quote suggests that for feminism to *be* African, it must, in a roundabout sense, *become* African. It must *become* intimate: with Africa, with feminism, and ultimately with itself. It must attend to its complex nature, examining and dissecting, unstitching, reassembling, observing, seeing, conscientiously knowing and feeling where to seek answers.

African Feminist Individuation

Individuation is in many ways already applied in African feminist world-making. For example, in the work of the radical scholar and ecofeminist Patricia McFadden, who writes that: 'despite the seemingly dire state of the world and of our continent in particular, the power of imagining and actually living a life of Freedom and Dignity through Feminist consciousness and activism is the most precious gift that each of us can give ourselves'.[13] In her essay, McFadden speaks, among other things, about the complicated process of 'feminist becoming' and how that process is intermittently a source of joy, transformation and discovery of new communities, but also equally involves despair, risk and the loss of communities once cherished.

When I first read McFadden's essay 'Contemporarity', during lockdown, I found it invaluable for reminding me that it is necessary to become 'contemporary' in times of piercing urgency. To put it briefly, and in my own words, becoming contemporary is ultimately about finding ways that can help us to live radical African feminist politics in real time. Although McFadden reimagines 'the contemporary' as the present temporality in which we can critically restructure our thought patterns, relations and environments, the essay is not primarily preoccupied with debates about the 'modern' or the 'Western'. Of course, modernity and the West are themes that McFadden has engaged with extensively in her body of work. But 'becoming contemporary' is honing and nurturing contemporary feminism specific to black women's challenges on the continent and in the diaspora. In this sense, it is a process of individuation, of becoming, that does not centre the 'Master' or the oppressor.

Similarly, in her most famous book, *Segu*, an engrossing and epic 1986 novel of history, love, loss and conquest, Maryse Condé tells a story of African precolonial history through fiction. Loved by Africans of all walks of life – and non-Africans too, of course – Condé is primarily known as a novelist. But from her memoir, *What Is Africa to Me?*, it becomes clear that she is one of the past centuries' beacons of Pan-Africanist social criticism (although in the Andro-Africanist world of Pan-Africanism, this is of course not how she is viewed).[14] The memoir tackles Conde's politicisation into both a feminist and an African intellectual in 1960s West Africa (where she moved to, inspirited by Aimé Césaire, whose poetic writing about Africa planted a seed of curiosity about the continent within her).

Condé describes her encounters with an assortment of powerful men, with whom she formed varying degrees of intimate closeness while living in Ivory Coast, Guinea, Ghana and Senegal; men such as Amilcar Cabral, Kwame Nkrumah, Ousmane Sembène, Sékou Touré, Laurent Gbagbo and Agostinho Neto. They were freedom fighters, legends and heroes who shaped the course of Africa. To Condé, however, they mostly lacked political integrity. Of the giant icon, Kwame Nkrumah, she provocatively said: 'Nkrumah cannot be considered either an astute philosopher or a serious political pundit. At the most, an astute juggler of shock formulas.'[15]

Condé not only wrote against the powerful male elites that she personally engaged with, but also towards 'their' communities. In Guinea, she encountered a 'series of gestures and mandatory dictates' that exasperated her soul. 'The world was composed of two distinct hemispheres,' she observed, 'that of men and that of women.'[16] She resisted this reductive compartmentalisation by defying expectations that were cast upon her to, for instance, learn her husband's language, Malinké, wear wrappers, or to braid her hair. Instead, she insouciantly learned the rival language Fulani, wore trousers and unapologetically styled her hair in an Afro.

She was, of course, punished for her defiance. Men whom she refused to go to bed with, both figuratively and literally, cost her jobs, her home, even her children. She was punished for living an anti-establishment life, a feminist life, a life that didn't put 'the community' before herself as an individual.

Yet, although Condé experienced the dark side of power relations in West Africa, she also harboured a profound love of the continent, as is evident in her many novels. Despite her irreverent expositions of the hypocrisies and dramas that unfold around Africa's leading men and her love-hate relationship with the male sex – one that perfectly mirrors the love-hate relationship to Africa that Condé came to harbour – Africa was the site of her politicisation, the place where her voice emerged, and where she learned to express her ideas, and escape European racism. Even if Africa's hypocrisies and deceptions overcame her with sorrow, it was also Africa that was the place of her becoming. 'More than the theoretical discourses of my friends,' she said, 'it was this country that taught me compassion and the importance of the people's well-being ... And it was here that I was becoming a very different human being.'[17]

There are other black feminist theories that are in conversation with individuation. 'Socially responsible individualism', a notion presented by the black feminist sociologist Patricia Hill Collins, is a way of thinking and acting that also aligns with individuation, as it balances personal autonomy and individual rights with a commitment to the collective good.[18] In Collins's view, socially responsible individualism honours individual agency and freedom but situates these within a framework of social responsibility and interconnectedness. Like individuation, her concept challenges the notion that personal success must come at the cost of collective well-being or vice versa. The phrase 'communities of individuals', often used in sociological and philosophical contexts to describe a social structure that focuses on the community as a whole and the individuality of its members, is another example of a perspective that involves the spirit of individuation on a societal scale, as it implies a social ecology where each person's individuality is the most exciting thing about the community.[19]

Kwame Nkrumah once said that: 'The basic organisation of many African societies in different periods of history manifested a certain communalism and that the philosophy and humanist purposes behind that organisation are worthy of recapture.'[20] Does this mean that you must choose community values over your own perspectives to be truly African?

I don't think so. I believe that a healthy community is indeed a community of individuals who honour the individuality of each person, including non-humans. As Nkrumah went on to say, too, what his work sought to recapture was 'not the structure of the "traditional African society" but its spirit, for the spirit of communalism is crystallised in its humanism and in its reconciliation of individual advancement with group welfare'.[21] This sentiment is one that PAWNers could do well to adopt.

To be who you are you must first know who you are, and to know who you are, you must first undergo a process of becoming. That is a key difference between 'becoming who you are', as Pindar instructs, and 'being who you are'. The notion of becoming is an unfurling, it is active, whereas the notion of *being* is both temporally and temperamentally more immediate. If African social values are communitarian, as they indeed are, then becoming who you are is an act that must disturb the binary between individualism and communitarianism. Rather, than a locked gate, this tension provides an opportunity for African feminist individuation. There are possibilities to become (active process) and to be (present) free of ressentiment (imprisoned by the Master/Slave dualism). It is to emerge like Mgudlandlu's flower, still rooted in the same soil as every other flower, but reaching far, far up, to experience the highest thrill of the rewarding processes of becoming and being.

Conclusion: Can Feminism Be African?

We have become these new women in ways that neither of us imagined.

– Patricia McFadden[1]

In the introductory chapter of this book, I suggested that the question: can feminism be African? could be interpreted in (at least) three ways.

Firstly, it could be asked with a silent 'already' at its end, to convey the oversight of African feminism in mainstream 'intersectional' feminist discussions. Can feminism be African *already*?

Secondly – although I hadn't yet introduced the concept of Andro-Africanism – the book's main question could be seen as an interrogation of what it means for feminism to be African if Andro-Africanism defines Africanness.

Lastly, I proposed that the question speaks to the paradoxical nature of the questions that African feminism grapples with, by itself being paradoxical.

Now that we have reached the end of the book, we can assess the threefold nature of the question again.

The first two interpretations present the 'question' in the sense of 'a problem'. And so even though I have written this book in response to problems such as Othering, patriarchy, eurocentrism, and so on, it was never within the book's remit to provide solutions to any of these problems, or it would be performing miracles. But I hope that it has uncovered the depth of these problems – always the first and most important step for true and lasting change.

Speaking of miracles, although I posited from the get-go that this would not be a book about humanitarian causes, or one providing an encyclopaedic description of African feminism, there are some topics relevant to the conceptual journey this book has taken, which I have only briefly touched on. Most specifically: religion.

Africa is the most devout continent in the world, with 89 per cent of its inhabitants claiming to be religious (compared to 59 per cent in the world at large[2]). The deep entanglement with religion, whether Judaeo-Christian, Muslim or traditional and indigenous belief systems within the continent, intersect with and complicate many of the issues that this book has addressed. These are value systems that both collide and collude with African feminism as they offer empowering communities for women but also strengthen androcentrism. In the early stages of researching this book, I had intended to identify these entanglements, but I soon realised they were so knotty that they'd need a book in their own right to decipher.

Having raised the issue of religion here, I will nevertheless say the following: I believe, like many feminists, that we ought to speak critically of religion insofar as religious doctrines are discriminatory against women and Africans. Yet, I also think that we need to create spaces for feminism to be in dialogue with the many variations of religious life in Africa. There will be no miraculous end to Superiorism or patriarchy, but spirituality is likely to play a crucial role in the journey of emancipation.

There are many other important topics that I have not addressed: *Are black feminism and African feminism interchangeable? If not, what are the differences and similarities between them?*

And there are themes that I have addressed broadly, and others barely. I have set out to discuss a range of difficult topics in this book, from metaphysics to decolonisation, to paradigm shifts to Pan- Africanism, to individuation, among others, and I am aware that the themes of the book require a lot of further analysis and attention. But this is in some sense the book's aim: to place African feminism on the agenda.

As for the third (paradoxical) implication of the question: 'Can feminism *be* African?' I can only respond in a correspondingly inconclusive and unsolvable manner. Consider the following: is the question asking whether feminism fits Africa? Or if it can be *from* Africa? Can feminism be from anywhere, if so? Do ideologies come from places? Moreover, the verb 'be' implies a future, but isn't feminism already an established movement? Can a movement be both from the past and the future simultaneously? And could you flip the question around to ask: 'Can Africa be feminist?' What kind of impact would that have?

I could also have asked: can *feminisms* be African? – as it has become increasingly common to speak of African feminisms in the plural. 'Feminisms' acknowledges the movement's diverse cultures, regional differences and nuances. It is a gesture of dialogue and mutual respect. I value the gesture – and different contexts or considerations might call for other choices – but I have not pluralised the term in this book as it suggests that feminism in Africa is plentiful and established when, instead, it is nascent. The pluralisation feminisms gives the sense that the movement has already spread broadly and widely into multiple strands,[3] from urban to rural environments, and to the African working class. As for differences within the movement, they certainly exist. But the singular notion of 'African feminism' conveys these nuances and is strategically important.

Also, for whom are we pluralising the word 'feminism' anyway? It should be obvious that there are different experiences and stances across Africa's feminist movement. Using the plural seems to be in service of those who dismiss African feminism on cultural grounds and who modify feminism to fit tradition. Plus, the small 's' in African *feminisms* has the effect of making it sound, to the writer in me, clunky and apologetic – even if my critical mind understands the motivation behind it.

In *The Book of Questions*, the Chilean poet Pablo Neruda presents us with questions 'that refuse to be corralled by the rational mind'. Neruda asks perplexing questions such as: 'How many bees are there in a day?', 'Is there anything sillier in life than to be called Pablo Neruda?', and 'Why wasn't Christopher Columbus able to discover Spain in a day?' These koan-like questions without clear answers invite the reader to move through 'intuitive perceptions, beyond rehearsed patterns of feeling and thinking'.[4]

Can feminism be African? is also a question that is not intended to be settled. It was never my intention to prescribe a specific kind of African feminism. In asking a question with uncertainty baked into it, it was not my intention to cause confusion but rather to find a way to jolt the mind out of the mechanic and linear reasoning of Europatriarchal Knowledge, and embrace a more intuitive, experiential form of understanding. By taking us out of the dominant empirical methodologies of Europatriarchal Knowledge, the question is itself a critique of Europatriarchal Knowledge. Through its paradoxical nature, I hoped that the question would irradiate the possible worlds residing in the glitches of the social imaginary, of ghosts, tricksters, spiders and sangomas.

Can feminism be African? This question marks the history of African feminism. Many have said: no, feminism is unAfrican. Others have insisted that feminism is indigenous to Africa. Both are wrong. As this book has shown, both Africa and feminism are in flux and thus cannot be neatly placed into geographical and temporal categories.

However, what this book has also shown, I hope, is that Africa is enriched by feminism, and feminism by Africa. Feminism is one of the most crucial conceptual tools with which we can reimagine Africa for Africans' advantage, and vice versa; Africa's position in the global order: its relationship to Nature, history, whiteness, technology and the human body brings questions to the fore that twenty-first century feminism cannot ignore.

We have asked the question emphasising different elements.

Can feminism be *African*?

Can *feminism* be African?

Can feminism *be* African?

So, can feminism be African?

In the end the question is like a matchstick: scraping the norm, crackling with possibility and igniting ... well, you tell me, I'd genuinely like to know.

Epilogue: A Pedagogy of *Shakara*

The police are like members of my family now. They are in my house everyday.

— Winnie Madikizela-Mandela[1]

God told me if I painted that mountain enough, I could have it.

— Georgia O'Keeffe[2]

In 2014, at a feminist leadership workshop in Banjul, the Gambia, I met a woman called Rashidat. She was one of the participants of the four-day event at which I and several African feminists facilitated workshops on feminism. We covered topics such as leadership, activism, empowerment and self-care. But the energy reverberating in the atmosphere was less heavy-duty than these topics suggest. It was defiant, brazen and mischievous. If I were looking for one word to characterise it, it would be: *shakara*, the Nigerian word that I previously translated in Chapter 9 as insouciance.

A memorable conversation with Rashidat confirmed this. A fellow Nigerian, Rashidat had left the country to escape a polygamous and brutishly abusive husband. This act had since been followed by alienation from her birth family and persecution from her husband.

The wickedness that she recounted shocked and infuriated me, and yet as we strolled under the palm trees as though we had known each other for years rather than days, life somehow felt light and full of possibility. Woman to woman, we explored what I now would describe as the process of African feminist individuation. We exchanged views on the immaturity of men, on their incredulous violence and destruction, but also about features which we each appreciated about men, such as how protected one can feel around honest and caring men. We tried to unpack what this protection was from – other men? The world? Ourselves? We also examined the social myths that uphold patriarchal power, introspected on the challenges and the wonders of striving for joy as an African woman, and acknowledged the ways that each of us had defied societal expectations. I was there as a workshop leader, and Rashidat had been consulting me for advice and support. But I was also being liberated, through her bravery and, despite it all, her appetite for life. I had the sense that Rashidat and I had bonded because we had glimpsed in each other that stubborn and autonomous quality of *shakara*. She had an unshakable spirit with no whiff of the 'victim trope' that is so quickly, so erroneously and so reductively imposed on African women.

There is nothing offensive in being a victim. Rashidat indeed had been a victim of unjustifiable violations. What is offensive are the assumptions of misfortune that accompany the victim narrative, as though the victim is only ever the victim and incapable of possessing a complex range of shifting registers.

The word *shakara* has a unique cadence in the context of African feminism. African women from the north, south, east, or west, the continent or the diaspora, cis or trans, poor or wealthy, have had to collectively persist in things that they should not have had to: the toils of the social order, the makings of history, the peregrinations of men, the hollowing of ancestral lands, the impoverishment of our countries, the physical violation and sociocultural judgement of our bodies…

History is flush with the injustices that the daughters of Africa have encountered – from Kemet, where they burned the monuments of

Hatshepsut, to Ife, Timbuktu and Bulawayo, where they relegated women to subservience. Through the twists and turns of the human story, African women resolutely endured. In Ethiopia, women raised their white flags to demand an end to violence; in America, they enmeshed lamentations into the rhythms and blues of concert halls, while recalling that they put us in zoos and sanatoriums; that they experimented on and violated our bodies under scrutiny and inspection, with the conviction that we were not human as they were human, even when they did not mind being entertained and nurtured by us, and even loving us despite the danger. In Octavia Butler's speculative novel *Kindred*, the lead character Dana time-travels to the past, where she encounters an enslaver, Rufus, who has just raped an enslaved black woman with whom he is in love. Dana reflects: 'I was beginning to realise that he loved the woman – to her misfortune. There was no shame in raping a black woman, but there could be shame in loving one.'[3]

In all these circumstances, we have been expected to rise above the constant and unflinching tsunamis of emotional warfare and political upheaval. Superiorists anticipated that we would wring buckets of forgiveness, patience and dutifulness from the heavy clouds they placed above our heads. They assumed that we would show loyalty to the priests, the husbands, the colonial masters, the corporations, the Big Men politicians ... We were not supposed to raise our flags, own our bodies, protect our minds, take up arms, bare our breasts, raise our fists, shout at the gates of the palaces of chiefs and their accomplices that: 'King, for a long time you have used your penis as a mark of authority that you are our husband. Today we shall reverse the order and use our vagina to play the role of husband' – as Funmilayo Ransome-Kuti nevertheless did when she gathered a group of women to demand the surrender of a patriarchal king of her town (and mine), Abeokuta, in 1949.[4]

They took it for granted that we would patiently heed when our brothers dismissed feminism and said, look: 'There will be time for me and time for you to share the cooking and change the nappies ... when Africa at home and across the seas is truly free ... till then, first things first!'[5] But the weight of appeasing, conciliating and preserving the peace showed up in our hearts, our gait, our gestures, and how our bodies aged, curled and bent. Acceptance of the unacceptable made us prioritise every struggle but our own; it kept us in relationships that bruised us. It encouraged us to stay – for the children, the husband, the boss, the nation – Arise, O Compatriots!

During those four days in Banjul, we were dancing (literally, on a few fabulous occasions) in the glitches of the Europatriarchal and Andro-African foundations that had structured our lives into norms from which we needed to escape, to find freedom, power and joy. It is still stamped into my mind that, just as the sun radiates through and in between a tree's branches, we were alive, present, gracious, supple and warm. Each of us little suns of *shakara* shining through the stodgy weight of the patriarchal nightmare that has the world in its grip.

Our demeanour was not unique to the gathering in the Gambia. *Shakara* is one of the defining qualities running through the course of African feminist history. It is embodied by real characters, who we have come to love and laud. Women like Winnie Madikizela-Mandela, Miriam Makeba, Wambui Otieno, Ama Ata Aidoo; and by fictional characters such as Ramatoulaye in Mariama Bâ's *So Long a Letter*, Enitan in Sefi Atta's *Everything Good Will Come*, Tambu in Tsitsi Dangarembga's *Nervous Conditions*, and the twin sisters Kainene and Olanna in Chimamanda Ngozi Adichie's *Half of a Yellow Sun*. These nonconformist, living-life-on-their-own-terms women, with their depth, resolve, humour and wit, are as enchanting as the fullest of full moons.

At my session in the Gambia, I shared a mind-trick that I had committed to: I would become incrementally more fearless, five per cent at a time. 'What would you do,' I asked them, 'if you were just five per cent more fearless?' After a period of personal reflection, and when the floor opened for everyone to share what they would do, I glowed when Rashidat responded: 'I would share my journey with feminists more.'

Dear readers, I pose the same question to you: what would you do if, from the moment you close this book, you were just five per cent more fearless? What would you do if you could not necessarily give a straightforward account for why feminism was African, but you were one hundred per cent sure that at least you were feminist and no longer in the duty of Andro-Africanism, or any variant of Superiorism? What would you do?

By suggesting the term *shakara* as a language to embody the African feminist lexicon, I am not suggesting that other qualities, such as grace, humility and care are not helpful. These are important feminist qualities, at least to me.

Ultimately, *shakara* is only one additional concept to be explored in an African feminist milieu. My broader point is to expand the lexicon in a way that responds to the urgency of our times, which is what I have tried to do with this book's conceptual explorations.

Yes, feminist work, by and large, requires grit and resolve. But we cannot constantly be toiling. We must also allow the irreverent lightness and insouciance of *shakara* into our lives, not only as knowledge production and political reality, but far and wide – into engineering, history, biochemistry, political studies, agriculture, anthropology, philosophy, literature, you name it.

So that's it. That's my hope for African women of today and tomorrow. Stir things up – in five-per-cent segments at a time if needs be.

Remember, feminism is not a rulebook. Feminism is a key to a non- patriarchal understanding of the world. There are no heavy duties and obligations you're required to perform as a feminist, and should anyone make you feel burdened by feminist duties, remember *shakara*, and live your life as fully and boldly as possible. But recall that you live in a world by and for men, and although feminism isn't a rulebook, simply labelling yourself as 'feminist' probably won't provide the key to escape that 'man's world'. Embodying feminism is to turn the key in the door and realise it was never locked. It is to paint the mountain. And have it.

Acknowledgements

This book was born from a long journey, made possible by the contributions of many, to whom I am deeply grateful. Firstly, my late mother, who instilled in me curiosity, defiance and love for the world, and which motivate my feminism and writing. I thank my father for fostering my appreciation of Yoruba history and Pan-Africanism. His influence brought the wisdom of this archive into this book.

Thank you to my wonderful agent, Georgina Capel, for your unwavering support in bringing this book to life. I'm grateful for your vigour, patience and diligence, and of course for helping me find my publishers, William Collins, who ultimately made the publication of this book possible. Thank you to Kate Johnson, Eve Hutchings and especially my editor, Arabella Pike, for helping guide this book to completion with your valuable insights and vision.

The research that laid the foundation for this book was formed during the years I spent writing my blog, *MsAfropolitan*. I am grateful to the many readers – some of whom have become colleagues and friends – and to all those I have learned from through events, comments, emails and tweets. The connections formed through *MsAfropolitan* were crucial to this book, and I am deeply thankful to all my readers for being part of this journey.

Thank you to the #AfriFem community, a critical group where African feminists shared conversations, knowledge and resources over the years. This book owes so much to you. A special shout out to Amina Doherty, Nana Sekyiamah, Hakima Abbas, Jessica Horn, Ainehi Edoro, Françoise Moudouthe, Rainatou Sow, 'Spectra Speaks', Lesley Agams, Rosebell Kagumire, OluTimehin Kukoyi, Mona Eltahawy, 'Sugabelly', Fungai Machirori, Saratu Abiola, Iheoma Obibi, Rainatou Sow, and everyone who contributed to nurturing this vibrant space of African feminist brilliance.

A special thank you goes out to The New Institute, the forward-thinking platform where I am a Senior Fellow and Research Chair,

and where I wrote most of this book. Thank you for providing the space
to think and create, which facilitated deep research and meaningful
collaboration alongside brilliant minds. Thank you, Erck Rickmers,
for creating this incredible space. Thank you, Anna Katsman, for
the inspiring rigour and zeal you bring to our community. Thank
you, Markus Gabriel, for your support, guidance, and for being an
inspiring intellectual companion throughout this journey, whose
thought-provoking discussions enriched my perspective. Huge thanks
to the fellows of Black Feminism and the Polycrisis for your invaluable
feedback: Pumla Dineo Gqola, Maha Marouan, Abosede Priscilla
Ipadeola, Akwugo Emejulu, Adenike Titilope Oladusu, and Kathryn
Sophia Belle. Your insights profoundly shaped my thinking throughout
the book. Thank you to the staff at The New Institute, especially Britta
Padberg, Jannic Welte, Ina Krug, Alice Gustsson, Christiane Mueller,
and Britta Neuman, for your support. To the many colleagues who
directly and indirectly impacted this book – Bayo Akomolafe, Avram
Alpert, Madhulika Banerjee, Tobias Mueller, Ruth Chang, Bruno
Leipold, Laszlo Upor, Ece Temelkuran, Wakanyi Hoffman, Maki
Sato, Anthea Behm, Fritz Breithaupt, and many others – I'm grateful
for your incredible work and the opportunity to engage with it.

To my dear aunty, Päivi Miettinen, whose comforting support,
particularly during late-night writing sessions, kept me motivated
through the writing process. To friends and family, Doudou, Ronke,
Hazel, Lara, Gopika, Robin, Sarah, Danielle, Emma, Ivelina, Rotimi,
Sidibe, Tim, Reiko, Hana, Andreas, Kunbi, Andy, Myriam, Jonathan,
Joke, Funke, Tayo, Cef, Lise, Angel – your insights, presence and
support has been a rock.

There are so many others, especially within the feminist movement,
whom I have not mentioned here, but who have contributed to the
knowledge pool from which this book draws its spirit. Thank you for
being part of the most inspiring movements I know – one defined by
a relentless commitment to a more just and beautiful world, which
continuously inspires my work and thinking.

Select Bibliography

The African Union, *Speeches and Statements Made at the First Organization of African Unity (OAU) Summit, 1963*: https://au.int/en/speeches/19630508/speeches-and-statements-made-first-organisation-african-unity-oau-summit-1963

Ahmed, S., *The Feminist Killjoy Handbook*, New Delhi: Allen Lane (2023)

Aidoo, A. A., *Our Sister Killjoy*, London: Longman (1997)

Akob, E., 'The Dangers of Western Feminism to Africa Women', TEDx Talks, 13 May 2022, (Youtube video, 14: 33): https://www.youtube.com/watch?v=4EbiVAfoGmo

Akomolafe, B., 'May your road be rough', (no date), Bayoakomolafe.net: https://www.bayoakomolafe.net/post/may-your-road-be-rough

'Arawak', *Britannica* (no date): https://kids.britannica.com/students/article/Arawak/316474

Arndt, S., *The Dynamics of African Feminism: Defining and Classifying African-feminist Literatures*, Africa Research and Publications (2001)

Baldwin, J., *Notes of a Native Son*, London: Penguin Classics (2017) *James Baldwin: Collected Essays*, edited by Toni Morrison, New York: Library of America (2014)

Barnes, J., (ed.), *Aristotle's Politics: Writings from the Complete Works: Politics, Economics, Constitution of Athens*, Princeton: Princeton University Press (2016)

Bauman, Z., *Theory and Society: Selected Writings, Volume 6*, edited by M. Davis et al.; translated by K. Bartoszynska, Oxford: Polity Press (2023)

Brezina, C., *Sojourner Truth's 'Ain't I a Woman?' Speech: A Primary Source Investigation*, New York: Rosen Publishing Group (2005)

Césaire, A., *Discourse on Colonialism*, New York: Monthly Review Press (2000)

Chazan, R., *Cambridge Medieval Textbooks: The Jews of Medieval Western Christendom: 1000–1500*, Cambridge: Cambridge University Press (2012), doi: 10.1017/cbo9780511818325

Chimakonam, J. O., 'What is conversational philosophy? A prescription of a new theory and method of philosophising, in and beyond African philosophy', *Phronimon*, 18 (2018), 115–30, doi: 10.25159/2413-3086/2874

Collins, P. H., *Black Feminist Thought: Knowledge, Consciousness and the Politics of Empowerment*, London: HarperCollins (1990)

Condé, M., *What Is Africa to Me?: Fragments of a True-to-Life Autobiography*, translated by R. Philcox, Greenford: Seagull Books London (2017)

Culshaw, P., 'Fela Kuti: Africa's Bob Marley – or an African Handel?', BBC, 18 August 2014: https://www.bbc.com/culture/article/20140818-fela-kuti-africas-bob-marley

Cumhaill, C. M., and Wiseman, R., *Metaphysical Animals: How Four Women Brought Philosophy Back to Life*, New York: Anchor Books (2023)

De Beauvoir, S., *The Ethics of Ambiguity*, Los Angeles: Kensington Publishing (2002)

— *The Second Sex*, London: Vintage Classics (2015)

Delap, L., *Feminisms: A Global History*, London: Pelican (2021)

Dickinson, E., *The Complete Poems of Emily Dickinson*, London: Little, Brown & Company (2007)

Diop, C. A., *Precolonial Black Africa*, translated by H. J. Salemson, New York: Lawrence Hill Books (1987)

Edwards, P., *Through African Eyes: Volume 1*, Cambridge: Cambridge University Press (1966)

Esbjorn-Hargens, S., and Zimmerman, M. E., *Integral Ecology*, Boston: Integral Books (2010)

Fanon, F., and Markmann, C. L., 'The fact of blackness', in *Theories of Race and Racism*, London: Routledge (2022)

Freeland, C. A., (ed.), *Feminist Interpretations of Aristotle*, University Park: Pennsylvania State University Press (1998)

García Márquez, G., *One Hundred Years of Solitude*, New York: HarperCollins (2016)

Garver, E., *Aristotle's Politics: Living Well and Living Together*. Chicago: University of Chicago Press (2012)

Geggus, D. P., *Haitian Revolutionary Studies*, Bloomington: Indiana University Press (2002)

'Global Pineapple Market to Reach $36.80 Billion by 2028, Fueled by Rising Health-Conscious Consumer Demand', *Yahoo Finance* (2023): https://finance.yahoo.com/news/global-pineapple-market-reach-36–103300173. html

Graeber, D., and Wengrow, D., *The Dawn of Everything: A New History of Humanity*, Harlow: Penguin Books (2022)

Head, B., *A Woman Alone: Autobiographical Writings*, Oxford: Heinemann International Literature and Textbooks (1990)

Higginbotham, E. B., *Righteous Discontent: The Women's Movement in the Black Baptist Church, 1880–1920*, London: Harvard University Press (1994)

Hobbes, T., *Leviathan*, Oxford: Oxford Paperbacks (1996)

Holland, T., *Dominion: The Making of the Western Mind*, London: Abacus (2023)

Hunt, J., *On the Negro's Place in Nature*, General Books (2012) Huntington, S. P., *The Clash of Civilizations: and the Remaking of World Order*, New York: Simon & Schuster (2002)

Instagram post: @Chimamanda_Adichie (2023): https://www.instagram.com/p/Cm_88ehossM/?hl=en

James, W., *The Principles of Psychology, Vol. I*, New York: Henry Holt and Co. (1890)

Jung, C. G., *Collected Works of C. G. Jung, Volume 6: Psychological Types*, edited and translated by Gerhard Adler and R. F. C. Hull, Princeton: Princeton University Press (1971)
    — *The Essential Jung: Selected Writings: Introduced by Anthony Storr*, edited by A. Storr, Princeton: Princeton University Press (2019)

Klein, N., *Doppelganger: A Trip into the Mirror World*, New York: Farrar, Straus and Giroux (2023)

Kundnani, H., *Eurowhiteness: Culture, Empire and Race in the European Project*, London: C. Hurst (2023)

Kupemba, D. N., 'Seventy-year-old Ugandan woman gives birth to twins – hospital', BBC News, 30 November 2023: https://www.bbc.com/news/world-africa-67577038

Latané, B., 'The psychology of social impact', *American Psychologist*, 36(4), (1981), 343–56. doi: 10.1037/0003-066x.36.4.343

Lerner, G., *The Creation of Patriarchy: The Origins of Women's Subordination, Women and History, Volume 1*, New York: Oxford University Press (1987)

Lorde, A., *Sister Outsider: Essays and Speeches*, Berkeley: Ten Speed Press (2007) Mbiti, J. S., *African Religions and Philosophy* (2nd edition), Harlow: Heinemann (1990)

McFadden, P., 'Becoming Contemporary African Feminists: Her-Stories, Legacies and the New Imperatives', Feminist Dialogue Series, Fórum Mulher and Friedrich-Ebert-Stiftung, Maputo, 2016: https://library.fes.de/pdf-files/bueros/mosambik/13028.pdf

— 'Contemporarity: Sufficiency in a radical African feminist life', *Meridians*, 17(2) (2018), 415–31: https://www.muse.jhu.edu/article/710137

Meadows, D. H., *Thinking in Systems: A Primer*, White River Junction: Chelsea Green Publishing (2015)

Mignolo, W. D., *The Idea of Latin America*, Chichester: Wiley-Blackwell (2009)

'Miriam Makeba Addresses the UN Special Committee on Apartheid', 1964, Youtube: @adeyinkamakinde6164: https://www.youtube.com/watch?v=WlIM3msOJcc

Morrison, T., *Sula*, London: Vintage (1998)

Mugo, M. G., *My Mother's Poem and Other Song, Songs and Poems*, East African Educ. Publ. (1998)

Muldoon, P., *Moy Sand and Gravel*, New York: Farrar, Straus and Giroux (2004)

Neruda, P., *The Book of Questions*, Copper Canyon Press (1991)

'Nigeria's Buhari says wife "belongs in the kitchen"', (no date): https://www.reuters.com/article/idUSKBN12E1GS/

Nkrumah, K., 'African Socialism Revisited', paper presented at the Africa Seminar, Cairo, 1967: https://www.marxists.org/subject/africa/nkrumah/1967/african-socialism-revisited.htm

— 'African Socialism Revisited by Kwame Nkrumah 1967', (nodate): https://www.marxists.org/subject/africa/nkrumah/1967/african-socialism-revisited.htm

— *Ghana: Autobiography of Kwame Nkrumah*, International (1989)

Offen, K., *Globalizing Feminisms, 1789–1945*, London, Routledge (2009)

Payton, M., 'Nigerian Senate votes down gender equality bill due to "religious beliefs"', *Independent*, 17 March 2016: https://www.independent.co.uk/news/world/africa/nigerian-senate-votes-down-gender-equality-bill-due-to-religious-beliefs-a6936021.html

Philosophy Overdose: 'Aristotle's philosophy, discussed with Martha Nussbaum and Bryan Magee, 1987: YouTube video, 2023: https://www.youtube.com/watch?v=pJC9o3bpujI

'Press release by the White House', Trumanlibrary.gov: https://www.trumanlibrary.gov/library/research-files/press-release-white-house

Ratele, K., *The World Looks Like This from Here: Thoughts on African Psychology*, Johannesburg: Wits University Press (2019)

Rich, A., *Of Woman Born: Motherhood as Experience and Institution*, London: Virago Press (1977)

Rousseau, J. J., *A Discourse on Inequality*, translated by M. Cranston, London: Penguin Classics (1984)

Salami, M., 'A historical overview of African feminist strands, Feminism and Social Criticism by Minna Salami', (2022), *MsAfropolitan*: https:// msafropolitan.com/2022/08/a-historical-overview-of-african-feminist-strands.html

Schwarzer, A., and de Beauvoir, S., *Simone de Beauvoir Today*, translated by M. Howarth, London: Chatto & Windus (1984)

Selassie, B. H., 'The Bumpy Road from Accra to Addis Ababa: Recollections of an Observer/Participant La route bosselée d'Accra vers Addis Ababa El camino bacheado de Accra a Addis Ababa', *Societies Without Borders*, 2(1), 49–62 (2007), doi: 10.1163/187188607x163257

Solnit, R., *Men Explain Things to Me: And Other Essays*, London: Granta Publications (2023)

Soyinka, W., *Of Africa*, New Haven, CT: Yale University Press (2014)

Srinivasan, A., *The Right to Sex*, London: Bloomsbury Publishing (2022)

Steinberg, J., *Winnie & Nelson: Portrait of a Marriage*, London: William Collins (2023)

Stewart, J., *Quotable African Women*, Parklands: Penguin Group (2005)

'Sudan: One year since conflict began, response from international community remains woefully inadequate', Amnesty International, 2024: https://www.amnesty.org/en/latest/news/2024/04/sudan-one-year-since-conflict-began-response-from-international-community-remains-woefully-inadequate/ (accessed: 12 April 2024)

Taylor, M., *Imaginary Companions and the Children Who Create Them*, New York: Oxford University Press (2001)

Tisdall, S., 'The global outlook is perilous. But here are three things Labour can do to make the world a safer place', *Guardian*, (no date): https://www.theguardian.com/commentisfree/2024/mar/12/global-outlook-perilous-labour-trident-aid-iran (accessed: 12 March 2024)

Vera, Y. (ed.), *Opening Spaces: Contemporary African Women Writing*, Harlow: Heinemann (1999)

Vico, G., *New Science*, London: Penguin Classics (1999)

Vincent, T., *Seventeen Black and African Writers on Literature and Life*, Lagos: Centre for Black and African Arts and Civilization (1981)

Wallace, M., *Black Macho and the Myth of the Superwoman*, London: Calder Publications (1979)

Ward, L. F., *Pure Sociology: A Treatise on the Origin and Spontaneous Development of Society*, The Classics (2013)

Woolf, V., *A Room of One's Own*, London: Chatto & Windus (1991)

Yacob-Haliso, O., and Falola, T. (eds.), *The Palgrave Handbook of African Women's Studies*, Cham: Springer Nature (2021)

Zinn, H., *The Real Christopher Columbus*, *Jacobin*: https://jacobin.com/2015/10/the-real-christopher-columbus (2015)

Notes

Epigraphs

[1] Attributed to Maya Angelou, see: https://www.washingtonpost.com/life style/style/lonnae-oneal-a-possible-misquote-that-may-last-forever/2015/04/04/41f937a4-da3c-11e4-b3f2–607bd612aeac_story.html

[2] Graeme Ewens, 'Miriam Makeba', *Guardian*, 11 November 2008: https://www.theguardian.com/music/2008/nov/11/miriam-makeba-obituary (accessed: 19 September 2024).

[3] Patricia McFadden, 'Contemporarity: Sufficiency in a Radical African Feminist Life', *Meridians: feminism, race, transnationalism*, 17(2), 415–31, 2018: https://www.muse.jhu.edu/article/710137 (accessed: April 2024).

Preface to the Cornell University Press Edition

[1] Martin Luther King Jr., *"Letter from Birmingham Jail,"* 1963.

[2] Avery F. Gordon, *The Hawthorn Archive: Letters from the Utopian Margins* (New York: Fordham University Press, 2018).

Prologue: The Glitch

[1] Wole Soyinka, *Of Africa*, New Haven: Yale University Press, 2014.

[2] Alice Walker, 'Edwidge Danticat, the Quiet Stream', 23 January 2010: https://alicewalkersgarden.com/2010/01/edwidge-danticat-the-quiet-stream/ (the official website for US novelist and poet Alice Walker) (accessed: 6 September 2024).

Introduction: Questions and Paradoxes

1 Bessie Head, *A Woman Alone: Autobiographical Writings*, Oxford: Heinemann International Literature and Textbooks, 1990.
2 Audre Lorde, *Sister Outsider: Essays and Speeches*, Berkeley: Ten Speed Press, 2007.
3 Simone de Beauvoir, *The Second Sex*, London: Vintage Classics, 2015.
4 Virginia Woolf, *A Room of One's Own*, London: Chatto & Windus, 1991.
5 Corona Brezina, *Sojourner Truth's 'Ain't I a Woman?' Speech: A Primary Source Investigation*, New York: Rosen Publishing Group, 2005.

PART I. AFRICA

1. Metaphysical Africa

1 Maryse Condé, *What is Africa to Me?: Fragments of a True-to-Life Autobiography*, translated by R. Philcox, Greenford, London: Seagull Books, 2017.
2 Julius K. Nyerere, 'A United States of Africa', *Journal of Modern African Studies*, Vol. 1, Issue 1 (1963): 1–6, http://www.jstor.org/stable/158780
3 Elaine Welteroth, 'Tyla Isn't interested in Being "The Next Rihanna" Actually', *Cosmopolitan*, 30 April 2024: https://www.cosmopolitan.com/entertainment/celebs/a60500279/tyla-interview-2024/ (accessed: 23 September 2024).
4 Countee Cullen, 'Heritage', in *My Soul's High Song: The Collected Writings of Countee Cullen*, New York: Anchor Books, 1991.
5 Maya Salam, 'Women's History Myths, Debunked', *The New York Times*, 1 March 2019.
6 Karen Offen, *Globalizing Feminisms, 1789–1945*, London: Routledge, 2009.
7 Antonio Gramsci, *Prison Notebooks: Selections*, edited by Quintin Hoare, translated by G. Nowell-Smith, London: Lawrence & Wishart, 1998.
8 M. Wheeler, 'Martin Heidegger', in E. N. Zalta (ed.), *The Stanford Encyclopedia of Philosophy* (online).
9 Kevin Shillington, *History of Africa*, revised edition, New York: Palgrave MacMillan, 1995.
10 Giambattista Vico, *New Science*, London: Penguin Classics, 1999.
11 Sophie B. Oluwole, *Socrates and Ọ̀rúnmìlà: Two Patron Saints of Classical Philosophy*, Lagos: Ark. 2017.

[12] There are thorough debates concerning periodisations of African history. See, for example, the work of people like: G. A. Akinola, Toyin Falola, Sophie Bosede Oluwole, Omar Gueye, Nakanyike Musisi, Nwando Achebe and Judith Byfield.

[13] Philosophers such as Abosede Ipadeola, Jonathan Chimakonam and Aribiah David Attoe are some who have written about this topic.

[14] Jonathan. O. Chimakonam, 'What is conversational philosophy? A prescription of a new theory and method of philosophising, in and beyond African philosophy', *Phronimon*, 18, (2018), doi: 10.25159/2413-3086/2874.

[15] Lorraine Code, *Ecological Thinking: The Politics of Epistemic Location*, Oxford: Oxford University Press, 2006.

[16] Quoted in Julia Stewart, *Quotable African Women*, Parklands: Penguin Group, 2005.

[17] Head, *Woman Alone*.

[18] Gabriel García Márquez, *One Hundred Years of Solitude*, London: Penguin Classics, 2000.

[19] Head, *Woman Alone*.

[20] Paul Edwards, *Through African Eyes: Volume 1*, Cambridge: Cambridge University Press, 1966.

[21] Simone de Beauvoir, *The Ethics of Ambiguity*, Los Angeles: Kensington Publishing, 2002.

[22] Aimé Césaire, *Lyric and Dramatic Poetry, 1946–82*, translated by C. Eshleman and A. Smith, Charlottesville: University of Virginia Press, 1990.

[23] UN Climate, 'Africa Climate Week 2023: Charting a Fresh Course for Climate Action', 4 September 2023.

[24] Boris Johnson, 'The Boris archive: Africa is a mess, but we can't blame colonialism', *Spectator*, 14 July 2016: https://www.spectator.co.uk/ article/the-boris-archive-africa-is-a-mess-but-we-can-t-blame-colonialism/ (accessed: 10 September 2024).

[25] Adrienne Rich, *Of Woman Born: Motherhood as Experience and Institution*, London: Virago Press, 1977.

[26] Edgar Morin and Anne Brigitte Kern, *Homeland Earth: A Manifesto for the New Millennium*, New York: Hampton Press, 1999.

[27] Palo-Närhinen, K, 'The radical politics of intimate spaces: Akwugo Emejulu on bell hooks', *ELM, European Lifelong Learning Magazine*, 15 November

2022: https://elmmagazine.eu/the-radical-politics-of-intimate-spaces-akwugo-emejulu-on-bell-hooks/ (accessed: 20 September 2024).

[28] Clearly, I have an interest in topics of a philosophical nature, and to assign someone the role of a philosopher, however misguidedly (in my own estimation), is to acknowledge that the person has in some way shone a light on a previously obscure element of knowledge; and that is a compliment that I modestly embrace.

2. Superiorism

[1] Nnamdi Azikiwe, 'Anti-god editorial jails two in Africa', *Afro-American*, 1 August 1936.

[2] Frantz Fanon, *The Wretched of the Earth*, translated by Constance Farrington, London: Penguin Classics, 2002.

[3] Hans Kundnani, *Eurowhiteness: Culture, Empire and Race in the European Project*, London: C. Hurst, 2023.

[4] Kundnani, *Eurowhiteness*.

[5] Robert Chazan, *Cambridge Medieval Textbooks: The Jews of Medieval Western Christendom: 1000–1500*, Cambridge: Cambridge University Press, 2012: doi: 10.1017/cbo9780511818325.

[6] Donella Meadows, *Thinking in Systems: A Primer*, White River Junction: Chelsea Green Publishing, 2015.

[7] Press release by the White House, 6 August 1945, Trumanlibrary.gov: https://www.trumanlibrary.gov/library/research-files/press-release-white-house (accessed: 29 March 2024).

[8] Clare Mac Cumhaill, and Rachael Wiseman, *Metaphysical Animals: How Four Women Brought Philosophy Back to Life*, New York: Anchor Books, 2023.

[9] Cumhaill and Wiseman, *Metaphysical Animals*.

3. The Trickster Dualism

[1] Bayo Akomolafe, 'May your road be rough', (no date), Bayoakomolafe.net: https://www.bayoakomolafe.net/post/may-your-road-be-rough (accessed: 20 April 2024).

[2] James Hunt, *On the Negro's Place in Nature*, New York: Van Evrie, Horton & Co., 1866.

[3] Sanche de Gramont, *Strong Brown God: Story of the Niger River*, Glasgow: HarperCollins, 1975.

4   SVB, Silicon Valley Bank, 'Half of startups have no women on their leadership team', 2019: https://www.svb.com/trends-insights/reports/wom en-in-technology-2019/ (accessed 15 September 2024).

5   de Beauvoir, *The Second Sex*.

6   Wande Abimbola, *Ifa Will Mend Our Broken World: Thoughts on Yoruba Religion and Culture in Africa and the Diaspora*, Boston: Aim Books, 1997.

7   Sophie B. Oluwole, *Womanhood in Yoruba Traditional Thought*, Bayreuth: Iwalewa-Haus, 1993.

8   Bayo Akomolafe, 'Black lives matter, But to whom? Why We Need a Politics of Exile in a Time of Troubling Stuckness (Part 1)', Democracy and Belonging Forum: https://www.democracyandbelongingforum.org/ forum-blog/black-lives-matter-but-to-whom-part-1 (accessed 2023).

9   *Portrait of a Lady on Fire*, directed by Céline Sciamma, 2019.

4. Ally Fever

1   Richard H. Bell Jr. (ed.), *Simone Weil's Philosophy of Culture: Readings Toward a Divine Humanity*, Cambridge: Cambridge University Press, 1993.

2   See for instance Biko in Sean Esbjorn-Hargens, and Michael E. Zimmerman, *Integral Ecology*, Boston: Integral Books, 2010.

3   Abimbola, *Ifa Will Mend Our Broken World*.

4   As shared by my friend, the author and babalawo, Leye Adenle.

5   Amia Srinivasan, *The Right to Sex*, London: Bloomsbury Publishing PLC, 2022.

6   Aimé Césaire, *Discourse on Colonialism*, New York: Monthly Review Press, 2000.

7   Akomolafe, 'Black lives matter'.

5. The Ghost of Whiteness

1   Zygmunt Bauman, *Theory and Society: Selected Writings, Volume 6*, edited by M. Davis et al.; translated by K. Bartoszynska, Oxford: Polity Press, 2023.

2   Kopano Ratele, *The World Looks Like This from Here: Thoughts on African Psychology*, Johannesburg: Wits University Press, 2019.

3   D. Field, J. Joyce, and D. McBride (eds.), *James Baldwin Review: Volume 1*, Manchester: Manchester University Press, 2015.

[4] Emily Dickinson, *The Complete Poems of Emily Dickinson*, London: Little, Brown & Company, 2007.

[5] Toni Morrison, *Beloved*, London: Vintage, 1998.

[6] *There Will Be Blood*, directed by Paul Thomas Anderson, 2007.

[7] Bayo Akomolafe, 'When you meet the monster, anoint its feet', *Emergence Magazine*, 2018, Available at: https://emergencemagazine.org/essay/when-you-meet-the-monster/ (Accessed: 25 November, 2024).

6. The Human Illusion

[1] Instagram post, 2023.

[2] 'Arawak', (no date) Britannica: https://kids.britannica.com/students/ article/Arawak/316474 (accessed 16 September 2024).

[3] Howard Zinn, *The Real Christopher Columbus*, Jacobin, 2015: https://jacobin.com/2015/10/the-real-christopher-columbus

[4] 'Global Pineapple Market to Reach $36.80 Billion by 2028, Fueled by Rising Health-Conscious Consumer Demand', Yahoo Finance, 2023: https://finance.yahoo.com/news/global-pineapple-market-reach-36–103300173.html

[5] Bertolt Brecht, 'To Those Born Later', *Bertolt Brecht Poems* 1913–1956, edited by John Willett and Ralph Manheim, London: Methuen, 1987.

[6] Other contemporary key concepts such as purpose and essence can easily be traced to Aristotle's too (*telos* and soul respectively). Among many others, he also coined the terms energy, kinesis and metabolism, still central to discussions on purpose. These are only some of the reasons why Aristotle's story is central if we seek to understand the values instilled into the human narrative today.

[7] Lorde, *Sister Outsider*.

[8] Eugene Garver, *Aristotle's Politics: Living Well and Living Together*, Chicago: University of Chicago Press, 2012.

[9] Jonathan Barnes (ed.), *Aristotle's Politics: Writings from the Complete Works: Politics, Economics, Constitution of Athens*, Princeton: Princeton University Press, 2016.

[10] *Philosophy Overdose*: 'Aristotle's philosophy', discussed with Martha Nussbaum and Bryan Magee, 1987: YouTube video, 2023: https://www.youtube.com/watch?v=pJC9o3bpujI (accessed: 28 January 2024).

[11] Cynthia A. Freeland (ed.), *Feminist Interpretations of Aristotle*, University Park: Pennsylvania State University Press, 1998.

12 Thomas Hobbes, *Leviathan*, Oxford: Oxford Paperbacks, 1996.

13 Although the 'noble savage' is what later interpreters of Rousseau's work termed it.

14 Jean-Jacques Rousseau, *A Discourse on Inequality*, translated by M. Cranston, London: Penguin Classics, 1984.

15 David Graeber, and David Wengrow, *The Dawn of Everything: A New History of Humanity*, Harlow: Penguin Books, 2022.

16 Graeber and Wengrow, *The Dawn of Everything*.

17 Donna Haraway, 'Situated Knowledges: The Science Question in Feminism and the Privilege of Partial Perspective', *Feminist Studies*, 14, No. 3 (1988): 575–99, https://doi.org/10.2307/3178066

18 Arlene B. Tickner and David L. Blaney, *Claiming the International*, London: Routledge, 2013.

19 David Patrick Geggus, *Haitian Revolutionary Studies*, Bloomington: Indiana University Press, 2002.

20 There were decolonisation attempts prior to these examples, such as the Bayano Wars versus Spanish colonists in 1550s Panama; the Irish versus the English in Ireland, and the Anglo–Powhatan wars, both in the seventeenth century. I start with Boukman's speech and the decolonisation struggles that followed it as they took place in a concentrated period of time. This period also has a specific relation to events in Africa.

21 Samuel P. Huntington, *The Clash of Civilizations: And the Remaking of World Order*, New York: Simon & Schuster, 2002.

22 Walter Mignolo, *The Idea of Latin America, 1st edition*, Chichester: Wiley-Blackwell, 2009.

23 African Studies Association of Africa, *Africa and the Human: Old Questions, New Imaginaries*, 2022: https://2022conference.as-aa.org/2020/10/27/asaa2022/ (accessed: 13 September 2024).

24 Naomi Klein, *Doppelganger: A Trip into the Mirror World*, New York: Farrar, Straus and Giroux, 2023.

25 Klein, *Doppelganger*.

26 Thomas S. Kuhn, *The Structure of Scientific Revolutions, Volume 2, No. 2*, 2nd edition, Chicago: University of Chicago Press, 1970.

27 *We Dare To Dream: Angelina Jolie on the Double Standards in the World*, Islam Channel, 2023, YouTube: https://youtube/zzMBcO80dZY?si=zNmXG4u7FbItOx94

[28] Instagram post, 2023.

[29] James Baldwin, *Notes of a Native Son*, London: Penguin Classics, 2017.

PART II. FEMINISM

7. Spider Mentality

[1] Louise Bourgeois, in Jean Frémon, *Now, Now, Louison*, translated by C. Swensen, London: Les Fugitives, 2018.

[2] Nyerere, 'A United States of Africa'.

[3] F. Anshen, and M. Aronoff, 'Using Dictionaries to Study the Mental Lexicon', *Brain and Language*, 68(1–2), 16–26, 1999.

[4] Quoted in Evelyn Brooks Higginbotham, *Righteous Discontent: The Women's Movement in the Black Baptist Church, 1880–1920*, London: Harvard University Press, 1994.

[5] Alice Schwarzer and Simone de Beauvoir, *Simone de Beauvoir Today*, translated by M. Howarth, London: Chatto & Windus, 1984.

[6] Danai Nesta Kupemba, 'Seventy-year-old Ugandan woman gives birth to twins – hospital', BBC News, 30 November 2023: https://www.bbc.com/news/world-africa-67577038 (accessed: 8 April 2024).

[7] Instagram post 2024.

[8] Bibb Latané, 'The Psychology of Social Impact', *The American Psychologist*, 36(4), (1981) 343–56, doi: 10.1037/0003-066x.36.4.343.

8. Harmony Feminism

[1] McFadden, 'Contemporarity'.

[2] Ryan Coogler, in *The Art of Marvel Studios: Black Panther*, United States: Marvel Entertainment, 2018.

[3] Coogler, in *The Art of Marvel Studios*.

[4] John S. Mbiti, *African Religions and Philosophies*, New Hampshire: Heinemann Educational Books Inc., 1990.

[5] C. G. Jung, *The Essential Jung: Selected Writings Introduced by Anthony Storr*, edited by A. Storr, Princeton: Princeton University Press, 2019.

[6] Jung, *Essential Jung*.

[7] J. J. B. Eliastam, 'Exploring *ubuntu* Discourse in South Africa: Loss, Liminality and Hope', *Verbum et Ecclesia*, 36, (2015).

[8] World Giving Index 2022, Charities Aid Foundation, October 2022

[9] Susan Arndt, *The Dynamics of African Feminism: Defining and Classifying African-Feminist Literatures*, Trenton, NJ: Africa World Press, 2002.

[10] @adeyinkamakinde6164 (YouTube): 'Miriam Makeba Addresses the UN Special Committee on Apartheid, 1964': https://www.youtube.com/watch?v=WlIM3msOJcc

[11] Sara Ahmed, *The Feminist Killjoy Handbook*, New Delhi: Allen Lane, 2023.

[12] Eliastam, 'Exploring *ubuntu* discourse in South Africa'.

9. Andro-Africanism

[1] Yvonne Vera (ed.), *Opening Spaces: Contemporary African Women Writing*, Harlow: Heinemann, 1999.

[2] Quoted in R. Keith Schoppa, *Twentieth Century China: A History in Documents*, Cary: Oxford University Press, 2004.

[3] Speeches & Statements Made At The First Organization Of African Unity (O.A.U) Summit, African Union Report.

[4] Bereket Habte Selassie, 'The Bumpy Road from Accra to Addis Ababa: Recollections of an Observer/Participant, La route bosselée d'Accra vers Addis Ababa El camino bacheado de Accra a Addis Ababa', *Societies Without Borders*, 2(1), 49–62, (2007), doi: 10.1163/187188607x163257.

[5] T. Falola, in Ademole Araoye, *The Ghettos of Pan-Africanism*, Ibadan: Pan-African University Press, 2021.

[6] C. L. R. James

[7] Julius K. Nyerere, *Ujamaa – Essays on Socialism*, London: Oxford University Press, 1968.

[8] The African Union, 'Speeches and Statements Made at the First Organization of African Unity (OAU) Summit, 1963': https //au.int/en/speeches/19630508/speeches-and-statements-made-first-organisation-african-unity-oau-summit-1963

[9] Lester F. Ward, *Pure Sociology: A Treatise on the Origin and Spontaneous Development of Society*, New York: The Macmillan Company, 1903.

[10] Toni Morrison, *Sula*, London: Vintage, 1998.

[11] Kwame Nkrumah, *Ghana: Autobiography of Kwame Nkrumah*, New York: International Publishers, 1971.

[12] Nwando Achebe, *The Female King of Colonial Nigeria: Ahebi Ugbabe*, Bloomington: Indiana University Press, 2011.

[13] Peter Culshaw, 'Fela Kuti: Africa's Bob Marley – or an African Handel?', BBC, 18 August 2014: https://www.bbc.com/culture/article/20140818-fela-kuti-africas-bob-marley (accessed: 16 April 2024).

[14] 'Nigeria's Buhari says wife "belongs in the kitchen"', (no date) Reuters. com: https://www.reuters.com/article/idUSKBN12E1GS/ (accessed: 29 July 2023).

[15] Maryse Condé, *What is Africa to Me?: Fragments of a True-to-Life Auto-biography*, translated by R. Philcox, Greenford, London: Seagull Books, 2017.

[16] Michele Wallace, *Black Macho and the Myth of the Superwoman*, London: Calder Publications, 1979.

[17] Gerda Lerner, *The Creation of Patriarchy: The Origins of Women's Subordination, Women and History, Volume 1*, New York: Oxford University Press, 1987.

[18] Kate Manne, *Entitled: How Male Privilege Hurts Women*, Harlow: Penguin Books, 2021.

[19] M. Payton, 'Nigerian Senate votes down gender equality bill due to "religious beliefs"', *Independent*, 17 March 2016: https://www.independent.co.uk/news/world/africa/nigerian-senate-votes-down-gender-equality-bill-due-to- religious-beliefs-a6936021.html (accessed: 29 April 2024).

10. Homegrown Feminism

[1] One of the earliest instances of explicitly named 'African feminist' discourse is *Black Sisters, Speak Out*, by Awa Thiam. Other early books include Filomina Steady's *African Feminism: A Worldwide Perspective* and Carol Boyce Davies and Ann Adams Graves's *Ngambika: Studies of Women in African Literature*.

[2] Olajumoke Yacob-Haliso and Toyin Falola (eds.), *The Palgrave Handbook of African Women's Studies*, Cham: Springer Nature, 2021.

[3] Theo Vincent, *Seventeen Black and African Writers on Literature and Life*, Lagos: Centre for Black and African Arts and Civilization, 1981.

[4] Instagram: @ChimamandaAdichie (2023): https://www.instagram.com/p/Cm88ehossM/?hl=en (accessed: 20 April 2023).

[5] McFadden, 'Contemporarity'.

[6] McFadden, 'Contemporarity'.

[7] Nancy Berke, 'The World Split Open: Feminism, Poetry, and Social Critique', in *A History of Twentieth-Century American Women's Poetry*, Cambridge: Cambridge University Press, 2016.

[8] Lorde, *Sister Outsider.*

[9] Woolf, *A Room of One's Own.*

[10] Rina Goldenberg, 'Germany sees high numbers in femicide', *Deutsche Welle*, 2020: https://www.dw.com/en/germany-sees-high-numbers-in-fem icide/a-55555702 (accessed: 23 September 2024).

[11] Lucy Delap, *Feminisms: A Global History*, London: Pelican, 2021.

PART III. BEING

11. Individuation

[1] Susan Sontag, 'Of courage and resistance', feature in *The Nation*, 17 April 2003: https://www.thenation.com/article/archive/courage-and-resis tance/ (accessed: 14 September 2024).

[2] Mariama Bâ, *So Long a Letter*, translated by M. B. Thomas, Oxford: Heinemann International Literature and Textbooks, 1989.

[3] Richard Wright, *Black Power, Three Books from Exile: Black Power: The Color Curtain; White Man, Listen!* London: HarperCollins, 2010.

[4] Baldwin, *Collected Essays.*

[5] YouTube video (14: 33): *TEDx Talks*, Elma Akob, 'The Dangers of Western Feminism to African Women', TEDx University of Pretoria, 2022: https://www.youtube.com/watch?v=4EbiVAfoGmo

[6] *TEDx Talks*, Akob, 'The Dangers of Western Feminism…'.

[7] Klein, *Doppelganger.*

[8] Abimbola, *Ifa Will Mend Our Broken World.*

[9] Cheikh Anta Diop, *Precolonial Black Africa*, translated by H. J. Salemson, Chicago: Chicago Review Press, 2012.

[10] Kopano Ratele, *The World Looks Like This from Here.*

[11] Jung, *Collected Works.*

[12] C. G. Jung, *On the Nature of the Psyche*, translated by R. F. C. Hull, Abingdon: Taylor and Francis, 1960.

[13] Patricia McFadden, 'Becoming Contemporary African Feminists: Her-Stories, Legacies, and the New Imperatives', Feminist Dialogue Series, Fórum Mulher and Friedrich-Ebert-Stiftung, 2016: https://library.fes.de/ pdf-files/bueros/mosambik/13028.pdf

[14] Condé, *What is Africa to Me?: Fragments of a True-to-Life Autobiography*, 2017.

[15] ibid.

[16] ibid.

[17] ibid.

[18] Patricia Hill Collins, *Black Feminist Thought: Knowledge, Consciousness and the Politics of Empowerment*, London: HarperCollins, 1990.

[19] ibid.

[20] Kwame Nkrumah, 'African Socialism Revisited by Kwame Nkrumah, 1967', (no date): https://www.marxists.org/subject/africa/nkrumah/1967/african-socialism-revisited.htm (accessed: 25 April 2024).

[21] Nkrumah, 'African Socialism Revisited by Kwame Nkrumah, 1967'.

Conclusion: Can Feminism Be African?

[1] McFadden, 'Contemporarity'.

[2] The Global Index of Religiosity and Atheism.

[3] Though I have written about the 'multiple strands of African feminism' in the past – for instance, see Minna Salami, 'A historical overview of African feminist strands, Feminism and Social Criticism', 2022, *MsAfropolitan*: https://msafropolitan.com/2022/08/a-historical-overview-of-african-feminist-strands.html (accessed: 25 April 2023) – I still contend, even in this essay, that the observation of these strands is at its earlier stages.

[4] Pablo Neruda, *The Book of Questions*, Washington: Copper Canyon Press, 1991.

Epilogue: A Pedagogy of *Shakara*

[1] Jonny Steinberg, *Winnie & Nelson: Portrait of a Marriage*, London: William Collins, 2023.

[2] Laurie Lisle, *Portrait of an Artist: A Biography of Georgia O'Keeffe*, Seaview Books, 1980.

[3] Octavia E. Butler, *Butler: Kindred, Fledgling, Collected Stories*, edited by G. Canavan and N. Shawl, New York: Library of America, 2021.

[4] Cheryl Johnson-Odim and Nina Emma Mba, *For Women and the Nation: Funmilayo Ransome-Kuti of Nigeria*, Illinois: University of Illinois Press, 1997.

[5] Asante, Samuel Yaw. *In My Mother's House: A Study of Selected Works by Ama Ata Aidoo and Buchi Emecheta*, Ottawa: National Library of Canada, 2001.

Index